THE ASCENSION IN KARL BARTH

This book explores the doctrine of ascension, and Barth's ascension thought in particular. First, it examines the doctrine of Jesus Christ's ascension into heaven, presenting a sustained discussion of Karl Barth's approach to this doctrine and the significance of the doctrine within his theology as a whole. Secondly, through examining Barth's ascension thought and dialoguing with three other theologians (Torrance, Farrow and Jenson), a clearer understanding of Barth and his theology is achieved. The treatment of issues related to Christ's ascension across a broader (protestant) perspective increases the relevance and usefulness of this unique study.

Andrew Burgess presents the doctrine of the ascension as an important and undervalued doctrine and encourages Christians to see how, like Barth, they might benefit in their ability to think coherently about the present age and about Jesus in relation to this age, enabling further thought about the work of the Holy Spirit, the church, and Christian ethics.

Barth Studies

Series Editors

John Webster, Professor of Theology, University of Aberdeen, UK
George Hunsinger, Director of the Center for Barth Studies,
Princeton University, USA
Hans-Anton Drewes, Director of the Karl Barth Archive, Basel,
Switzerland

The work of Barth is central to the history of modern western theology and remains a major voice in contemporary constructive theology. His writings have been the subject of intensive scrutiny and re-evaluation over the past two decades, notably on the part of English-language Barth scholars who have often been at the forefront of fresh interpretation and creative appropriation of his theology. Study of Barth, both by graduate students and by established scholars, is a significant enterprise; literature on him and conferences devoted to his work abound; the Karl Barth Archive in Switzerland and the Center for Barth Studies at Princeton give institutional profile to these interests. Barth's work is also considered by many to be a significant resource for the intellectual life of the churches.

Drawing from the wide pool of Barth scholarship, and including translations of Barth's works, this series aims to function as a means by which writing on Barth, of the highest scholarly calibre, can find publication. The series builds upon and furthers the interest in Barth's work in the theological academy and the church.

Other titles in this series

Barth on the Descent into Hell
God, Atonement and the Christian Life
David Lauber

Ecclesial Mediation in Karl Barth
John Yocum

The Ascension in Karl Barth

ANDREW BURGESS
All Saints Anglican Church, Nelson, New Zealand

ASHGATE

Published by
Ashgate Publishing Limited
Gower House
Croft Road
Aldershot
Hampshire GU11 3HR
England

Ashgate Publishing Company
Suite 420
101 Cherry Street
Burlington, VT 05401-4405
USA

Ashgate website: http://www.ashgate.com

British Library Cataloguing in Publication Data
Burgess, Andrew
   The Ascension in Karl Barth. – (Barth studies)
   1. Jesus Christ – Ascension 2. Barth, Karl, 1886–1968 – Views
   on the Ascension
   I. Title
   232.9'7

Library of Congress Cataloging-in-Publication Data
Burgess, Andrew R. (Andrew Robert), 1969-
      The Ascension in Karl Barth / Andrew Burgess.
          p. cm. – (Barth studies)
      Includes bibliographical references.
      ISBN 0-7546-3874-X (alk. paper)
          1. Jesus Christ–Ascension. 2. Barth, Karl, 1886–1968. I. Title. II. Series.

   BT500.B87 2003
   232'.7–dc22

                                                                    2003057770

ISBN 0 7546 3874 X

Printed and bound by Athenaeum Press, Ltd.,
Gateshead, Tyne & Wear.

To Rebecca: with all my love and thanks

Contents

Acknowledgements

Exerpts from Barth's *Church Dogmatics*, and from Douglas Farrow's *Ascension and Ecclesia*, are reprinted by permission of The Continuum International Publishing Group.

> Barth, Karl, *Church Dogmatics*, volumes I-IV, Edinburgh: T&T Clark, 1936-1969. Copyright T&T Clark.

> Farrow, Douglas, *Ascension and Ecclesia: On the Significance of the Doctrine of the Ascension for Ecclesiology and Christian Cosmology*, Edinburgh: T&T Clark, 1999. Copyright D.B. Farrow 1999.

My especial gratitude must be expressed to John Webster who supervised my work at Oxford. I have nothing but admiration for John as a Christian and as a theologian. Stephen May was an inspirational first teacher of theology, and I, like many of his students, remain very much in his debt.

Introduction

The doctrine of Jesus Christ's ascension is currently somewhat in vogue. Douglas Farrow's recent work on the doctrine[1] has stimulated interest in this *locus* of theology, even though previously in the modern period it has not often received large amounts of attention, at least for its own sake. This is not to say that Jesus' ascension has not received *any* distinct and focussed treatment, even in the twentieth century. Behind Farrow's work we may discern the influence of Thomas Torrance, who dedicated half of his book *Space, Time and Resurrection*[2] to a treatment of the ascension. Torrance is noted for an emphasis on the vicarious humanity of Christ, and this readily leads to an interest in Jesus' ascended life and activity. Nonetheless, the doctrine of Jesus' ascension has not featured very strongly within the theological framework of most modern protestant theologians. What is it that the ascension has to offer theology, and the church, if we incorporate it more fully into our thought?

Theology has the task of reflecting, obediently, on the reality of God revealed to us in Jesus Christ, the man of Nazareth and the Saviour of the world. Thinking about Jesus therefore exercises control over all other thought, in the sense that the attitude with which we approach all reality must be shaped and over-ruled by faith in Jesus Christ. So for example, Christian thought about the present age of the world – even the belief that there is such a thing as the present age of the world, existing between ascension and Christ's return! – must be formed by attending to Jesus and what impact His reality has upon this age. Dietrich Bonhoeffer was quite right to ask 'Who is Jesus Christ for us today',[3] but the answer must be found in attending to Jesus Himself, rather than in obedience to the fashions of our time, as so many seem to have taken Bonhoeffer to mean. If Jesus of Nazareth is the risen and active Lord, the One whom Christians are to worship and adore above all others, and moreover the One whose reality is the measure of all other reality, then knowledge of Him is knowledge of the highest and most powerful truth. Thus, to return to our example, to understand the present age of the world it is necessary to understand Jesus' ascension and ascended life – for it is these theological *loci*, in full partnership with doctrines such as that of the incarnation, reconciliation, and revelation, that give us the tools to think 'Christianly' about this age. In a time when many feel that Christianity, at least in the west (or north), is in

---

[1] *Ascension and Ecclesia: On the Significance of the Doctrine of the Ascension for Ecclesiology and Christian Cosmology* Edinburgh: T&T Clark, 1999.

[2] *Space, Time and Resurrection* Edinburgh: Handsel Press, 1976, republished by T&T Clark, Edinburgh, 1998.

[3] Bonhoeffer, Dietrich *Christ the Center* trans. E.H. Robertson, San Francisco: Harper and Row, 1978.

crisis, or suffering a crisis of confidence, reflection on Jesus' lordship and activity in the present time, as well as upon the limits of the church in what Barth calls the 'time between' ascension and *eschaton* (Jesus' return at the end), may serve the church very well. Moreover, reflection upon Jesus' history as moving toward the end of this age, and the full revelation of His saving power in that ending, can and must also serve to reframe our awareness of Jesus of Nazareth as the one Lord whom we need to know and to serve. If Jesus is the risen and ascended lord, then the future is in His hands, and we do well to seek it there and not elsewhere.

A theology of Jesus' ascension is therefore not concerned only, or perhaps even primarily, with a discussion of the event of Jesus' ascending itself. Rather, Jesus' ascension requires theological attention because it tells us a great deal about whom Jesus is, 'where' He is, and what He is doing in the present age. A theology of the ascension belongs with and informs a theology of Jesus Christ's 'heavenly session' (Jesus' activity and authority as they are exercised now that He is ascended), so that together these two form more or less one *locus* of theology. As they are developed together theological thought about Jesus' ascension, and about the outcome of His ascension in the heavenly session, come to exercise considerable influence on thought about the present age of the world. If Jesus is ascended, then the event of His ascension may be argued to inaugurate the present age and to provide the conditions that frame the age. Of course, understanding of the ascension does not come independently of a raft of theological material. To state that Jesus has ascended to the 'right hand of the Father' might be a simple thing, but to think about what that ascension might mean involves consideration of a great deal more than that. Jesus' ascension can only be understood in relation to His being as the 'God-man'- that is, we must also have in mind an examination of God becoming human in the incarnation, of what Jesus may be claimed to have accomplished on the cross, of the shape of His resurrection, and not least at all, of what eschatology has to do with it all.

This book addresses this set of issues, and does so by examining the theology of Karl Barth, and then more briefly engaging three other protestant theologians. It is therefore hoped that the work will have something to offer in two ways: firstly in opening up further discussion of the ascension and its importance within the framework of dogmatic theology, especially for a church struggling with its faith, and; secondly in addressing a significant aspect of Barth's thought in such a way as to contribute to contemporary Barth studies and discussions. Jesus' ascension is significant in shaping Barth's vision of the present age – Barth specifically calls this age the 'time between' ascension and eschaton. In so shaping the conditions and nature of the present age Jesus' ascension and ascended life become very important for Barth's understanding of the current role of the Spirit, of the church as existing in the 'time between', for his eschatology, his theology of the Christian life, and so on. Significantly, many of these aspects of Barth's thought are controversial, and the particular insight into them that attention to Barth's ascension thought can offer may well contribute usefully to the current debate. So, for instance, the debate regarding Barth's attitude to Christian life (ethics), and to the Christian as an agent within God's economy, may benefit from attending to the way in which Barth describes Christian life as 'between the times'. Barth is very clear that while Jesus is absent via ascension, and awaited in the eschaton, Christians have a distinct calling that fits these circumstances. Christians are seen as living out a genuine redeemed existence, and as ethical agents in obedience to God, but this existence is clearly delimited by the fact that in the 'time between' redemption is still 'on its way', and faith is not yet replaced by sight, the corruptible not yet swallowed up by the incorruptible. This particular set of commitments occupies central place in chapter four.

In tracing the ascension in Barth, and in dialoguing with other thinkers, I do not simply intend to study Barth's theology as an end in itself – although examination of Barth's thought dominates the discussion. Rather, I propose to open up the doctrine of Jesus' ascension and present agency as significant for theology as we undertake it afresh in our own generation. If theology serves the church by ever reminding us of the truth of Jesus and that no other reality has any claim upon us that can compete with His claim, then Jesus' ascension is extremely important for understanding ourselves and our age in relation to Him. He is Himself the truth we need to know and the life we need to live – He does not represent an idea we must adhere to, rather He is the living Lord before whom we bow even as He graciously gives us life. Theology will benefit greatly from taking Jesus' risen and ascended life seriously. Barth stands out as a theologian who has attempted to work out a dogmatic theology in considerable detail, and by enquiring into the role of the ascended Christ within the framework of his theology we may be able to investigate the import of Jesus' ascension and session as they function *within* a complex theology. In other words, the task is to explicate the function of Jesus' ascension and of key aspects of His ascended being, as it is worked out within the complex of Barth's doctrinal affirmations, all of which bear fruit in varying ways throughout the development of the dogmatic task. The ascension is thus found to influence the handling of other doctrines, while at the same time Barth's thought about Jesus' ascension is clearly controlled by his commitment to the Chalcedonian creed, to the cross as the high point of Jesus' history, and so forth. The result is, I think, a treatment which is richer and more laden with connections than a discussion of the doctrine in isolation could be.

Barth does not devote large amounts of space to discussion of Jesus' ascension, or to its outcomes, in isolation – even though *Church Dogmatics* is a vast work, few pages are given over to discussion of Jesus' ascension alone. However, at significant points Barth claims that Jesus' ascension, or the shape of the present age, which in turn is predicated in part upon Jesus' ascension, is shaping his discussion. It is very interesting, and of great value, to trace the influence of Jesus' ascension in this way. For this reason, Barth's explicit and implicit reference to Jesus as ascended will occupy our attention. Barth certainly refers explicitly to Jesus' ascension and being in heaven, and part of the task of this work is to demonstrate that this is so, but more than that, the explicit references are backed up by the role Jesus' ascended life has in his theology. This means that we can learn from Barth something of the way in which Jesus' ascension must play its part in shaping our thought as a whole. In particular, significant links between incarnational theology and ascension theology are uncovered, most plainly in the dialogues with three other thinkers which occupy the second half of the book. The doctrine of the ascension, like any significant aspect of the faith, cannot simply be tacked onto an existing theology – it must be allowed free rein to play its part within the whole. Barth reveals something of how this may occur.

Nonetheless, in assessing Barth's contribution, I do not wish to defend Barth at every point. Barth is surely wrong at times – his treatment of baptism is often recognised as extremely problematic, even by Barth sympathisers, and will need to be addressed in relation to the present topic. Even so, I consider that Barth's work regarding Jesus' ascension and life 'between the times' has a great deal to recommend it. Dialogue with others largely reinforces the point. I wish to commend Barth's achievement at this point, and invite others to draw further upon it.

In order to develop an understanding of the place of Jesus' ascension, and of Barth's particular treatment of it, three other protestant theologians are engaged in relation to Barth and to Jesus' ascension. This engagement takes the form of three chapters which are essentially essays in themselves. Thomas Torrance is a renowned and significant theologian, who, although 'one of Barth's foremost disciples in the English-speaking world',[4] remained critical of Barth specifically in regard to the ascension. Torrance undertakes a more 'sacramental' reading of the relationship between the creation and the Creator, and alongside his emphasis on the vicarious humanity of Christ, this undergirds a set of concerns regarding Barth's treatment of Jesus' ascended life. Moreover, Torrance has himself offered a significant discussion of Jesus' ascension which is itself important for the discussion of this doctrine. Torrance's critique of Barth is engaged, and some return questions are offered to Torrance's work, particularly in relation to his theology of the incarnation.

Douglas Farrow is a much younger theologian than Torrance, but he has written in some depth on the doctrine of the ascension, and has been critical of Barth's treatment of the doctrine. Farrow therefore offers a significant dialogue partner. His treatment of the church and the eucharist contrast with Barth's, and open up an important area of contemporary thought for discussion. It is notable that many contemporary protestant theologies are emphasising more and more the eucharist as the centre of church existence, and even embracing Zizoulas' version of the Orthodox claim that the eucharist constitutes – or in some way brings into being – the church. Farrow may be argued to take something of this line, and turns to the ascension in order to do so. Barth's treatment of the ascension, and his understanding of Jesus'

---

[4] R. D. Williams 'Barth on the Triune God' in S. W. Sykes ed. *Karl Barth: Studies of his Theological Method* Oxford: Clarendon Press, 1979.

ascended life, direct him to argue in quite the opposite direction to Farrow, and so the debate is lively and contemporary.

Finally, like Torrance, Robert Jenson is another theologian of considerable note and stature. Jenson is of interest in relation to the work before us, not because he directly engages with Barth in discussion of the ascension, but because his view of the ascension is very different, as is his description of the being of the church and his vision of the present age. Where Barth, Torrance, and Farrow all see the ascension as Jesus' bodily withdrawal into a heaven which is a place somehow separated from the earth, Jenson sees Jesus' ascension as into the church around the sacraments. Heaven is the church around the sacraments, and the church is the resurrection body of the Lord. Jenson therefore offers a very interesting counterpoint to Barth. Moreover, like Farrow, Jenson's emphasis on church and sacrament reflects a significant strand of theological fashion, especially in ecumenical circles, and interaction with Jenson increases the relevance of the discussion in relation to current theological circumstances. Some strenuous criticism of Jenson is the result of the dialogue, especially with regard to his idea of Jesus' body, and his thought about the Trinity.

Finally, and speaking very broadly, it is noticeable that many other theologians pay little or no particular heed to Jesus' ascension. At the same time, if one reads various theologies with the question of Jesus' current existence and life in mind, two options often seem to be supposed. Sometimes Jesus is simply assumed to be absent, although not necessarily via ascension. Whatever may be stated regarding faith in the resurrection, Jesus' living agency appears to be lacking, at least in any way that would make a difference. On the other hand, Jesus can appear to have risen and ascended into the church itself, although few theologians are as explicit or as nuanced as Jenson on this. Reminiscent of Bultmann's description of Jesus as rising into the *kerygma* (gospel proclamation), Jesus' ascended life seems to be simply assumed, or subsumed, in the life of the community. This may be in a (supposedly) more 'protestant' emphasis upon the individual believer existing in faith, or a (allegedly) more 'catholic' emphasis on the institution of the church across time. Thus, in both cases, the focus of a theology of the church and of the present age tends to be upon human agency somewhat in isolation from any specific agency of Christ, or upon human agency *as* the agency of Christ. Talk of the Spirit's work among His people may thereby lack any definition in terms of Christ's agency and lordship as transcendent of human agency, particularly in the church.

Interestingly, and importantly, neither of these ways of thinking about Jesus and the church is available to us if we take something like the line that Barth takes regarding Jesus' ascension. In Barth we find a tremendous emphasis on Jesus as the living and active Lord of the church, of Christians, and indeed of the whole cosmos. Barth therefore rejects both the options above, and instead seeks to explicate the agency of the Lord as predicated upon his absence according to His risen flesh, and the claim that His presence is mediated in the Spirit until He returns. Barth develops a very clear notion of the church as both glorious in Christ and at the same moment profoundly limited by His absence. In the same way, Christians, as Jesus' people between the times, are both glorified in Him, and at the same time those who suffer and struggle within an age shaped by His absence. Christian existence is existence in Christ, and thus it is glorious, but while His return is yet awaited it is entirely a life of faith and hope, of suffering and of expectation of joy. It is to the basis of Barth's reading of all this in the ascension that we turn in the succeeding chapters.

PART I

KARL BARTH

ON

JESUS' ASCENSION

AND

HEAVENLY SESSION

Chapter 1

The Shape of Barth's Theology

Karl Barth's theological achievement is very impressive. Attention can be drawn to the sheer size of his mammoth work in the *Church Dogmatics*,[1] but the volume of his writing alone is not enough to indicate greatness. At the heart of Barth's achievement are some fundamental commitments, for instance, to the creed of Chalcedon, to the Lordship and agency of God, to the claim that God alone reveals God, and that the absolute reality of the gospel profoundly relativises human knowledge *apart from the enlightening power of God*. These fundamental commitments are worked out in such a fashion as to yield a theology which expresses utter faithfulness to Jesus Christ, and to the good news about Him. The *Church Dogmatics* is a large scale reworking of the theological tradition, in which the various doctrines of the church interweave with each other, and mutually condition one another – it is a thoroughly *theological* work, in which the church's proclamation of Jesus Christ taken up, critiqued and measured through extended reflection upon Jesus Christ. So great is Barth's emphasis upon Christ that he has been accused of *christomonism*, that is, of making Christ the sum total and measure of God, and of reducing the Father and the Spirit to the vanishing point. While it is not true that Barth loses sight of God's tri-unity – indeed Barth's ascension theology will help explicate his theology of the Spirit, for instance – Douglas Farrow is correct when he notes that the 'works of Barth breathe a loyalty to the Man of Nazareth that none can mistake'.[2]

Because of the thoroughly interlinked nature of Barth's theology we cannot isolate out the ascension from the achievement as a whole. Any attempt to examine the treatment of one doctrine in isolation from its larger context will fail to do justice to the material. However, it is not possible to offer a full introduction to Barth's thought in this brief chapter. Other authors offer excellent introductions to Barth, and a more general account may be

---

[1] Barth, Karl *Church Dogmatics* vol. I-IV, Edinburgh: T&T Clark, 1936-1969. Copyright T&T Clark, 1936-69. Reprinted by permission of The Continuum International Publishing Group. Now *CD*.

[2] Farrow, Douglas *Ascension and Ecclesia: On the Significance of the Doctrine of the Ascension for Ecclesiology and Christian Cosmology* Edinburgh: T&T Clark, 1999, p.229. Copyright D.B. Farrow, 1999. Reprinted by permission of The Continuum International Publishing Group.

found in their works.[3] What can be achieved in this chapter is an outline of several key aspects of Barth's theological project – particularly where his thought is more distinctive – so that the focus upon the ascension which follows is not abstracted from its ground in his particular thought. The brief interaction with aspects of Barth's thought below is therefore not intended to be representative of his theology as a whole, so much as to prepare the ground for a discussion of the ascension. Some key aspects of Barth's work which impinge particularly forcefully on his ascension thought – such as his reworking of the themes of humiliation and exaltation in the light of Chalcedon – will be examined in depth within the discussion of the ascension, and so are not treated here.

Introduction to Key Themes

The Lordship and Agency of God

That 'God reveals Himself as the Lord' is the central claim of Barth's prolegomena with which he introduced (in two large 'tomes'!) his *Church Dogmatics*. Indeed, God's lordship is central to the entire *Dogmatics*. Barth knew – the gospel ever impressed upon him – the wonderful authority and majesty that belong to God as Creator and Redeemer. The rule of God is vital to the matter of revelation, which lies at the heart of so much of *Church Dogmatics*. In the prolegomena, with its focus upon the self-revealing power of God there is a tremendous emphasis upon the authority of God exercised in the act of self-revelation. God does not simply reveal the *fact* of lordship, rather revelation is God acting – acting in lordship, in rule and authority. As the promulgation of the kingdom of God (βασιλεία τοῦ Θεου) revelation is simply God the Lord acting as Lord in relation to humans. That is, to be Lord is to act as God *does* in acting upon humans in self-revelation.[4] God's lordship is revealed in His freedom for His creatures, the power of His grace to reconcile and redeem, even when those creatures have destroyed their own capacity for relationship with God. At issue is God's freedom to reveal Himself to His creature, and further, God's freedom in His creature to make redemption the reality of the creature's being and act. The reality of this freedom is the basis of all Christian theology, all dogmatics. Nothing can or will deny God this freedom – the freedom of lordship. Any disjunction between God's deity and our humanity, or even between God's holiness and our sin, is not adequate –

---

[3] See especially: George Hunsinger's *How to Read Karl Barth: The Shape of His Theology* Oxford: Oxford University Press, 1991; Geoffrey W. Bromiley's *An Introduction to the Theology of Karl Barth* Edinburgh: T&T Clark, 1979; Thomas F. Torrance's *Karl Barth, Biblical and Evangelical Theologian* Edinburgh: T&T Clark, 1990; John Webster's *Barth* London: Continuum, 2000.

[4] *CD* I/1, p.306.

on any basis – to limit the freedom of God to be for us, and even to be free 'in us'. Both christology and pneumatology speak clearly of this.[5]

This freedom, which we call lordship, is God's ability to achieve what God wills, to act and have God's action agree perfectly with God's being and intention. 'Lordship means freedom'.[6] God in freedom is unconditioned and autonomous, and this freedom is exercised in such a manner that in God's decisions (which is the same as to say 'in God's act') such things as righteousness, holiness, mercy, and truth, are revealed as the realities they are in God.[7] These notions of freedom are therefore not to be taken abstractly. Their basis is not an idea of lordship, or of freedom, or even creaturely experience of what we call lordship and freedom. Rather, all is founded upon the concrete and particular reality of God's action toward us in Jesus Christ. God reveals Godself as the Lord: 'All else we know as lordship can only be a copy, and is in reality a sad caricature of this lordship'.[8]

To recognise the lordship of God in all dealings with creation is therefore to affirm, in the strongest fashion, God's agency – God is Lord in action. In all his work Barth is deeply concerned with God's agency: in elucidating the reality of God's self-revelation he is at pains to emphasise that God is the all-sufficient agent. Self-revelation is an act of the Lord, who in sovereignty becomes revelation in the Word. God in freedom *decides*, and decision means actualisation, the exercise of God's freedom. God's Word is therefore not 'mere possibility' but God's decision for humanity, 'a choice taking place'.[9] The freedom of God, God's free agency, is therefore manifest in the Word. This is what Barth calls the 'root of the doctrine of the Trinity': that the lordship of God is manifest in the second person of the Trinity, God in God's Word, God the Son. 'God's freedom for us men is a fact in Jesus Christ, according to the witness of Holy Scripture'.[10] Thus the first part of Christology, the doctrine of the Word of God, is 'the part which answers the question: How does the encounter of His revelation with man become real in the freedom of God?',[11] and this Christological centre is the axle upon which Barth's entire theology turns.

The Doctrine of Revelation

So we see that Barth understands revelation doctrinally, from a centre in Christology and with further elaboration in the doctrine of the Trinity, rather than from any anthropological centre. Jesus Christ as the incarnate Son of God is the one reality of revelation, attested in the New Testament, and His

---

[5] *CD* I/2, pp.2-3.
[6] *CD* I/1, p.306.
[7] *CD* I/1, p.307.
[8] *CD* I/1, p.306.
[9] *CD* I/1, p.157.
[10] *CD* I/2, p.25.
[11] *CD* I/2, p.3.

reality alone is the matter with which we are confronted, and which determines all our thought of God. No prior anthropology or philosophy can offer us an understanding of God's revelation in Jesus of Nazareth. There is no 'general idea' which can shed light on the New Testament's naming of the Son of God as this man of Galilee. It is the reality which the New Testament attests that sheds light upon itself – that is, the reality of Jesus Christ can only be understood only from the perspective of the witness to Him.[12]

We may well expect a modern theologian to show an *epistemological* interest in revelation, (given the doubt cast upon knowledge of God in the modern period), but although revelation is necessarily a matter of knowledge of God, Barth's concern is not to develop an epistemology, or even address epistemological issues as such. Rather he claims to be driven by the nature of God's self-disclosive activity itself, as God in lordship and authority takes hold of fallen humans, addressing them in the one Word of life. What this means is that epistemology is not a necessary prolegomena to theology proper – it is not a piece of independent philosophical work which must be undertaken *before* theology can begin. Rather, theology itself offers the grounds upon which it proceeds – the knowledge of God itself reveals how God may be known. If the doctrine of revelation offers an epistemology, and provides a prolegomena, then in doing so it is *already* theology. It is as God takes hold of humans in the power of divine self-revelation that speech about God becomes possible – not upon the basis of a prior epistemological enquiry. Barth is renowned for the 'actualism' of this approach, as he describes God's being as in God's act, and God's act as the straight-forward reality of God's being. Revelation occurs as the event, the act, of God's acting in order to become manifest, and revelation is therefore neither a datum of our experience, nor a deposit of knowledge we have received. In fact, revelation is the very being of God toward us – God's being in God's act of reconciliation. Barth's prolegomena is thus founded upon his description of God's self-revelation in Jesus Christ, and this is simply based upon the assertion that this is how God has and will be revealed.

Within the Trinitarian dynamic of all of God's work, Jesus Christ and Jesus alone is the revelation of God – He is the objective reality to whom we attend if we are to know God, even as the Spirit realises that knowledge in us. 'The content of the New Testament is solely the name Jesus Christ, which, of course, also and above all things involves the truth of His God-manhood. Quite by itself this name signifies the objective reality of revelation'.[13] Thus all knowledge of God is to be understood as knowledge of Jesus Christ. It is in relation to Jesus Christ that we can think and speak under the aegis of God's truth, and no other source of knowledge or relationship can stand next to Him.

What is more, it is only within this revelation of God in Jesus, the Word of God, that we learn that we are sinners and fallen, that we are lost and ignorant of God, and that reconciliation in Jesus is our one hope of life. It is the same

---

[12] *CD* I/2, pp.14-15.
[13] *CD* I/2, p.15.

revelation of Jesus Christ as the forgiveness of our sins which also reveals our status as enemies of God – the Word of God reveals that humans have placed themselves outside of fellowship with God.[14] As the Word become flesh Jesus is the living bridge between God and lost humanity, recreating in Himself a whole new humanity, even a whole new creation. It is here that we learn that we are not privileged with a prior competence for knowledge of God, even God in the person of the Word, but that all is grace. All claims that humans are unable to know God *apart from God's* grace are not made *a priori* (before) but *a posteriori* (after), in the light of the grace received in Jesus Christ, within whose 'Yes' to us and to human knowledge and speech of God we must recognise a preceding 'No'.

So we must attend to the considerable emphasis Barth places upon the living and personal character of Jesus Christ as the objective content of revelation. We do not have to do with an inanimate object within our world, within creation, which we can appropriate and possess like any other fact. If for a moment we look ahead to Chapter Three, even the church as His body does not simply 'have' Jesus, and knowledge of the truth in Jesus is not a donation that can be held and maintained. Church proclamation cannot claim immediacy with the Word of God in Christ. 'The human impossibility of the church's proclamation consists simply in the impossibility of the attempt to speak of God'.[15] But, in the agency of Jesus Christ, this inadequacy is not the end of the story. Jesus Himself can and does speak in and through inadequate human words. Grace is therefore revealed as grace indeed, and Jesus Christ is known to be present in the power of His risen life wherever humans genuinely speak of God.[16]

As the incarnate Word Jesus Christ is the revelation of God to us because He is present in our flesh, and yet precisely in this flesh He remains veiled, as He undergoes humiliation in weakness and lowliness. So, although knowledge of God in Christ turns upon the humanity of the Son, the very incarnation is a veiling of God in flesh, a *kenosis* and Jesus' life is also His passion.[17] Even in this supreme condescension of incarnation, Jesus remains utterly 'other' – in fact, it is in His likeness to us that He is most unlike us. It is as the sinless One found in the likeness of sinful flesh that He is closest and yet most distant from us.

What Barth therefore describes are two 'moments' in the history of Jesus Christ, the movement of veiling, of *kenosis*, in the incarnation, and that of unveiling which he locates in the resurrection and ascension. The way of Jesus Christ from one moment to the other is the history at the heart of revelation, a history that turns upon God's becoming flesh. 'If God's revelation is the way from veiling of the eternal Word to His unveiling, from crib and cross to resurrection and ascension, how can it possibly be anything else than God's

---

[14] *CD* I/1, pp.407-8.
[15] *CD* I/2, p.750.
[16] *CD* I/2, p.752.
[17] *CD* I/2, p.36.

becoming man, His becoming flesh?'[18] The movement from birth, culminating at the cross is one of humiliation. But, (as explicated in great detail in volume IV), it is highly significant that Barth does not follow the theological tradition in assigning humiliation to one period of Jesus' history and exaltation to another such as resurrection or ascension. Humiliation and exaltation are ever present, accompanying each other – they are functions of the very nature of incarnation, of the union of the Son of God with the Son of Man. This union does not cease to be the reality of Jesus Christ's being. So also the glorification of the Son of Man in union with the Son of God, and the humiliation of the Son of God in being united with the Son of Man, does not cease. Rather this being of Jesus Christ in humiliation and exaltation is the reality of His existence for us into eternity – the truth of His reconciliation of God and humanity in His own self.

Thus, as he considers the relationship between Jesus and humans living in the 'time between' – that is, this present time between ascension and eschaton – Barth maintains that the same dynamic of veiling and unveiling is at work while we stand at a temporal distance from the events of His life. Jesus ascended is neither more nor less veiled in His identity as the God-Man, nor more or less unveiled through His own activity of self-revelation. The Holy Spirit, as we shall see, is the power of God at work in us to bring about the subjective reality of revelation, but the presence of Jesus in the Spirit is no less obscure to us than His being as the Son of God was obscure to His earthly contemporaries. The risen and ascended Jesus is present in the Spirit, but not in such a way that the distinction between Him and us is dissolved, or so that we simply possess Him. Rather, the Son of God who has come in Jesus of Nazareth remains the coming one, and the present time of the church awaiting His return is the age of faith and hope. 'Not a line of the real New Testament can be properly understood unless it is read as the witness to finally achieved divine revelation and grace and therefore as the witness to hope'.[19]

Looking back to the Reformation, Barth confirms Calvin's view that affirming Christ's presence to the believer as a pure unmediated presence 'meant abolishing the remaining difference between us and Christ. True, in Christ all salvation was present, but in Christ Himself, not as already mediated to us, not as proper to us in any other way than in the act of His giving'.[20] Indeed Barth is sure that any dissolution of the difference between Jesus and us will in fact remove all meaning from faith in Christ, and distort the doctrine of revelation into something false. Revelation does not become a 'revealed state' but rather as revelation remains identical with Jesus Himself, so the power of revelation consists in the otherness with which Jesus always confronts even the believer such that the believer is not left alone with only her own faith to fall

---

[18] *CD* I/2, p.43.
[19] *CD* I/2, p.117.
[20] *CD* I/2, p.118.

back on, but is instead ever in relation to the living Lord. Christ's being for us, and power within us, consists also in His difference from us.[21]

God's agency in revelation therefore remains primary, even after Jesus' resurrection and ascension, and during the age of human faith – God is the active subject in revelation – and as God's self-revelation Jesus Christ is the one in whom this agency confronts us. Jesus Christ as the agent in revelation is key in Barth's understanding, and both the possibility and the nature of this agency will be further explicated with direct reference to the doctrine of resurrection and ascension, especially with reference to Barth's particular description of time, and various 'times', within a broad eschatological framework.

The Ascension as the Foundation of Eschatological Expectation

Although direct reference to eschatological expectation is limited in the *Church Dogmatics* it is nonetheless an important theme. Jesus is ascended and in some senses absent, but at the same time we expect His promised return, and the interplay of presence and absence in the 'time between' always involves faith and hope as the activity of looking forward to Jesus' future immediacy. Thus, for example, when we explore the relationship between the time of Jesus and our present time we will see that revelation in the present age is the in-breaking of the time of God which is the only true time, and yet which is only present now in the mediate presence Jesus Himself adopts. Jesus' immediate presence at the *eschaton* will also bring the immediacy of His time and the end of the age.

The reality of the 'time between' is that it is the age of grace and faith, of the absence as well as the presence of the ascended Lord. This is the age of penultimate knowledge, both of God and of ourselves as God's redeemed people, the age defined by eschatological expectation, in which our limited knowledge of God and experience of salvation can only be fully explicated in contrast to Jesus' expected advent. The age of grace (*regnum gratiae*) is such that faith dominates – faith and not sight – and we are not yet with the Lord in the *eschaton* (the *regnum gloriae*). We cannot see the reality of our redemption from God's side, but only from within the tension of faith, ever seeking the resolution that lies on the other side of the divide.[22]

This eschatological orientation of the 'time between' colours every aspect of the age. The presence of the Word is always to be understood as an eschatological presence, so that although Barth does not need to repeat this claim at every turn, nonetheless it lies at the heart of his understanding. The Word of God is God's announcement to humanity that He is the reality of our future – the only future we have. God's presence in the Word is ever as the coming Lord, whose *parousia* will be the consummation of both creation and

---

[21] *CD* I/2, p.118.
[22] *CD* I/1, p.462-3.

redemption.   Everything that God says and may say belongs within this eschatological relation.[23]

In what follows the eschatological dimension, as a function of the *ascended* and therefore also *awaited* state of the Lord, is not to be forgotten.   The eschatological future of God is determinative of all reality now, in the age of anticipation and expectation.   The being of the church, and indeed of the Christian, is wholly eschatological being.   Everything that can be said about the human filled with the Spirit is said eschatologically.   Not that such speech is in some way vague or false, but rather it is eschatological in the sense that it ever relates to the coming *eschaton* and thus to divine fulfilment of all things. Far from unreality such eschatological speech relates to the one true reality of the living and coming God, and this speech is therefore the truth in relation to temporal reality also.[24]

Addressing the Ascension in Barth

It is clear, then, that Jesus Christ is the overwhelming focus of Barth's attention as he pursues the various aspects of his theological programme. The reality of Jesus is determinative of all creaturely reality – He *is* the new creation, and in Him resides the only creaturely reality that will persist beyond His return in the *eschaton* – and this being so, Jesus' ascension has a great deal to say regarding the shape of the present age, as noted already. By examining the ascension within Barth's thought certain issues within his approach to contemporary reality may be made clear, and this will be made more explicit below. In the mean time, how are we to pursue the ascension and heavenly session within Barth's massive project?

Douglas Farrow has recently described volume IV of Karl Barth's *Church Dogmatics* as 'one of *the* major works of ascension theology',[25] and rightly so. Indeed, the comment may be safely applied to the whole of Barth's *Church Dogmatics*. Although phrases such as 'Jesus' ascension' and 'Christ ascended' are absent from many of the pages of *Church Dogmatics*, nonetheless throughout his work Barth draws heavily upon belief in Jesus Christ as risen and ascended in order to make sense of theology as focussed upon *humanity with God*. The importance of the ascension for Barth, and the shape it lends his thought, especially with regard to the redemption of humanity, is at the centre of this thesis. Of course, it must be admitted that a claim of *comparative* greatness for Barth's treatment of the ascension is relatively easy to make, simply because the theological tradition of the West, especially in recent centuries, has paid little obvious attention to ascension theology. The fact remains, however, that

---

[23] *CD* I/1, p.142-3.

[24] *CD* I/1, p.464.

[25] Farrow, Douglas 'Karl Barth on the Ascension: An Appreciation and Critique' *International Journal of Systematic Theology* 2 (2000) p.127. Emphasis original.

this much-neglected doctrine of the creeds receives significant attention from Barth – not in isolation from the rest of his theology, but in a typically interlinked fashion, which yields an equally typical circular exposition.

Barth draws extensively upon his understanding of Jesus as the risen and *ascended* Lord in order to make sense of the form in which His transcendent agency is expressed in the 'time between'. On this basis we will treat Jesus' ascension, and His heavenly session as the outcome of ascension and the description of His ascended state, as more or less one doctrinal theme. Barth's own interest in Jesus' ascension is not in the notion of movement, or perhaps better, in a change in Jesus' location in space, so much as His transcendent *destination* – that Jesus, in His risen humanity, goes to the Father's side and enters the hiddenness of God. It is this location of Jesus in the hidden, 'Godward', side of creation that lends shape to the present age as the age of expectation and revelation.

The fact that ascension and the being of Christ as the *ascended* Lord are somewhat conflated, both in Barth's work and therefore in our own exploration of it, lends a particular shape to our examination of ascension and heavenly session as a theme. The ascension as event is significant in that it initiates the age in which Jesus' transcendent Lordship and agency take a peculiar form – that is, a form shaped by the fact that Christ is ascended and present only mediately in the Holy Spirit, and in such concrete forms as scripture and church proclamation. That Jesus is ascended therefore often functions as a presupposition underlying the particular account Barth gives of Jesus' 'post-history', and the various matters related to that continued existence of Jesus as the ascended Lord. Our exploration of Barth's thought will often involve examination of areas where a particular understanding Christ's current existence as ascended is crucial to the discussion, although only implicit within it.

Many of the important themes of Barth's theology are therefore strongly related to his understanding of the ascension, and of what it means that Jesus is ascended. Not least among these themes are some of the more controversial aspects of his thought, such as the continuing agency of Jesus Christ, pneumatology, ecclesiology, eschatology, and the being of the Christian (including anthropology and the subjectivity of humans in relation to God). Barth is frequently accused of lacking an adequate pneumatology, and of failing to give due space both to human agency in relation to salvation (sanctification), and to the church as God's graced community. So, for instance, the criticisms of Barth levelled by Thomas Torrance and Douglas Farrow, with whom we interact in later chapters, involve the complaint that humanity is devalued in Barth's theology. This is argued to apply firstly in the case of Jesus Himself, yielding the claim that Barth is at least a little *docetic* (that is, downplaying or even ignoring Jesus' humanity), and subsequently therefore that he devalues our own humanity also. Robert Jenson, too, critiques Barth on this point and attempts to put forward a theological programme in which humans and the church play a far greater positive role in the mystery of salvation than Barth will allow.[26] However, what Barth *does* have to say on these matters can be clarified in the process of examining his treatment of the ascension.

As has already been made clear, the breadth of Barth's approach makes his work very rich, but at the same time creates some difficulties for an analysis of the role of any particular doctrinal affirmation, such as that of Jesus' ascension and heavenly session. Furthermore, in order to address the question of the ascension within Barth's thought we cannot strictly (or naïvely) ask what

---

[26] See *Unbaptized God: The basic flaw in ecumenical theology* Minneapolis: Fortress Press, 1992. Moreover, it is to pneumatology that these writers turn in order to explicate a stronger place for human agency in the work of redemption. For a current example see Reinhard Hütter's 'Karl Barth's 'Dialectical Catholicity': Sic et Non' *Modern Theology* 16:2, April 2000, pp.137-57. See also his comparison of Barth and Stanley Hauerwas, *Evangelische Ethik als kirchliches Zeugnis: Interpretationen zu Schlusselfragen theologischerEthik der Gegenwart* Neukirchener, 1993, and 'The ecclesiastical ethics of Stanley Hauerwas: a Lutheran responds' *Dialog* 30 (Summer 1991), pp.231-41. Hütter draws upon Nicholas M. Healy, 'The Logic of Karl Barth's Ecclesiology: Analysis, Assessment and Proposed Modifications' *Modern Theology* 10:3, July 1994, pp.253-70. Healy describes Barth's ecclesiology as 'reductionist' in that the human reality is underplayed, and the Spirit's work bifurcated from the practices of the community. Other accounts of Barth as failing in this regard are offered by, e.g., Colin Gunton in *Christ and Creation* Carlisle: Paternoster Press, 1992, pp.48-51, where a weakness in Barth's treatment of Jesus' human career is claimed to turn upon a lack of attention to the Spirit as the eschatological agent of God's work of perfecting the creation. For a fuller treatment of similar issues worked out in relation to God's threeness and the freedom of His creatures see 'The triune God and the freedom of the creature' in S. W. Sykes ed. *Karl Barth: Centenary Essays* Cambridge: Cambridge University Press, 1989. Gunton offers a more nuanced commentary in 'Salvation' in Webster, John B. ed. *The Cambridge Companion to Karl Barth* Cambridge: Cambridge University Press, 2000, pp.143-58. Interestingly he locates his (moderated) complaint with a glance at Jesus' ascension, claiming that it does not play a significant role within the structure of Barth's thought: 'that the doctrines of the Holy Spirit and the ascension play so little structural part in [Barth's treatment of Christ's threefold office] is a symptom that something somewhere has gone astray'. ('Salvation', p.157). This thesis offers a different reading. R. D. Williams in 'Barth on the Triune God' in S. W. Sykes *Karl Barth: Studies of his Theological Method* Oxford: Clarendon Press, 1979, also offers a certain level of complaint regarding Barth's failure to become a genuinely incarnational theologian. This is drawn largely from the significant work of Gustaf Wingren, *Theology in Conflict: Nygren, Barth, Bultmann* trans. Eric H. Wahlstrom, Edinburgh: Oliver and Boyd, 1958. Interestingly in relation to our later interaction with Torrance and Farrow, Wingren's own early work was on Irenaeus' theology of the incarnation. A related criticism is made by A. E. McGrath, who claims that Barth's emphasis on revelation displays his lack of interest in soteriology, and thus a lack of interest in sinful humanity. See *Iustitia Dei: volume II, from 1500 to the present day* Cambridge: Cambridge University Press, 1986, pp. 170-84, especially pp.179ff. For a very brief response see Trevor Hart's essay 'Revelation' in Webster, John B. ed. *The Cambridge Companion to Karl Barth* Cambridge: Cambridge University Press, 2000, pp.37-56, especially pp.53-4.

difference this doctrine makes – that would involve speculation as to the shape of Barth's theology if he had chosen for some reason not to affirm the doctrine of Christ's ascension, and such speculation would finally be empty of genuine content. We cannot know what Barth would have thought if he had maintained something different from what he actually did. However, we can ask what function his description of Jesus as ascended does actually have, what influence or control it does concretely exercise. Further, we can examine the particular way in which Barth understands Jesus' ascension and how that understanding functions within his thought, recognising that certain other ways of understanding Jesus' 'location' and existence in the present age would necessarily involve very different convictions in related doctrines.

In particular the ascension informs a dynamic of *presence* and *absence* – Jesus Christ's coincident presence and absence during 'this time between', as the church and individual Christians occupy the space created for them by the 'unnatural' delay of the *eschaton*. This dynamic runs throughout Barth's theology, as he attempts to maintain a radical faithfulness to Jesus Christ, and to take Jesus seriously as the fully effective reconciliation of God with humanity. Barth finds in Jesus Christ the full presence of God with humanity, *and* of true humanity with God. Reconciliation in the person of Jesus originates in God, but nonetheless creates, calls forth and empowers a genuine, transformed, humanity. Barth was deeply concerned to be able to speak of the subjective human reality of reconciliation[27] (although an absence of this subjective realisation has often been the substance of complaint against Barth), and the understanding of Jesus Christ's risen and ascended agency which Barth develops is key to understanding the nature of human freedom and agency within the economy of salvation for both church and Christian.

Against a commonly held view of Barth as lacking adequate pneumatology, Philip Rosato offers a strong argument that he is a genuinely pneumatic theologian.[28] Rosato believes that throughout his career Barth is in fact deeply concerned with how we may say 'God' and 'humanity' together – Barth is undoubtedly a christocentric theologian, but precisely in his christocentrism he finds the resources to place *humanity with God* at the centre of his theology. It can be argued that Barth is occupied with the need to speak theologically about the subjective human pole of reconciliation. Thus Rosato sees Barth's life-long interaction with Schleiermacher, and his debates with Bultmann on the one hand and Roman Catholic theology on the other, as

---

[27] See Rosato, Philip J. (S.J.) *The Spirit as Lord: The Pneumatology of Karl Barth* Edinburgh: T&T Clark, 1981, especially pp.3-17. See also Thompson, John *The Holy Spirit in the Theology of Karl Barth* Allison Park, Pennsylvania: Pickwick Publications, 1991. Thompson takes issue with certain of Rosato's conclusions, in particular where Rosato seeks to press beyond Barth, but he is nonetheless in substantial agreement with Rosato's exposition of Barth's pneumatology.

[28] This is in no way to ignore the fact that Rosato finds Barth's pneumatology finally dissatisfying. His proposal is to gain ground by coordinating Word and Spirit Christologies, where he feels Barth's is too Word focussed.

turning upon questions of pneumatology. At the centre lies the necessary mediation between the objectivity of Christ's victory and its subjective realisation in the Christian.[29] Humanity with God is found in the being of Jesus Christ, who is ascended, and it is this humanity which is mediated to, and realised in, the Christian. But how? Barth, according to Rosato, finds his answer to this problem in a thoroughly christological pneumatology – and this, we will argue, is radically dependent upon the particular shape of Barth's acknowledgement of the ascension.

Argument for this emphasis upon the subjective human pole of reconciliation in Christ finds corroboration in the developing redescription of Barth's interest in ethics. Against another commonly held view of Barth, John Webster has urged that 'ethics was not a late discovery for Barth, nor did it involve him in retracting any of his major theological convictions: it was ingredient in those convictions from the first'.[30] Thus, for example, the fragment of the *Church Dogmatics* on the ethics of reconciliation (volume IV/4) and the posthumous material published as *The Christian Life*[31] 'showed – as perhaps no other section of the *Dogmatics* shows – how ethical concerns take us to the centre of what Barth is trying to do in his *magnum opus*'.[32] Humanity *is* taken seriously, and human agency is a key concern of Barth's entire theological project.[33] God is at work *creating*, not suppressing, human agency.

> We remember that it is due only to the free grace of God that as there can be
> dealings with God at all, so there can be the special dealings between God and

---

[29] For Barth's treatment of many of these issues see his *Protestant Theology in the Nineteenth Century: Its Background and History* London: SCM Press, 1972, especially pp.459ff. Barth views Roman Catholicism (or much thereof), Neo-Protestantism, and Rudolf Bultmann as all failing to adequately maintain the distinction between justification and sanctification.

> Sanctification is not justification. If we do not take care not to confuse and confound, soteriology may suffer, allowing justification (as in the case of much Roman Catholicism in its following of Augustine, but also of many varieties of Neo-Protestantism) to merge into the process of his sanctification initiated by the act of the forgiveness of sins, or by allowing faith in Jesus Christ as the Judge judged in our place (this is in my view the most serious objection to the theology of R. Bultmann) to merge into the obedience in which the Christian in his discipleship has to die to the world and to himself. *CD* IV/2, p.504.

[30] Webster, John *Barth's Moral Theology: Human Action in Barth's Thought* Edinburgh: T&T Clark, 1998, p.3.

[31] Barth, Karl *The Christian Life: CD* IV/4. *Lecture Fragments* Edinburgh: T&T Clark, 1981. See also the lectures collected as *The Holy Spirit and the Christian Life: The Theological Basis of Ethics* Louisville, Kentucky: John Knox Press, 1993.

[32] Webster, John *Barth's Moral Theology*, p.2.

[33] While remaining critical of Barth's 'command' ethics, Nigel Biggar still notes that 'Barth himself engaged in a systematic form of ethical deliberation about right conduct'. (*The Hastening that Waits: Karl Barth's Ethics* Oxford: Clarendon Press, 1993, p.25.)

[God's people], the history of their encounter, the concrete intercourse and exchange between them, a living relation in which not only God acts but these specific people may and should be truly active as well. The grace of God is the liberation of these specific people for free, spontaneous, and responsible cooperation in this history.[34]

Barth's desire to do justice to the reality of free, responsible humanity with and before God requires his affirmation of Jesus Christ's resurrection *and* ascension: both the positive affirmation of the being of the new humanity, and the limits that must be placed and hedged about that affirmation are explicable in terms of a pneumatology and ecclesiology founded upon and shaped by a strong doctrine of ascension. The dialectic of presence and absence provides the framework in which it is possible for Barth to attempt a biblical and thorough-going analysis of what it means to be those who belong to Jesus Christ and who exist as the first-fruit of His on-going *parousia*.

Note on the Sources of Material

The approach undertaken in Part I of this book is therefore primarily expository. Our focus is on primary texts, especially the *Church Dogmatics*. However, indications of key points, and significant emphases may be found in other published writings. In looking at Jesus' ascension and Jesus' ascended life in Barth's thought there are two aspects to the task. Firstly, there is the essential matter of Barth's explicit statements regarding Jesus as ascended and the event of His ascension. This material gives shape to the investigation as a whole, and without it any discussion of the role Jesus' ascended being plays within Barth's theology would remain highly speculative. But secondly, there is also the task of attempting to trace, and demonstrate the existence of, the influence of Christ ascended upon areas of Barth's thought where explicit reference to ascension or heavenly session are either rare or lacking. As it is worked out below, the investigation of Jesus' ascended being as important for Barth bears fruit, and large blocks of material from the *Church Dogmatics* could be usefully explored. However, rather than attempt to treat *every* section of the *Dogmatics* that has the potential to yield links to Jesus' heavenly existence, the material is utilised more selectively. Rather than consistently surveying large tracts of Barth's writing an attempt is made to focus more closely on certain sections. Thus for instance a (more) detailed examination of *Church Dogmatics* I/2 section 18, 'The Life of the Children of God', occupies a chapter to itself, while the material on Jesus' time and earthly time in interrelation found in volume III/4 receives no specific treatment at all,[35] and other sections which contain reference to Jesus as ascended also receive a less detailed inspection.

---

[34] Barth, Karl *The Christian Life*, p.102.

[35] This is, at least in part, because the material in *CD* III/4 provides little that is new compared to the discussion of time in I/2 and III/2, on which we do focus.

It is important to note that volume IV of the *Church Dogmatics* contains a great deal of material related to Jesus' *exaltation*, which initially looks likely to yield rich material relating to Jesus' ascension. However, while it is true that volume IV does contain significant material relation to Jesus' ascension, two considerations limit the attention given that material in this thesis. Firstly, as explicated below, Barth does not strictly align Jesus' ascension and exaltation: the ascension is not the event in which Jesus is exalted, but is rather the revelation of His exalted glory as the Son of God in union with the Son of Man. Secondly, the emphasis of volume IV is more clearly upon Jesus' heavenly session, and while glancing treatments of some issues related to Jesus' session will be offered, the centre of our concern is the dynamic of Jesus' presence and absence, rather than His heavenly reign *per se*. It is for this reason that the key material examined in relation to Barth's ecclesiology comes from *Church Dogmatics* I/2 with support from material drawn from volume IV, rather than the other way around. Nonetheless, the claim of this work is that by addressing the material that it does, and by varying the focus from a wide view to a closer examination, and back again, what is uncovered is representative of Barth's work as a whole.

Summary

This chapter has involved a 'ground-clearing' exercise prior to the introduction of Barth's doctrine of the ascension proper in Chapter Two. However, to draw the parts of this chapter together, before moving onward, a central theme is the fact that Jesus' ascension and His ascended life cannot be isolated out from the complex of doctrinal material which shapes Barth's work as a whole. Jesus' transcendence, the matters of His agency, the nature of the 'time between', revelation and eschatology, are all keys to the work that we undertake.

Thus, once again, we note that although Barth does have an explicit theology of the ascension, as we seek to trace out the impact of that theology within his thought as a whole we may often consider that Jesus' being as ascended is *presupposed* as much as named. Jesus' presence and absence provide a significant theme in Barth's vision of the present age. A key aspect of our investigation will therefore be the relation between the present age as the 'time between' and Jesus' ascension and session as the origin of that age. Theology that is itself worship of Jesus Christ, and which seeks to serve Christ's people as they worship Him, is necessarily concerned with Jesus' action and lordship as expressed in the current age. It is this that will dominate the following chapters, as Barth's witness to Jesus is unpacked in relation to Jesus' ascension to the Father's side.

Chapter 2

The Doctrine of the Ascension

Introduction

Given the shape of Barth's theology, as outlined in Chapter One, what does he think Jesus' ascension is about? That is, what does Barth think Jesus' ascension achieves, for Jesus and for us, and what influence does the ascension have on Barth's thought? These are the questions which most immediately require answer. The purpose of this chapter is to investigate Barth's understanding of Jesus' ascension, with its outcome in the heavenly session, and to introduce the ways in which this understanding is worked out in relation to other doctrines. Moving from the nature of Jesus' ascension as an event within His history, and the nature of His destination in the heavenly session, we will investigate further Barth's rejection of ascension as Jesus' glorification – and then examine the function that he does ascribe to it. Jesus' ascension is understood in relation to His *parousia*, that is, in relation to Jesus' coming, both at the end of the age, and during this age in the presence of the Holy Spirit. The dynamic of His presence and absence expresses the way in which this *parousia* is worked out in the current time, the 'time between'. So, finally, the Holy Spirit is identified as the agent of Christ's coming between the times, as He remains somewhat absent until the *eschaton*.

As a result of this we may see Jesus' ascension and heavenly session as key to Barth's vision of the present age as the 'time between'. Flowing out of the initial treatment of material explicitly relating to Jesus' ascended being, much of this chapter involves identifying ways in which the ascension and heavenly session *implicitly* inform Barth's understanding of Jesus' 'post-history' (His history beyond cross and resurrection). That Jesus is ascended may sometimes therefore appear as something like a presupposition in Barth's thought, and it is in this fashion that we will attempt to uncover its role. It is as just such a presupposition that Barth views the function of Jesus' ascension within the New Testament Epistles, for instance. In Barth's view the authors give very little direct attention to either the empty tomb, or the event of Jesus' ascension, but nonetheless presuppose the concrete reality of these signs to His being as our risen and ascended Reconciliation with God.[1] Barth's own theology of the ascension might be described in a similar vein: he gives the ascension only moderate amounts of direct attention, but if we take out the ascension then a significant aspect of his thought becomes lacking and the whole ceases to make

---

[1] See *CD* III/2, pp.452-3.

sense, just as the New Testament faith ceases to function if Jesus is no longer seen as risen and ascended. By investigating Barth's ascension thought we may hope to understand more of the role faith in Jesus as ascended should have in our own thought.

We will therefore move from Barth's explicit treatment of the ascension, and the New Testament ascension texts, and on into the role of the ascension as a presupposition and formative belief. In so doing we intend to uncover the significance and function of Jesus' ascension and ascended life, and also prepare the ground for the more detailed examination of the relation between these realities and Barth's accounts of the church and of the Christian in the 'time between' which will occupy chapters three and four.

The Ascension as Concrete 'Event'

How does Barth approach the New Testament witness to Jesus as ascended? Barth rejects any 'demythologisation' of the ascension – that is, the ascension cannot be reduced to a symbolic story or exemplary narrative. As explicated below, the ascension is a genuine event in the history of the man Jesus of Nazareth, and as such it is full of import for the Gospel of God's activity in Him. The New Testament witnesses record the empty tomb and the ascension as the poles of the Easter event – that is, of the forty days – and they are essential parts of their story,[2] in that they as the boundaries of the Easter event itself they cannot be discarded without seriously damaging the description of that event. However the New Testament testimony to these aspects of the story is limited and circumspect. Direct reference to both is somewhat vague, and even contradictory in detail, but this does not mean that they are to be disregarded – instead they are understood to function as signs of Jesus as the Resurrected, as we will explore below.

> The content of the Easter witness, the Easter event, was not that the disciples found the tomb empty or that they saw Him go up to heaven, but that when they had lost Him through death they were sought and found by Him as the Resurrected. The empty tomb and the ascension are merely signs of the Easter event ... Yet both signs are so important that we can hardly say that they might equally well be omitted.[3]

We may note that this attitude to both ascension and empty tomb as historical realities is not dependent upon a denial of the difficulties the texts offer an historical-critical approach. Barth is even prepared to describe the New Testament accounts of both as 'legend',[4] but care must be taken to understand his use of terms such as 'saga' and 'legend' in relation to the

---

[2] For Barth's fullest treatment of Jesus' ascension as an event see *CD* III/2, pp.451ff.
[3] *CD* III/2, p.453.
[4] See *CD* III/2, p.453.

biblical material. These terms are used to avoid the claim of 'history' as modernity understands historical writing, but this does not mean that Barth is denying concrete reality to the matters described. Barth sees it as *appropriate* that the New Testament descriptions of the events of Jesus' resurrection and ascension are somewhat vague, so that a historian must find them troubling, for they refer us to an event which is beyond historical research and description. The reason for this is that as events they are not the content of the witness *per se*, but rather function as signs of the Resurrected. The risen Jesus Christ is the content of the witness, and the empty tomb and ascension are signs which point to Him. If the witness to the ascension is weak, according to the canons of modern historical research, its strength lies in the self-attestation of the risen Lord, and the weakness is no impediment to the work of the sign in the hands of the Signified. That is: it is as Jesus acts to reveal Himself as the One who is ascended that the ascension event points to Him, and therefore it is His ability to reveal himself that underpins acceptance of the event as a corollary of faith in him as the ascended Lord.[5] Thus, as below, when Barth shows a lack of interest in the ascension as 'literal event', at least in the sense of 'space travel', he still maintains that Jesus was taken from the disciples sight 'before their eyes'.[6]

How then does the ascension function as a 'sign'? What is the shape it lends to the message of Easter? 'As the empty tomb looks downwards, the ascension looks upwards' – it 'points forwards and upwards, thus serving a positive function'.[7] Yet the intention is not spatial: Jesus goes into heaven, but heaven is not a realm of the sky. Rather heaven is the inaccessible realm of God's immediate presence to and within creation – inaccessible and even incomprehensible to humans because of our fallen condition. As the 'throne of God' heaven is opened up to human 'sight' only from within, that is, this creaturely realm of God's glory is only disclosed by God. Thus the point of the ascension is not spatial, but that Jesus was taken from sight and entered this inaccessible place of God the Father's immediate presence.[8] The issue is thus the (transcendent or eschatological) *destination* rather than the mode of 'travel'. The man Jesus, risen beyond death, goes to the right hand of the Father, revealed in His divinity, but not in such a manner that He ceases to be human – a creature like us. Rather, He is revealed as the creature – the man – who is also God, belonging with and acting in concert with, the Father, and belonging thus within the God-ward realm of creation which we call heaven.

Against docetic or 'demythologised' readings of Jesus' resurrection and ascension Barth insists upon the risen humanity of the Son as He ascends to the throne of God. The resurrection is of Jesus the man of Nazareth, and the reality of this event includes its 'physicality'. Jesus 'physically' rose, and so the

---

[5] See *CD* III/2, p.453.

[6] For more on 'saga' and 'legend', especially in contrast to 'myth', in the biblical material see *CD* I/1, pp.327-9.

[7] *CD* III/2, p.453.

[8] *CD* III/2, pp.453-4.

tomb is found to be empty, and thus He also departs 'physically' in the event of the ascension. The forty days – the extended Easter event, the revelation of God in Jesus Christ – are marked out in concrete particularity by their beginning in the empty tomb and their end in the ascension. Jesus' risen humanity is fully established, and He is revealed as the *divine* man in that from henceforth He is to be understood as God acting and working among His people – a revelation with full retroactive force.

Along these lines Jesus' disappearance into the cloud speaks of an absence that yields a new form of His presence – the 'whence' of Jesus' going speaks of revelation and *parousia*. Barth holds that in biblical language and imagery the cloud speaks of the hidden *presence* of God, and indeed of revelation penetrating hiddenness. Thus, the cloud signifies not merely a departure into a closed heaven, but rather a departure which initiates a new form of coming, of *parousia*. Heaven is not simply closed, but is open from God's side! The ascension is not, therefore, simply a farewell, but a revelation of Jesus as the Coming One and a sign of the *parousia*, pointing to His return out of all concealment and on the clouds of heaven.

Jesus therefore is to be sought and understood as this One, the One whose hiddenness is 'the hiddenness of God', and the hiddenness of God is to be understood 'in such a way as to suggest that it burgeons with the conclusive revelation still awaited in the future'.[9] Jesus is the One who belongs at the right hand of the Father, the One in whom God has taken flesh and made the whole creation anew, the One who comes now to make people new and the One who will return in all glory and power bringing the fulfilment of all time. The ascension is the sign of this Jesus. 'As this sign, the ascension is indispensable, and it would be injudicious as well as ungrateful on any grounds to ignore or reject this upward and forward-looking sign'.[10]

But, affirming the concrete reality of the ascension does not lead Barth to consider his work done at the point where such avowal is offered – he does not simply say that Jesus ascended and stop there, so that having established Jesus as the ascended One he may now forget about it. Rather faith in Jesus as ascended is required to play its part in the complex of doctrinal work which goes into the practice of dogmatics. Thus, the whole shape of Barth's doctrinal work, especially as it relates to the nature of the present age, is penetrated, at least implicitly, by the reality of Jesus' *ascended* lordship. Barth's concern, quite rightly, is to pursue dogmatics in such a fashion that who Jesus is, and what Jesus is doing, is always to the fore. It is the reality of God in Christ that is determinative for dogmatics – whether the discussion is of the incarnation, with obvious focus upon Christ, or of the present age of the world, which might be analysed according to the canons of all sorts of disciplines. As the Son of God united with the Son of Man, Jesus Christ is the absolute measure of all creaturely reality, and moreover, as the Saviour of the world,

---

[9] *CD* III/2, p.454.
[10] *CD* III/2, p.454.

what He is and does in the present is absolutely determinative of that present. So it is that the doctrine of Jesus' ascension works in partnership with other doctrines to determine the topography of the territory Barth explores – the import Jesus' ascension cannot be understood in isolation from the incarnation, or the cross, or indeed the resurrection. Equally, the application of these doctrines, especially in relation to the present age of the world, also relies upon the doctrine of the ascension, as the ascension helps describe the relationship between Jesus and the world we live in. This broader role of Jesus' ascended being is the matter to which we now turn, beginning with the ascension and heavenly session understood within Barth's chalcedonian approach to Jesus' incarnate being.

Chalcedonian Descent and Ascent

Christian theology has usually recognised two movements in the history of Jesus Christ: a descending movement attributed to God, located in the incarnation, and with reference to the cross; and a subsequent ascending movement of the human, located in Jesus' resurrection and/or ascension. The two movements have therefore tended to be divided temporally, and seen sequentially. Exaltation follows humiliation, as ascension follows incarnation, or as resurrection follows crucifixion. Thus, where it has been recognised, the doctrine of the ascension has often been seen as describing the return of Jesus full circle – having descended from the Father in humiliation, and borne humiliation *for a time*, He returns in exaltation to take up His place again. But Jesus does not return altogether unaltered: according to the different emphases of various theologians, Jesus' own exalted humanity is described more or less strongly as an exaltation of our humanity, and the Christian life as more or less a matter of sharing in the exaltation of the Son. [11] Barth, however, diverges strongly from the tradition at this point. The reasons for this have a great deal to do with the theology of the incarnation, and in particular Barth's strong adoption of the creed of Chalcedon.

Chalcedon affirmed that Jesus was fully God and fully human while yet being one person. The creed denied any attempts to describe Jesus' deity as attached to one part of His being – such as His mind alone – and His humanity to another – such as His body alone. But the creed also denied any attempt to describe deity and humanity as somehow 'mixed'. The way in which Barth adopts this creed into his own thought leads to a distinct reading of Jesus'

---

[11] Farrow identifies this with a strong tendency toward dualist Christologies, which are apt to emphasise the ascent of the mind, and pay less heed to Jesus' bodily ascension. (See *Ascension*, pp.89ff.) Farrow's account does appear a little tendentious however, characterising Irenaeus as the saviour of patristic theology, and Origen as the source of all evils that follow. Kierkegaard and Barth are then seen as, at least partial, redeemers of the situation. See Chapter 7 below.

exaltation and humiliation, and this in turn has considerable bearing on his ascension theology.

Barth adopts a very strong descent/ascent schema in his Christology, and Parts I and II of the fourth volume of the *Church Dogmatics* develop in considerable depth the themes of humiliation and exaltation respectively. Furthermore, Barth assigns descent to Jesus Christ as God, and ascent to Him as human, although the way he works these themes out diverges from other treatments such as Milligan's[12] – especially in his description of humiliation as a proper characteristic of deity, as explored below. There is no descent proper to the Son of Man, humanity already occupies the low place into which Jesus Christ descends in His being as Son of God. Fallen and sinful humanity, as rebellious against God, belongs in the place of rejection by God, and of death. Occupying this place is not a humiliation for sinful flesh, it is simply a matter of taking its rightful position. This is not to say that Jesus does not undergo a career of suffering, or that He does not descend from God in humiliation. What is claimed is that Jesus' descent is proper to His divinity – it is not as human that He is humiliated but as divine. The Son of God is humiliated in becoming united with sinful flesh, but the Son of man *is* sinful flesh.[13] Equally, Jesus Christ as Son of God is in no need of ascent, but as Son of Man it belongs to Him to ascend. 'As the Son of God He did not need to be exalted. In fact, He could not be exalted'.[14] But, saying this we immediately encounter the significant way in which Barth reworks the descent/ascent schema. For Barth the themes of descent and ascent as applied to the history of Jesus Christ have somewhat less to do with spatial categories, and far more to do with His very being in the incarnation. Descent and ascent belong with chalcedonian doctrine, and are present *throughout* the ministry of the One who is at once Son of Man and Son of God. It is precisely in assuming human nature that the Son of God descends – a *humiliation* that finds its *telos* and its full depth upon the cross – and it is the same adoption of human nature by the Son of God in which the Son of Man is *exalted*, and upon the same cross that this exaltation reaches its peak. In this treatment of descent and ascent Barth claims to have

> ... done justice to the doctrine of the humiliation and exaltation of Jesus Christ, not as a description of two different states, but to denote two opposed but strictly

---

[12] See Milligan, William *The Ascension of Our Lord* London: Macmillan, 1894, especially pp.151ff.

[13] It is not that Barth is assigning different aspects of Jesus' career to His humanity and divinity respectively – in fact Barth resists this strenuously. This is what is at issue when Barth holds together exaltation and humiliation as the two sides of one event, or of one history. Exaltation and humiliation occur together in the one history of Jesus, the Son of God in union with the Son of Man.

[14] *CD* IV/2, p.150.

related moments in that history which operate together and mutually interpret one another.[15]

But what does this say of the *event* of ascension that, in the biblical narrative, follows resurrection? While affirming an historical ascension, Barth refuses all senses in which this event might be seen as achieving something new for the being and identity of Jesus Christ – He does not achieve a new status, or reappropriate a significance previously renounced. Indeed, Barth is committed to the 'Calvinistic extra', as one aspect of his maintenance of the Lordship, priority, and agency of God in the incarnation.[16] According to this view, the divinity of the Son of God cannot be viewed as *reduced* or *limited* to His humanity – Jesus' divinity must be regarded as *extra* (beyond) as well as *intra* (within) His humanity. This is to say that Jesus' humanity is not a vessel for His deity. The two are united, but the one is not contained within the other – Jesus remains the Lord of all creation, even as He is a creature within that creation.

Barth is undoubtedly aware of the danger here – that we may speculate about the *logos asarkos* (the Son of God apart from the incarnation) or even another God behind the God present and incarnate in Jesus Christ, something he is utterly against. However, Barth does want to maintain the *full* divinity of the Incarnate One, and the agency of *God* throughout. Reconciliation is not the result of some equal partnership, or cooperation between Creator and creature, nor is it the realisation of some human potential for divinisation. The incarnation as a whole is a free act of the sovereign Lord – we must say; 'the Word became flesh', but we cannot and must not say; 'the flesh became Word'.[17]

God remains God even in His humiliation. The divine being does not suffer any change, any diminution, any transformation into something else, any admixture

---

[15] *CD* IV/2, p.106.

[16] Barth offers a discussion of the *extra Calvinisticum* and related incarnational theology in section 15.2 'Very God and Very Man', *CD* I/2, see pp.163ff and especially pp.168-71. Barth is sympathetic to the Reformed position, over the Lutheran, but acknowledges that the Reformed 'failed to show convincingly how far the *extra* does not involve the assumption of a twofold Christ, of a λόγος ἔνσαρκος alongside a λόγος ἄσαρκος, and therefore a dissolution of the unity of the natures and hypostatic union, and therefore a destruction of the unequivocal Emmanuel and the certainty of faith and salvation based thereon' (*Ibid* p.170). Barth's final decision is that the Reformed position puts the matter of the Incarnation more strongly than the Lutheran, and indeed provides a proper basis for the Lutheran emphasis upon the full presence of the Word in flesh – Barth's claim is in fact that only the Reformed position allows this. If one allows that Jesus' flesh is a 'vessel' containing the infinity of God then the genuineness of His humanity is laid open to question, and thus the Word's presence in the flesh is lost. Thus Reformed theologians must maintain the *extra* but also work harder to avoid the suspicion of a 'twofold Christ'.

[17] *CD* IV/1, p.179.

with something else, let alone any cessation. Any subtraction or weakening of it [Christ's divinity] would at once throw doubt upon the atonement made in Him.[18]

Issues to do with the incarnation of the Son of God are very much to the fore, and Barth is attempting to maintain the absolute reality of incarnation: the full and undiluted divinity, but also the genuine and complete humanity of Jesus of Nazareth. In speaking of a divine *extra*, he will not allow any limitation of God's full presence in Jesus Christ – indeed, the reverse. Jesus Christ is fully human, yet more than *just* human. The presence of the fullness of God in Christ – which necessarily includes and gathers up, but also *transcends* His humanity – reveals the true nature of God as the One who truly becomes the servant. Thus we recognise that the '*forma dei* consists in the grace in which God Himself assumes and makes His own the *forma servi*'.[19] It belongs to God's being that God can do this – in fact, humility is thereby revealed as the very nature of God's own character.

So for Barth, it belongs to the true *divinity* of Jesus Christ that He is also truly human – not because God must become human, but because God freely elects to become humiliated in order to exalt the creature. This is the God we encounter in the man Jesus, and there can be no other God in the background. In adopting our flesh, God is not reduced to our flesh, but nonetheless does truly adopt it. Sinful humanity stands in utter contradiction before God, and yet it is in the likeness, the form of flesh opposed to God that the Son of God is to be found. Can God thus be seen as in opposition to God? No, for in taking flesh the Son of God remains Lord (*extra*!) in reconciliation. Rather than make common cause with human contradiction before God, He destroys it. 'He acts as Lord over this contradiction even as He subjects Himself to it'.[20] It is *because* the Son of God is not reduced to sinful humanity that He is able to redeem it – as Lord He adopts sinful flesh in order to turn it back to the Father.

Barth's chalcedonian Christology will permit no breach between the divinity and humanity of the Reconciler, but also no confusion. Thus the man Jesus of Nazareth *is* the very presence of the eternal God, God with us, and at exactly the same time the presence of genuine humanity with, and in union with the eternal God. Resurrection and ascension cannot and must not be seen as altering the being of the Reconciler, via some sort of deification, or exaltation *additional* to the divinity and exaltation already present in the Crucified One. So, although the first two part volumes of *Church Dogmatics* IV deal with Jesus Christ as the humiliated and exalted Lord respectively, there is no sense in which the two aspects are seen as belonging to different periods of Jesus' history. Indeed, in the third part volume when Barth turns to a treatment of the themes raised by the unity of humiliation and exaltation he gives these themes – indeed the unity itself – logical priority. The third theme provides the only ground from which to approach and understand the first two.

---

[18] *CD* IV/1, p.179.
[19] *CD* IV/1, p.188.
[20] *CD* IV/1, p.185.

In this third volume Barth discusses the being and action of the Reconciler in terms of 'witness', and gathers up all that has been involved in parts one and two. Everything turns upon the interconnection of exaltation and humiliation, so that the exaltation is already fulfilled in and through humiliation, and equally so that the exaltation includes humiliation within itself, 'so that Jesus Christ is already exalted in His humiliation and humiliated in His exaltation'.[21] Jesus Christ as True Witness is the revealer of both the 'No' and the 'Yes' of God to humanity, and as the risen and ascended One He reveals that God's 'No' is the servant of His 'Yes'. This is to say, we are shown that reconciliation has been achieved in Jesus Christ – He is the Judge judged in our place, so that God's being toward us can become the Word of our lives.

Farrow describes the content of these three part volumes in vector, or directional, terms: they 'expound two vertical movements, descent and ascent, as the material content of the doctrine of reconciliation, and a third lateral movement, witness, as its formal content'.[22] However, this description hardens a set of distinctions that Barth attempts to keep more flexible, and divides too much what is intended to be interpenetrating. William Stacy Johnson is a better guide when he describes the third theme – Jesus Christ as True Witness, in His prophetic office – as the climax of the other two, but not in terms of a sequence, nor even as a third theme which is strictly other than the first two. The third theme is the *unity* of the first two, in which each always accompanies and informs the other.

> Jesus not only embodies true divinity and true humanity, but he makes these realities known in their togetherness. This third theme forms the climax of Barth's presentation of reconciliation ... The third aspect is not a third in sequence, for Barth spoke of the third theme explicitly as solidifying a union: it forms a mediating or intervening link between the first two.[23]

This explanation fits very well with Barth's own summary of the matter.

> The third christological aspect [Jesus Christ as the True Witness] ... is at once the simplest and the highest. It is the source of the two first, and it comprehends them both. As the God who humbles Himself and therefore reconciles man with Himself, and as the man exalted by God and therefore reconciled with Him, as the One who is very God and very man in this concrete sense, Jesus Christ Himself is one.[24]

This understanding of the history of Jesus Christ's humiliation and exaltation from a centre in their unity, yet without confusion of their difference (in

---

[21] *CD* IV/1, p.110.

[22] Farrow *Karl Barth on the Ascension*, p.128. What exactly the terms *material* and *formal* mean in this context is unclear.

[23] Johnson, William Stacy *The Mystery of God: Karl Barth and the Postmodern Foundations of Theology* Louisville, Kentucky: Westminster John Knox Press, 1997, p.112.

[24] *CD* IV/1, p.135.

parallel with the two natures of Jesus Christ Himself), informs Barth's understanding of every event and passage of this history – including the event of ascension.

The ascension finds its goal in the revelation of the unity of God and humanity, exaltation and humiliation, *which was always present* in Jesus Christ, although previously veiled. This revelation culminates in the presence of the God-Man with the Father: *sedet ad dexteram Dei Patris* (seated at the right hand of God the Father). This is the terminus and goal of the history of revelation that moves from resurrection to ascension, the forty days, and thus marks a new point in the history of the Saviour, but not a deification of the human, or a recovery of a previously abandoned glory. The glory of God remained present, yet profoundly veiled, throughout the career of humiliation and exaltation Jesus Christ undertook. As the Son of God His ascension cannot mean His deification – this is cannot be a requirement for Jesus as Son of God, and is surely impossible for Him as Son of Man. Instead what we see in the ascension is the placement of Jesus as *human* as the right hand of the Father, in full fellowship and participation.[25]

Barth in fact gives the entire post-resurrection history the character of revelation and is able to call every part of this history '*parousia*' – that is, Jesus' coming – from and including the resurrection, right up to and including the *eschaton*. This *parousia*, or coming, occurs primarily in three parts: resurrection and ascension, the (continued) coming of the Holy Spirit, and Jesus' awaited return at the *eschaton*. As such, the resurrection and ascension are two moments of one occurrence, with which the *parousia* may be said to begin. 'The resurrection and ascension of Jesus Christ are two distinct but inseparable moments in one and the same event'.[26] What is revealed in this event is that in this man Jesus Christ we have in fact to do with the eternal God – a fact utterly impenetrable to human eyes, especially as this man seemingly ends His career upon a cross, abandoned by God. Resurrection and ascension reveal a reality that is deeper than human apprehension of it allows – that God is here, reconciling and redeeming the world.[27] 'It is revealed and knowable even to human eyes in the event which terminates with the ascension, so that from this side too [i.e. of human perception] it is the exaltation of this man, and positively to the side of God, and fellowship in His work'.[28] That this particular human being has now gone to the place that is the source of all

---

[25] *CD* IV/2, p.153.

[26] *CD* IV/2, p.150.

[27] Of course, revelation is a key theme of Barth's whole theology, and to a certain degree he sees revelation occurring in the pre-Easter history. In this sense resurrection and ascension can be understood acting *retrospectively*. So, for instance, Barth regards the transfiguration as a glimpse, ahead of time, of the glory only later to be revealed in resurrection and ascension. See *CD* III/2, p.478.

[28] *CD* IV/2, p.154.

power, dominion, grace and love, 'is the hidden thing which is revealed in the ascension of Jesus Christ'.[29]

What then can be said of the relationship between the ascension and the continuing history of God's creation, bearing in mind the redemption of all creation that Barth sees Christ having achieved in His pre-resurrection history? Jesus' session, or rule and work, at the right hand of God describes a role and a function. It in no way implies a cessation of activity on Jesus' part. 'Rather it describes the continuance, the permanence of this function'.[30] So, for instance, Jesus continues to intercede (stand in) for us before God, and to represent God to us, in exactly the same way that He did upon the cross – the cross is the basis of all Jesus continues to do, and what He does is the effective work of reconciliation. 'It was His conducting of God's case with us sinners that brought Him to the cross, and His conducting of our sinner's case with God is the eternal effect, the victorious result of His suffering and death'.[31]

What is more, this event of His going 'to the Father's side' forms the origin of the community of Jesus Christ, and provides its ongoing impetus. Wherever, and whenever, there is knowledge of Jesus Christ there is knowledge of His homecoming as the Son of Man in the way of the Son of God into the 'far country', and this is revealed in the resurrection and ascension of Jesus. As we shall explore in Chapter Three, the being of the church turns very much upon the agency and activity of the ascended Lord, and upon the reality of redemption which Christ is pouring out in His Spirit. The question of the reality of the church must receive a pneumatological answer, and that answer must in turn be predicated upon the ascension of Jesus Christ as the basis of His ongoing work in sending His Spirit, and in uniting human beings to himself as His earthly-historical body.[32] Indeed, the entire reality of subjective justification (that is, the human side of justification, in the reception of transforming revelation) is predicated upon the activity of Jesus in His heavenly session, and worked out within the dynamic of His presence and absence.

> The reason, and the only reason, why man can receive revelation in the Holy Spirit is that God's Word is brought to his hearing in the Holy Spirit. ... Therefore in relation to revelation all capacity is concretely the capacity of the Word, the capacity of Jesus Christ. ... Jesus Christ creates the fact that we believe in Jesus Christ. Up there with him it is possible for it to be possible down here with me.[33]

Thus, to make further sense of the way in which the events of Jesus' past history have force in our ongoing history we must return to the unity of resurrection and ascension with the coming of the Spirit, and the *eschaton*.

---

[29] *CD* IV/2, p.154.
[30] Karl Barth *Credo* London: Hodder and Stoughton, 1964, p.106.
[31] *CD* I/2, p.113.
[32] *CD* I/2, p.221.
[33] *CD* I/2, p.247.

Ascension and the Present Age of the World

As we have seen, Barth understands Jesus Christ's *parousia* as a threefold coming – resurrection and ascension, the 'promise' of the Spirit,[34] and His final *eschaton*. As such, these three forms of Christ's coming are all forms of His being and self-revelation toward, in, and for the world. These stages of Jesus Christ's *parousia* mark out, and indeed create, specific periods in the post-Easter history of the creation and its redemption. The resurrection marks the beginning of the revelation of the Son of Man as the glorious Son of God, as above. The ascension, as the terminus of the forty days, marks the end of the particular the revelation which the apostles witnessed at first hand. There is a profound unity to the post-Easter history, and the three stages of Christ's coming. Resurrection and ascension are *parousia*, but the 'outpouring of the Holy Spirit is also the *parousia*. In this it has not only taken place but is still taking place to-day. And as it has taken place in the resurrection and is taking place to-day in the outpouring of the Holy Spirit, it is also true that it will take place at the end of days in the conclusion of the self-revelation of Jesus Christ'.[35]

Jesus' resurrection and ascension set up the conditions of the present age, and this may be expressed in two ways. Firstly, it is Jesus' resurrection and ascension that definitively reveal who He is, and what He has achieved. The present age is the time given to the world for the reception and acknowledgement of the reality of Jesus Christ. But secondly, in the very same way, the present age is revealed as the 'last time', the penultimate age, in which Jesus is awaited in the immediacy of His glory.

> In the Easter event as the commencement of the new coming of Jesus Christ in revelation of what took place in His life and death, it is also revealed that the time which is left to the world and human history and all men can only be the last time, i.e., time running toward its appointed end. In this sense the Easter event is the original because the first eschatological event. The impartation of the Holy Spirit is the coming of Jesus Christ in the last time which still remains.[36]

Thus in acting as terminus of one period of the history of Jesus Christ's self-witness, the ascension also acts as the necessary condition for the beginning of the next period. The present age, the 'time between', is therefore the time of Jesus' *parousia* in a particular form and manner. It is the age in which Jesus is ascended to the right hand of the Father, and in which He

---

[34] For Barth, 'promise' is the peculiar form of coming that corresponds to the being of the Spirit among humans. This should not be read as meaning that this being and presence is in some way tenuous, or questionable – rather the term 'promise' indicates the specifically eschatological orientation of the Spirit's being in the world, and the eschatological orientation of the community of the Spirit. See *CD* IV/3.i, pp.295ff.

[35] *CD* IV/3.i, p.295.

[36] *CD* IV/3.i, p.295.

comes in the Spirit. That is, the coming of the Spirit is dependent upon the resurrection and ascension as the beginning of post-Easter history, and in particular the gift of the Spirit is a gift from the risen and *ascended* Jesus Christ. Jesus, while absent via ascension, is not simply absent, and in grace continues to reach into the time of the fallen creation and bring saving transformation in the knowledge of salvation. He does not cease to save, but rather, in the Spirit, is present and active – *on the basis of His heavenly life and authority* – to mediate salvation and thus to make fallen humans into sharers with Him in His grace. However, before moving on to a closer examination of the relation between Jesus ascended and the work of the Spirit, the question of Jesus' relationship to time offers another insight into Barth's thought. The nature of the present age as the 'time between' is determined by the relationship between Jesus' time – the time He has as the risen and ascended human – and the continuing time of the old creation in which we live.

The Word and Time

If we take the incarnation seriously, as Barth does, then we must say that Jesus Christ, the Word of God, is also a man in time: 'If we say Jesus Christ, we also assert a human and therefore a temporal presence'.[37] As such He is the fulfilment of time. In Jesus of Nazareth God has taken time to Himself and made it anew, made it His own, and in so taking up creaturely time the Creator has fulfilled time – that is, God has redeemed time, made it what it was always intended to be, brought it back into congruence with God's own being and existence. Jesus of Nazareth's 'time is not only the time of a man, but the time of God, eternal time'.[38] Just as humanity is made altogether new in the event of Jesus Christ, so the time of God, present in Jesus, is altogether new time – it cannot be identified with, or reduced to, any other time. It is not time as we creatures normally have it, full of tensions and disparities – the time of Jesus does not collapse into a present, past and future which are incongruous, or disrupted, as the time of all fallen creatures must.

> Here there is a genuine present – and not now in spite of it but just because of it, a genuine past and future. The Word of God is. It is never 'not yet' or 'no longer'. It is not exposed to any becoming or, therefore, to any passing away, or, therefore, to any change. The same holds also of the Word of God become flesh and therefore time.[39]

'Thus, as the title ['Jesus, Lord of Time'] suggests, Jesus not only is in time and has time like other men, but He is also Lord of time'.[40] In Jesus the glorious future of the new creation has already taken time, Jesus is Lord of time because

---

[37] *CD* I/2, p.50.

[38] *CD* III/2, p.464.

[39] *CD* I/2, p.52.

[40] *CD* III/2, p.464.

He is the future of all things, and the only future possible is the future that comes in Him and exists in His time – everything else must perish.

What does this mean for the present age, the lingering remnant of the old creation with its doomed time? Firstly we must say that the presence of fulfilled time is found in the presence of Jesus the Word, as the Word is addressed to the church and individuals within the church in what Barth calls the 'time between', that is, as we are made contemporaries of Jesus through His act of self-revelation. That Jesus is ascended as the *incarnate* One implies His continued existence in time, and this has profound implications for the present age in which we find ourselves as those to whom the Word is addressed (the present age being the time in which Jesus is ascended, the age defined by His resurrection and ascension). A closer examination of these claims about Jesus' time will help show the way in which Barth's understanding of the present age as the 'time between' turns upon his conception of Jesus' ascension and session.

At the beginning lies the time of the forty days as a peculiar time, which to a certain degree stands on its own as an anticipation of the *eschaton*. Jesus' straightforward presence during this time, unveiled as the glorious One, although limited, prefigures His presence at the end when every eye will see, and every tongue will confess that He is Lord. It is in the event of the resurrection that Jesus is revealed as the incarnate Saviour – wherever He is known, he is known as the risen One – the resurrection does not add to His being as the only son of the Father, but it makes this being *visible*. The cry from the cross – 'It is finished!' – means what it says, that is, all is complete with Jesus' achievement of the journey to Golgotha. Thus the resurrection and ascension define and shape the faith given to Christians, as they reveal who Jesus is and what He has achieved and will completely unveil at the end.

> What the New Testament says about Jesus Christ is all said in the light of Easter and Ascension, that is, in the light of the union, achieved once and for all, between the eternal Word and the human existence assumed by Him. God's Son, so the Christian message runs, is now what we are for all time, nay for all eternity; He is Emmanuel, He is 'with us always, even unto the end of the world' (Mt. 28[20]) ...[41]

This Easter time, the forty days, reveals Jesus' Lordship over time – that all time belongs to Him, and furthermore that all other times exist in relation to His time. Indeed, all other times are shown to have their meaning and purpose in relation to the time of Jesus. He is the living God present in time and making it His own. It is on this basis, of the presence of the Creator within the created realm of time, that Jesus' time is the key to all others.

> Here, in this creature, in this man, who had His own time of life and death, and beyond this His time of revelation, God, the Creator and Lord, had already had time before His time, eternal time. ... It is the time which He willed to have for us

---

[41] *CD* I/2, p.165.

in order to inaugurate and establish His covenant. It is the time which is the time of all times because what God does in it is the goal of all creation and therefore of all created time. Since God in His Word had time for us, and at the heart of all other times there was this particular time, the eternal time of God, all other times are now controlled by this time, i.e., dominated, limited and determined by their proximity to it.[42]

Clearly the logic of election (as Barth understands it) provides a rationale for the understanding of Jesus' time as the eternal time of God. God elects His own Son from all eternity in the man Jesus of Nazareth, and this election – the covenant – provides the internal basis and goal of creation. In electing Jesus God elects Him in His historical reality, including His possession of, and existence within time. Jesus' time can be understood as the human time God has elected from all eternity as the true time, the saving and perfect time of the saving and perfect man. So Jesus' time is the goal and purpose of all time – the meaning of all time is found in the existence of Jesus and of His particular, contingent, history and time. The covenant of God with humans, and thus with the whole creation, is the goal of all time and history, and all of this finds its meaning in the time which God has taken up for this purpose.

How then do other times relate to the time of Jesus? How does the time before Jesus' coming find its meaning in His time? Or how does the time that comes after belong to His time? Or do we overcome the implied temporal progression and separation involved, by seeing Jesus' time as somehow 'non-historical', as not really the time of a man at all? On the contrary, for Barth everything relies upon the genuine humanity of Jesus, and therefore also upon the genuine nature of His time. The man Jesus of Nazareth has time like that of any other man – time that begins, endures, and ends – and which belongs to the movement of history in which we too live and move. It is a time that is past for us, was contemporary for others, and was future for yet others. Only a docetic Christ could be described as having any other time than this, and to deny His having time in this way would be to deny the incarnation.[43]

In an exegetical section relating to the New Testament notion of Jesus' time as 'the fullness of time', the 'Sabbath time' of God, Barth expresses very simply the orientation of this time 'before' and 'after' Jesus to His being at the centre of all time.

Mk. I makes it clear beyond all doubt that in the life of Jesus we have to do with a real event in time, but with a particular event and therefore a particular time, the time at the centre which dominates all other times. The fact that in His life all time comes to fruition means that all time before it moved towards it and all time after it moved away from it. In the last resort the only real reason why men had time at all was that – although they did not realise it, apart from the prophets who prophesied 'until John' – this day was to come. And the men after Christ have time only in order to orientate their lives in the light of this day which in the series

---

[42] *CD* III/2, p.455.
[43] *CD* III/2, pp.462-3.

of days has now appeared ἅπαξ and ἐφάπαξ and is proclaimed with an explicit imperative.[44]

To return to our key question, the age which follows upon the life and revelation of Jesus – our age – is simply the time which is given to humans in which to orientate their lives to the true time of Jesus Christ. The way in which Jesus' time is past transcends the normal sense in which another person is past to us, and the reason for this is that He is the risen One (a fact which is inseparable from His identity as the Son of God). The end of Jesus' life is such that it remains present and future, even though in ending it necessarily becomes past. Even in the present age, when Jesus is clearly a figure of the past, Jesus' time is such that all time remains the time of His coming – all time is derived from Him, and all time is His time.[45]

Again, an exegetical note explains what Barth is thinking: all times belong to Jesus because He is the Lord of time, as revealed in His being as the risen and ascended One.

> Jesus Christ belongs not only to yesterday, or to to-day, or an indefinite future. He belongs to all times simultaneously. He is the same Christ in all of them. There is no time which does not belong to Him. He is really the Lord of time. If we ask the author of Hebrews how he came to attribute to Jesus this extraordinary being in time, the only answer which he can give is to refer to the point indicated a few verses later (Heb. 13[20]). Who is 'our Lord Jesus'? He is the great Shepherd of the sheep in the blood of the covenant, whom the God of peace 'brought again from the dead.' He is the great High Priest who 'hath passed through the heavens' (4[14]) to sit down on the right hand of the majesty on high, i.e., God (1[3]; 8[1]; 10[12]; 12[2]).[46]

As we have seen before, the time in which Jesus is past (and future!), the 'time between', is therefore not a time of Jesus' pure absence. He is not 'past' in that manner. Jesus ascended, as the man who is bearer of the time of God, is the One who is active in bringing our time into relation with His own. Jesus is present in the Spirit in such a way that His past impinges upon every moment of the current age. Jesus' life at the right hand of the Father – a life already fulfilled through the death He undertook – means that Jesus is also present now (temporally). He gives His people His own Spirit, and thus is present in full reality Himself. Proclamation of Jesus is not mere recollection of the past, but undertaken in order that He may be present.[47] Jesus as agent of His own revelation and kingdom reaches into the lives of His people, and crucially, He does so in such a way that they are now made to share *His* time. The New Testament communities experienced Jesus interruption of their old time, and knew that they belonged to the new time of Jesus – the coming time.

---

[44] *CD* III/2, p.461.

[45] *CD* III/2, p.464.

[46] *CD* III/2, p.466.

[47] *CD* III/2, p.467.

This was not something they accomplished, but rather something that only Jesus Himself could do.

> These men do not make or feel or know themselves to be the contemporaries of Jesus. It is not they who become or are this. It is Jesus who becomes and is their Contemporary. As a result of this, His past life, death and resurrection can and must and actually do have at all times the significance of an event which has taken place in time but is decisive for their present existence. Hence they can and must and actually do understand their present existence as a life of direct discipleship; as their 'being in Christ'; as a being done to death with Him at Golgotha, renewed in the garden of Joseph of Arimathea, and on the Mount of Olives (or wherever the ascension took place) entering into the concealment of the heavenly world, or rather, into the concealment of God.[48]

Yet as earlier, this emphasis upon the presence of Jesus' time – Jesus' presence as the Contemporary – includes in the same breath the notion of absence. Christians are those who know their citizenship to be in heaven, 'as it is already actualised *proleptically* in the man Jesus'.[49] Fulfilled time becomes our real time, but our own time and Jesus' time never become simply identified, and general time does not simply become fulfilled time. Fulfilled time is present to us only in the special event of God's presence. 'At this point we must emphasise the fact that God has time for us because – and this is a fact, an act (and an incomparable act at that) of which God Himself and He alone is the Subject – He reveals Himself, i.e., proceeds out of a veiling and unveils Himself'.[50] In relation to time the 'veil of which we must speak in this context is general time, the old time, our time, so far as He assumes it in order to make it – and this is the unveiling – His own time, the new time'.[51] Through His incarnation, through the veiling of His glory within the fallen time of the world, He makes time anew.

Nonetheless, there remains the peculiar time in which we continue to exist, the 'time between' as Barth calls it. This current time involves an absence as well as a presence of fulfilled time – there is a gap between the institution of fulfilled time in the history of Jesus Christ and the full presence of that time in His *eschaton*, the already and the not-yet. The presence of Jesus as He invades the old time of fallen humanity in the 'time between' is always an eschatological presence. The form of Jesus' presence always drives toward the future – His revelation in the Spirit, although utterly genuine, always moves toward the final, future, and definitive revelation. In that sense Jesus' presence in the Spirit is an 'instalment' of that which is to come in Jesus' glorious return.[52]

---

[48] *CD* III/2, p.467.
[49] *CD* III/2, p.467, emphasis added.
[50] *CD* I/2, p.56.
[51] *CD* I/2, p.56.
[52] *CD* III/2, p.468.

Rather than a failure, or a negative feature, as it might appear, the current absence as well as the presence of Jesus' time is an act of God's grace. The event of Jesus Christ is the end of all other history, of all history that opposes His Lordship. When Jesus returns, every alternative life, every other time, will be destroyed by the sheer reality and glory of His being – the true being of the new creation. It is a work of grace that this end is not immediate, but delayed. In this age of waiting for and anticipating Jesus' return 'our time' is conserved – that is, inasmuch as the time of God is not yet the only time, and as the old time of the fallen creation is allowed to continue, a 'parallelism' is created between the two.[53]

This upholding of our time – the very time in which we resist God and continue in sin – is the space that God grants for response to His grace, that is, for repentance and belief. Thus Jesus elects to continue to be veiled in order that He may unveil Himself to us. Grace requires a continued veiling which in turn may be made to yield unveiling, revelation. Why is this so? Why must Jesus be veiled if there is to be grace? If Jesus were not veiled, if He were simply present in the fullness of His glory, the glory of the eternal Son of God, then His time would be simply present, and all other time would cease to exist. Apart from knowledge of reconciliation in Christ, apart from the Spirit's redemption of all things, the end of our time could only mean our death, our own end. We would no longer have any space within which we could exist – for unredeemed we are not able to stand in the presence of God, in His time, indeed we do possess time as our own right but exist always in the grace of God. The end of 'general time' will spell the end of those who belong to it, and so God remains veiled in order that in Jesus He may be revealed. 'God's revelation without this veiling or in the form of an unknown being from another world would not be revelation but our death. It would be the end of all things, because it would mean the abolition of the conditions of our existence'.[54] So for instance, as a significant example of the way this shapes his thought, Barth claims that our theologies cannot do away with all veiling, and escape the penultimate nature of our knowledge of God in Christ, for the present age is penultimate.

> [Christology] must keep constantly in view the fact that it is not chance but necessity that retains the penultimate sayings, the statements about God and man, about Jesus Christ, in their position of relative antithesis in the New Testament and in this very position makes them point beyond themselves to an ultimate Word, Jesus Christ, which as such can only be explained in terms of the reality thereby indicated and by nothing else. The realm of grace would have to be dissolved by the realm of glory if it were to be otherwise …[55]

---

[53] *CD* I/2, p.68.

[54] *CD* I/2, p.36.

[55] *CD* I/2, p.25.

This is simply to say that Jesus' immediate presence can only be the awaited end (and beginning) of all things, the *eschaton*.

But, as above, the time of Jesus drives toward this 'coming again', toward this future in which He will leave His current concealment and every eye will see and every knee will bow. The penultimate must give way to the ultimate. The time of Jesus is therefore in one sense interrupted by the present age, the 'time between'. There is a direct line from the forty days to the *eschaton*, and it is as if this line is stretched in order to give space for the time of the church[56]. As a time of His hiddenness the present age interrupts the movement from veiling to unveiling which began in the resurrection and will become complete at the *eschaton*.

> And so Jesus in His coming is simply the risen Jesus resuming and completing His coming and thus vindicating that beginning and promise. For what will take place at His return is just that the arch of His time which began with the revelation of His first coming, and then vaulted over the interim time of the community, of the Gospel and the Spirit, of faith and love, the time given for the conversion of the world, will then be completed.[57]

To be sure, the 'time between' is also very much Jesus' time – but the *manner* in which Jesus' lordship of this time is expressed is once more shaped by the reality of His ascension and hiddenness at the right hand of the Father. The 'time between' belongs to Jesus, but 'as His time it needs to be completed by Him as it was begun by Him as an interim time, a time of His invisibility'.[58] Thus the agency of Jesus in the time between is the agency of the *coming* Saviour.

Revelation and the Agency of Jesus in the 'Time Between'

Douglas Farrow has complained that Barth leaves nothing for Jesus to do after His ascension – on the basis that He has already achieved everything – but this claim may be disputed.[59] Barth certainly sees Jesus as very much active in the present age, as above. If Jesus Himself is the presence of fulfilled time, then His taking of that time to the Father's side – the place of all rule and authority – is the creation of that space for us delineated above. It initiates the time that Barth calls the time of recollection – the time in which there is witness to the revelation already achieved in Jesus, and in which Jesus Himself, risen and

---

[56] See below.

[57] *CD* III/2, p.489.

[58] *CD* III/2, p.490.

[59] A fuller treatment of this complaint follows in Chapter 7.

ascended takes up that witness to enact revelation afresh.[60] As the time of the church, this is also the time of the New Testament,[61] and of the voice of God through it. But even as we recognise the absence of the ascended Jesus, we also recognise that it is only the presence and agency of the ascended One that allows Barth to speak of revelation through recollection at all.

> Thus, while there is recollection and tradition from the standpoint of the action of the community, objectively and in fact He Himself is the acting Subject who lifts the barrier of yesterday and moves into to-day, making Himself present, and entering in as the Lord. This is the inner connexion between Easter and Pentecost.[62]

It is only the power of God in self-revelation that enables knowledge of God. Jesus' ascension to the Father's side – again, the place of all rule and authority – also creates the possibility of His presence, and therefore of revelation. 'In other words, even in relation to the New Testament's claim to revelation, we are pointed to Jesus Christ Himself, to the act of lordship in which He gives the Holy Spirit of hearing and obedience to whom He will'.[63]

Jesus ascended has indeed already achieved everything for the salvation of humanity, but that does not mean that He ceases to be active – rather His activity is precisely the activity of the One who has already reconciled humanity in Himself. Jesus is still working – not some other Jesus, but the same Jesus of Nazareth – and so the witness of the apostles and the recollection involved in that witness is centred on Jesus as the living Lord who continues to act as the Subject of that recollection.[64] In resurrection and ascension He does not become someone different, but rather continues in the eternity of God as the One He was upon the cross. This is our present salvation and life. 'It was His conducting of God's case with us sinners that brought Him to the cross, and His conducting of our sinner's case with God is the eternal effect, the victorious result of His suffering and death'.[65] Thus Jesus

---

[60] Thacker notes Barth's treatment of Jesus' appearance to Paul, and in particular the claim that after the forty days Jesus is evidently still a subject capable of action and self-revelation. Of course, the belated appearance to Paul, as a *resurrection* appearance, is regarded as differing from the normal post-ascension mode of revelation in that it does not rely upon apostolic authority but rather establishes it in Paul. (See *CD* III/2, p.471) Thacker, Anthony *Karl Barth's Understanding of the Resurrection: analysis, discussion and contrast.* Unpublished dissertation, University of Oxford, Faculty of Theology, 1983, p.152.

[61] See below, *The Church in the Service of the Ascended One*, pp.55ff.

[62] *CD* III/2, p.470.

[63] *CD* I/2, p.103.

[64] *CD* III/2, p.471.

[65] *CD* I/2, p.113.

is the One who sends the Spirit to mediate His presence, and the salvation which is contai ed in that presence.[66]

All this stands in opposition to any notion that the ascension simply results in the absence of Jesus and of His time. Rather, in His own agency Jesus creates the relation of faith in which His people inhabit His time and are made to be His contemporaries.

> It could not possibly be ... that now that His past had reached its fruition in the event of the forty days a kind of past had begun when the Bridegroom was taken from them, and could now only live in their hearts and minds, so that they had to do without Him in reality and truth, managing without His help. To think of the Resurrected, even when He was no longer seen, was to think of the living Lord, not absent but present to-day and every day to His own. It was to live in faith in Him, and therefore in love for Him, and therefore, even when the forty days were over, in His time, fulfilled time.[67]

Jesus promises His presence, and on the basis of His cross and resurrection, and His ascension, that promise is sure. Yet in this 'time between' He is also absent, and the limitation or veiled nature of His presence demands our response in hope and faith. A person grasped hold of by Christ is therefore one who needs must stretch forward to things hoped for – things that are apprehended in faith. This is the mode in which our present is united, on occasion, to the time of Christ and thus is life under the Word.[68] So in the following section we turn to a closer examination of the manner of this presence and agency of Jesus Christ, who is ascended to the right hand of the Father – His presence in the Holy Spirit.

The Holy Spirit as the *Parousia* of the Ascended Christ

For Barth the Spirit is always to be understood as serving the mission the Father undertakes in and through the Son. Thus, as below, the Spirit works in the 'time between' to enact Jesus' self-revelation among and to humans. The Spirit is Jesus' Spirit, and the Spirit's work is Jesus' work. This requires careful treatment in order to avoid the impression that Barth in some sense fails to offer a fully trinitarian theology by reducing the person of the Spirit to a mere instrument of the Son, and this matter will be treated below. However, it is essential to understand at the outset that in the person of the Spirit we have to

---

[66] Barth is very clear in maintaining that the present action of Jesus is always predicated upon, and an outworking of, His life, death, and resurrection. He is concerned to allow no space for an idea of Jesus' present agency in some way superseding His past, and of a Christian faith that feels free to alter the shape of its belief on the basis of such an idea. For Barth, Jesus' past has *equal* weight with His present and future. See *CD* III/2, p.474.

[67] *CD* III/2, p.487.

[68] *CD* I/2, p.119.

do with the mediated agency of the ascended Son, and thus pneumatology bears close relation to ascension theology.

Throughout the *Church Dogmatics* Barth sees the Spirit as the source of subjective faith, and Christian experience, but refuses to reduce the Spirit to this subjective reality. From volume I/1 onward the Spirit is the power of the Lord in revelation, grasping and transforming humans, becoming Lord of them in and through revelation.

> The Spirit of God is God in His freedom to be present to the creature, and therefore to create this relation, and therefore to be the life of the creature. And God's Spirit, the Holy Spirit, especially in revelation is God Himself to the extent that He can not only come to man but also be in man, and thus open up man and make him capable and ready for Himself, and thus achieve His revelation in Him. Man needs revelation, for He is certainly lost without it. He thus needs to have revelation become manifest to him, i.e., he himself needs to become open to revelation. But this is not a possibility of his own.[69]

Thus Barth can say: 'In the Holy Spirit and only in the Holy Spirit can man be there for God, be free for God's work on him, believe, be a recipient of His revelation, the object of the divine reconciliation'.[70] Reception of revelation is not a possibility of fallen humanity, but it is a reality of God's humanity in Jesus Christ, mediated in the Holy Spirit. The Spirit is thus not simply God's external presence to humans, but also God's presence 'from below, subjectively', so that in raising us into relationship with Himself God 'encounters Himself from man'. The freedom to do this is God's freedom in the Spirit.[71]

We have already referred to Philip Rosato's argument that Barth is a far stronger pneumatologist than he is usually recognised to be. Indeed, Barth is often considered to be too weak in his treatment of the entire third article of the creed. However, with Rosato and more recently George Hunsinger,[72] we maintain a more positive reading of Barth at this point.[73] It is not that Barth has little or no pneumatology, or ecclesiology, or even anthropology – rather, it is that these areas of his thought are often not recognised or accepted by

---

[69] *CD* I/1, pp.450-1.

[70] *CD* I/2, p.198.

[71] *CD* I/1, p.451.

[72] Hunsinger, George 'Karl Barth's doctrine of the Holy Spirit' in Webster, John B. ed. *The Cambridge Companion to Karl Barth* Cambridge: Cambridge University Press, 2000, pp.177-94. 'Barth intended to develop a doctrine of the Holy Spirit's saving work that would be rigorously Christocentric, yet without becoming deficient in its grasp of essential trinitarian relations. [Salvation is achieved in Christ] yet no "subordinationist" displacement could be allowed of the Spirit's own special work of redemption'. *Ibid.* pp.178-9.

[73] As earlier, Rosato is not entirely positive about Barth's pneumatology. The third and last part of *The Spirit as Lord* offers an attempt to go beyond Barth, from an expressly Roman Catholic point of view.

commentators (perhaps because the shape he gives them is not what is expected). Barth is thoroughly pneumatological, but his pneumatology is typically *christocentric*.

Rosato views pneumatology as the particular arena within which Barth struggles to overcome the liberal theology he rejects,[74] and also to oppose the aspects of Roman Catholic thought he finds unacceptable. At the centre of Barth's struggle is his desire to be able to do justice to the overwhelming 'Yes!' of God to humanity in Jesus Christ – he wants to be able to speak meaningfully and powerfully of the *subjective* reality of God's reconciling work. The key for Barth, however, is to be able to maintain both poles of the relation, or as Rosato[75] has it, both foci of the ellipse, without them collapsing into one – the lordship, and indeed the 'otherness' of the Spirit must be maintained, while at the same time the subjective human reality of reconciliation must be affirmed. The Holy Spirit works to create the free and active participation of humans in the objective work of God.

> It would be comfortless if everything remained objective. There is also a subjective element; and we may regard the modern exuberance of this subjective element, which had already been introduced in the middle of the seventeenth century, and was brought by Schleiermacher into systematic order, as a strained attempt to bring the truth of the third article into force.[76]

Schleiermacher gave human consciousness the mediating role between the objective reality of Jesus Christ and the subjective experience of the believer, but Barth claims that this role belongs solely to the Holy Spirit – according to Rosato Barth regards pneumatology as at the heart of Schleiermacher's failure.[77] Thus the work of the Spirit is central to Barth's response: 'In reacting to excessively anthropological conceptions of the Spirit, Barth concentrates from now on exclusively on the Spirit's soteriological function'.[78]

> Though Barth is usually considered a Christologist, pneumatology plays a key role in every aspect of his thought, and especially when it is a question of man's correspondence to the person and work of Jesus Christ. Barth clearly intends to

---

[74] Hunsinger makes a similar claim, see 'Karl Barth's doctrine of the Holy Spirit', p.181.

[75] Rosato borrows the image from Barth's chapter on Schleiermacher in *Protestant Theology in the Nineteenth Century*. Barth describes Schleiermacher (and Bultmann in his turn) as unable to protect the integrity of the objective pole of the Christ-Christian relation, so that the greater pull of the subjective pole gradually draws the objective pole onto itself, yielding a circle fully centred upon and formed about the subjectivity of the Christian. See pp.460ff.

[76] Barth, Karl *Dogmatics in Outline* London: SCM Press Ltd., 1949, pp.137-8.

[77] For confirmation of this view see Barth's chapter on Schleiermacher in *Protestant Theology in the Nineteenth Century*, especially pp.460-63.

[78] Rosato, pp.30-31. Thus, Rosato sees Barth's pneumatological, and anthropological emphases and interest as stemming from very early in his career.

write a theology of the Christian which is not christianocentric but pneumatocentric.[79]

As above, throughout the *Church Dogmatics* Barth sees the work of the Spirit as focussed upon the subjective pole of revelation – the Spirit works to bring about human response to the revelation and reconciliation objectively achieved in Jesus Christ. However, the work of the Spirit is in no way independent – the Spirit does not bring another revelation, or a different salvation from that achieved in and by Jesus Christ. Even Barth's designation of the Spirit as Redeemer relies upon his understanding of Jesus Himself as Redeemer. Rather the Spirit 'is still to be regarded wholly and entirely as the Spirit of Christ, of the Son, of the Word of God'.[80] The instruction and illumination the Spirit brings is entirely 'the instruction, illumination and stimulation of man through the Word and for the Word'.[81]

How are we to understand the relation between the Spirit, the Word of God, and Jesus Christ? It might be tempting to see a simple form of identity in Barth's thought at this point (and, of course, he has been accused of christomonism), for there is a strong unity expressed between Jesus and the Spirit. Jesus Christ is described as the one Word of God, whom humans need to hear, and no rival word can either compete with Him, or be tolerated. Yet at the same time, the *subjective* reality of this Word simply *is* the Holy Spirit, as an act of God in and amongst humans (not to mention the concrete forms of the Word in scripture and proclamation). Barth argues that without the work of the Spirit Jesus' being as the Word of God remains objectively real, but is not subjectively realised in the being of humans – Jesus is not made *manifest* apart from the work of the Spirit. Revelation as the manifestation of God is not simply the givenness of the facts, but is also, and necessarily a specific act of the Godhead – which is to say, of the Spirit.[82]

Nonetheless, the Spirit is not merely the subjective *human* aspect of revelation – Barth's whole discussion of the role of the Spirit in revelation maintains the independence and sovereignty of the Word, even as God gives Godself most radically to the creature. Jesus Christ is God's Word, but the Spirit is God at work opening up, transforming, and empowering the human subject. The very ability of the Spirit to create a relation between the creature

---

[79] Rosato, p.43. Thompson agrees with much of Rosato's exposition of Barth, but disagrees with Rosato's critique of Barth and attempt to press beyond him. Rosato maintains the christocentric nature of Barth's pneumatology – pneumatology is precisely what enables Barth to maintain the present Lordship of *Jesus Christ*. Rosato's attempt to press beyond Barth involves a less christocentric emphasis. See *The Holy Spirit in the Theology of Karl Barth*, especially the final chapter interacting with Rosato, pp.197-211. Hunsinger too emphasises the christocentric nature of Barth's pneumatology, see 'Karl Barth's Doctrine of the Holy Spirit'.

[80] *CD* I/1, p.452.

[81] *CD* I/1, p.453.

[82] *CD* I/1, p.449.

and Creator is what marks the Spirit as other than the creature – for the relation of creature to Creator is beyond the ability of the creature to establish, or to restore. God alone creates the relation, and the Spirit is God's presence in and to the creature in such a mode that as God the Spirit creates the capacity for knowledge of God, for relationship with God.[83] Jesus' history from Bethlehem to Golgotha *is* continued – but on the basis of its already having been completed upon the cross. 'It is in the form of suffering, as the wholly Rejected, Judged, Despised, Bound, Impotent, Slain and Crucified, and therefore as the Victor, that He marches with us and to us through the times, alive in the promise of the Spirit.'[84] He is not witness to an independent truth, but as the True Witness He is the mediator of the reconciliation achieved in His own being and action.

Barth emphasises that his talk of subjective and objective revelation does not designate two separable entities, but rather involves two ways of looking at the one event. On the one side he sees objective reconciliation achieved in Jesus – whether humans know it or not – and on the other side the necessary work of the Spirit in bringing this reconciliation to life in us. Yet Barth acknowledges that even this way of talking implies too much separation. There are not two events of revelation, the one objective and the other subjective; there is only the one reality of Jesus Christ.

> Subjective revelation is not the addition of a second revelation to objective revelation. ... Subjective revelation can consist only in the fact that objective revelation, the one truth which cannot be added to or bypassed, comes to man and is recognised and acknowledged by man. ... Here, too, we must remember that the Holy Spirit is the Spirit of the Father and also of the Son. He is not a Spirit side by side with the Word. He is the Spirit of the Word itself who brings to our ears the Word and nothing but the Word.[85]

It is at this point that many commentators have found cause for criticism. Barth is often perceived as so emphasising both human incapacity for God and the lordship of the Spirit in revelation, that the human disappears altogether from view and human subjectivity is altogether lost. However, even in the material quoted above we can perceive that it is not necessarily so. Barth's point is precisely that in the Spirit God creates a subjective and *genuinely human* reality that corresponds to the objective reality of Jesus Christ. '[For Barth], as disclosed by the Spirit, in other words, the knowledge of Jesus is not something merely cognitive, for it claims those who are addressed by the gospel as whole persons'.[86] In the Spirit fallen humans attain to a measure of genuine subjectivity before the Father. So Barth takes a title that is normally purely Christological and applies it to the Spirit: the Spirit is the *Redeemer*. The

---

[83] *CD* I/1, p.450.
[84] *CD* I/1, p.390.
[85] *CD* I/2, p.239
[86] Hunsinger, 'Karl Barth's doctrine of the Holy Spirit', p.182.

redemptive work of Jesus Christ is now in the process of being accomplished in the presence and power of the Holy Spirit. To speak of the Holy Spirit is therefore to speak of a particular form of the presence of Jesus Christ. Jesus is ascended and that means that He is not present as He was – not even as He was in the forty days – and He cannot be located in time and space.[87] But nonetheless Jesus' absence in this way (His presence with the Father) also creates the possibility of His continued presence and agency in the world. It is Jesus presence at the right hand of the Father which grant Him the authority of action that belongs to the Father Himself. Jesus exercises that authority – the very grace of God – in the 'power of His resurrection and the promise of the Spirit'.[88] In the Spirit we have to do with the genuine coming and presence of the Reconciler; an ongoing coming no less genuinely His *parousia* than His coming at the nativity, or in the resurrection. Jesus takes hold of humans in His Spirit in such a way that they are transformed, and come to belong to and with Him.

The Presence of the 'True Witness'

Farrow has criticised Barth for failing to allow the ascended Jesus enough role as 'Priest'. Barth's reorganisation of the *munus triplex* is well known, but Farrow believes that Barth appropriates the two offices of Priest and King to a descent/ascent schema in *Church Dogmatics* IV parts 1 and 2 respectively, and that of Prophet to His being as the risen Lord, and that this detracts from His agency once ascended.[89] However, as we noted earlier,[90] Farrow reads Barth at this point in terms of three distinct but related movements – descent, ascent, and a third lateral movement in witness. As before, we maintain with Johnson that Barth does not see these movements in this way at all. Descent and ascent are not followed by a third movement, but rather find their ground and meaning in the unity of Jesus Christ, expressed and developed in His being as the True Witness.

It is extremely important to understand that, even though reconciliation is completed at Golgotha, the third theme of Witness – Jesus' being and action as Prophet – does not spell the absence of Jesus' activity as Priest and King. Rather these two offices are gathered up and brought to bear on human subjectivity in the third. It is precisely *as* the True Witness that Jesus Christ is present as both Priest and King – thus existing and acting in, among, and for His own. As He remains the Son of God united with the Son of Man, we cannot think of Jesus ascended as in some way no longer united with us in our humanity, and even the weakness of our flesh. This is the outworking of Barth's rejection of a sequential description of humiliation and exaltation: just as Jesus' ascension cannot be regarded as a new exaltation, because as the Son of God He is and was *always* exalted, so His ascension cannot be seen as

---

[87] *CD* IV/3.i, pp.356-7.

[88] *CD* IV/3.i, p.357.

[89] See *Karl Barth on the Ascension*, p.128 and pp.141-3.

[90] See pp. 42ff. above.

leaving behind His humiliation, or His humanity. If this were so Jesus ascended would indeed be of no benefit to us. The revelation of sin and guilt, and of the way in which the penalty is paid, all of this would be more than humans could bear. But Jesus also tells us that He *still* bears our burdens and carries our infirmities, and therefore enables us to walk with Him.[91] He is still the One who suffers for us, befriends the weak and the broken, the sinner and fool. He remains the One who is rejected and reviled. 'All this is behind Him, yet it is also continually before Him'.[92] The once for all of Jesus' actions and suffering in His passion is not once and for all in the sense that He no longer acts for us in this way – rather the once and for all involves Him as Risen Lord in taking 'it to heart with undiminished severity'. [93] It is in this way that Jesus acts as His own witness and meets us even today. Revelation is a matter of powerful agency in the midst of our humanity, and of the transformative self-giving of God.

If Jesus is heard – if humans find themselves to be those whom He has reconciled, and to whom He comes in the promise of the Spirit – then the 'power of our hearing was simply the power of His speaking, as the power of His speaking became that of our hearing. It was the work of the Spirit that we heard, and therefore that we could hear'.[94] The presence of Jesus Christ in the Spirit and as the True Witness is not passive, or even simply *noetic* – He is present as agent of His reconciliation being worked out in redemption. Barth describes this in terms of Jesus Himself being 'on the way' from resurrection to *eschaton*: His being is not static, but the being-in-action of an agent, and the goal of His history and agency is the fullness of revelation (and therefore transformation) which will be achieved in the *eschaton*. This process of redemption is a process in which the history of Jesus Christ is brought to bear in and upon the history of the world. As ascended Lord He comes to the world in the Spirit, and as the True Witness He mediates reconciliation through the redemption of humans into His own history. What He has achieved is quite simply made present and effective in the Spirit. Present time and history – with all the appearance that it has of rolling on undisturbed – is consistently the sphere of Jesus' work in the presence of the Spirit. In this history and time Jesus encounters humans, offers them His promise and claims them irrevocably.[95] Thus a great deal can be said about humanity in communion with the Son. As Rosato notes, much of what Schleiermacher said can be affirmed: 'even Schleiermacher is right provided that man is what he is only because the Spirit causes him to become such through eschatological grace'.[96]

---

[91] *CD* IV/3.i, p.395.

[92] *CD* IV/3.i, p.396.

[93] *CD* IV/3.i, p.396.

[94] *CD* IV/3.i, p.420.

[95] *CD* IV/3.i, p.420.

[96] Rosato, *The Spirit as Lord*, p.37.

To return to our question: does this mean that the Holy Spirit is simply and purely to be identified with Jesus, with the Word of God, with no remainder or distinction? Quite simply: No. The resurrection and ascension disclose a completed revelation, achieved in the way of the Son of God into the far country, and concluded in the exaltation of the Son of Man. Jesus Christ's *parousia* in the Spirit is as this exalted Lord, and the faith created in humans by the Spirit is faith in Him as exalted. But it is not the Spirit who has travelled into the far country as the Son has; it is not the Spirit who has united human nature to divine nature in His own person.

> We have seen already that Christ is the revelation of the Father in His passage through death to life. Those who believe in Him and confess Him believe in Him and confess Him as the exalted Lord. Thus the Spirit in whom they believe and confess and He who is the object of this faith and confession stand as it were on two different levels.[97]

The Holy Spirit as revealing agent is God at work in this time between Christ's *parousia* in resurrection and His *parousia* in the *eschaton* – He is God present in the third mode of His being, the Spirit of the Father and the Son. But the work of the Spirit in this time is entirely predicated upon and an outworking of the accomplished and continuing history of Jesus Christ. There is a profound unity, but also a difference between Word and Spirit: 'The Holy Spirit is not identical with Jesus Christ, with the Son or Word of God'.[98] Nonetheless, in all the work of the Spirit, He is present as the Spirit of the Word, of the Son.[99] In His being as the One who has reconciled the creation to the Father, and the One who will deliver the creation to Him, Jesus is the rule and ruler of all history. In this time between His first and last coming all history belongs to Jesus Christ – it is His history, and therefore the history of God. 'The existence of the man Jesus is the first and basic and controlling factor to the extent that it supplies the initiative which makes the whole possible and actual, and which determines and fashions it'.[100]

Concluding Comments

At the heart of the previous section is the determination of the Spirit's activity by the reality of Jesus as ascended and present at the Father's side – from whence He sends the Spirit as the form of His agency in the 'time between'. The ascended Lord is the active and present Saviour in the action and presence of His Spirit. As *ascended* Lord He holds our future in the absolute reality of

---

[97] *CD* I/1, pp.451-452.

[98] *CD* I/1, p.451.

[99] This is the basis of Barth's preference for the presence of the filioque in the creed, over its absence. See the extended small print section in *CD* I/2, p.250f.

[100] *CD* IV/2, p.336.

His being with the Father – even as this age allows the continuation of sin and evil, so that the whole creation may rejoice in its final redemption.[101]   As ascended *Lord* He lives and reigns even in the midst of this age, coming by his Spirit, the Redeemer, who is also the Spirit of the Father, the Spirit who also is Lord.   In the Spirit Jesus creates a new people to belong to Him, and moves them inexorably within his own movement toward the *eschaton*.   This leads us on to the matter of the next chapter, and the particular way in which Barth envisages Jesus' presence as the True Witness will offer a way into his ecclesiology. In the present chapter, by moving from Barth's conception of the ascension as an event, and the relationship of Jesus' ascended time and the 'time between', through to the nature of Jesus' presence and absence as worked out in the agency of the Spirit, we have gradually moved deeper into the dogmatic function of the ascension and Jesus' ascended being.   This has involved both Barth's explicit mentions of the ascension, and his implicit reliance on the doctrine, as noted at the beginning.

Unsurprisingly, Jesus' ascension, and the particular way in which Barth envisages both ascension and heavenly session, informs very clearly the way in which Jesus' relationship with the present age of the world is worked out. The great strength of this is that Barth moves from dogmatic description of Jesus Christ into dogmatic description of the present age, and not *vice versa*. Jesus' being as the risen and ascended One, firmly grounded in a doctrine of the incarnation, and of the cross, is allowed to determine a theological assessment of the present age. It is thus that Barth describes this age as the 'time between' – for the limits 'between' which the present age continues are Christological limits, and determined by Jesus' history as the one true history which is determinative of all others.   The present age is that between ascension and eschaton. Moreover, the conditions of this age are described in more detail on the basis of Jesus' continuing life and action. It is Jesus' presence and absence that give the 'time between' its particular shape, and it is Jesus' intentions for the age which give it meaning. That being so, as we turn to the nature of the church – traditionally a primary locus for the outworking of a theology of the Spirit – we will be able to focus in further upon Barth's work, elucidating both his ascension theology and his ecclesiology as we examine them together. In particular, we will see that the church functions specifically within this age as Jesus' body as it is related to His *heavenly and ascended body*. Moreover, Barth derives the limitations and the glory of the church precisely from his understanding of Jesus' ascension and the shape of His availability in the Spirit, and His heavenly existence in its own right.

Barth's ascension theology is thus very significant for his thought, and that significance should be made even more explicit in the succeeding chapters. It is my judgement that this theology 'works' – Barth has managed to integrate his doctrine of the ascension with his theology as a whole in such a way that it

---

[101] For more on this see the succeeding chapters, especially Chapter Four with its discussion of the purpose Barth sees in the 'delayed' *eschaton*.

functions appropriately in that whole. A particular achievement here is Barth's ordering of his ascension thought within a strongly chalcedonian theology of the incarnation.[102] Barth overturns the tradition at this point, and the result is a coherent account of Jesus' career that includes a strong doctrine of the ascension without any falsification of the relationship between humiliation and exaltation in Jesus' earthly career. In the New Testament, John is particularly clear in describing Jesus' suffering and death as 'glorification', and Barth is able to maintain exactly that emphasis. It is otherwise tempting to see Jesus' ascension as His glorification, but at that point it immediately becomes difficult to comprehend the glory of His incarnate suffering and death. In the dialogues of Part Two book the matter of kenotic theory – that is, of the nature of Jesus' humiliation in the incarnation – will often be to the fore, and at this point we may see why this is so. Barth's rejection of kenotic theory, combined with a strong reading of the ascension is a strength of his theology. The following material should serve to reinforce this claim.

Furthermore, it should be plain that Jesus' ascension has a great deal to say to those who wish to faithfully serve the church as theologians. As we investigate the church and Christian life in the 'time between' we may see further how our thinking needs to be conditioned by responsible attention to Jesus' ascended life. To live as Christ's people, as follows, both corporately and individually is solely a matter of belonging to Jesus in the 'time between', but the shape of that belonging, and in particular, the expectations that we may rightly have of the church and ourselves as Christ's must be formed with a view to Jesus as ascended and awaited. To be worshippers of Jesus Christ – the man of Nazareth – means being worshippers of this man ascended to the throne of God. It also means being those who receive the Spirit of this same Saviour, sent from the father with whom He lives. This is the rich fruit of Jesus' ascension in dogmatics as reflection upon the good news of this Lord.

---

[102] This is, of course, what Farrow likes least about Barth's theology. See Chapter 7.

Chapter 3

Ascension and the Church

Jesus Christ is the risen, living and active Lord. That is the heart of Barth's theology as unpacked in Chapters One and Two. As He is risen and living, Jesus Christ is also ascended, and the present age of the world is inaugurated in His resurrection and ascension, and bounded at its final terminus by His return. For Christian faith these facts are not neutral, or merely interesting, but are filled with an extraordinary significance. This significance may be seen with a particular clarity in Barth's ecclesiology (theology of the church) and in his thought about Christian life. The church exists in the present age, and Christians live in the present age. The nature of the age, and more specifically, the nature of Christ's presence and absence, the ways in which He exercises His lordship in the present age, are all very much tied up with His ascension and His heavenly life.

It will be obvious to readers that there are many theological approaches available, both to the church as an institution, and to Christians as God's people. Some ecclesiologies emphasise the glory of the church – the ways in which the church experiences Christ's presence, and has access to the mysteries of salvation – often with a stress upon the eucharist as the place or event in which Jesus is present. (The eucharist, of course, being very much something that happens in and for the *church*, rather than outside the church's boundaries.) So, for instance, many protestant denominations appear to be more and more focussed upon the eucharist as the central rite of the church's existence.[1] Other ecclesiologies include views of the Christian as the dominant agent in the present age, and therefore the accent falls upon the faith of the individual and thus the faith of the church. Faith is seen as somewhat triumphant, marching through the age and on into a future in which the *eschaton* may or may not feature. Of course, others pay little heed to the church as a matter of *theological* investigation at all, and one suspects that outside of academic theology many people within as well as without the church do not see the church in a very positive light. The church is a human institution which suffers many scandals, and makes many mistakes, and Christians must necessarily feel the shame attached to the church's failures. It is easy to conclude that the church is simply a society of like-minded persons who benefit

---

[1] For example, Chapter 7 will include the claim that Farrow's emphasis on the eucharist is too great, with little justification for it, and that his work suffers as a result, and Chapter 8 will highlight the eucharist as a determinative feature within Jenson's theology.

from the mutual support and encouragement of belonging together, but who are not 'the body of Christ' in any sense different from that in which we might speak of the 'body of football fans', or of 'workers'.

How are we to view the church under God in this 'time between'? It is very clear that in Barth's thought it is the dynamic of the presence and absence of Jesus Christ that is most significant. The reality of the entire creation is determined – somewhat invisibly in this age! – by Jesus and His death and resurrection, but this is particularly clear in the case of Christians and the church into which they are called. In rejecting both an overly optimistic view of the church – as somehow possessing the mysteries of God – *and* an overly limited view of the church – as merely human society – Barth draws explicitly on his theology of the ascension. The result is that he sees the church as genuinely and fully Jesus' body in the world – a human institution with dimensions that transcend those of all other human institutions because the living Jesus Christ pours out His Spirit upon it and makes it also His own concrete presence to the whole creation. Barth sees that the church is very much a creature of this age – it is a work of God during and for the 'time between'. More than this, he even argues – forcefully – that the 'time between' finds its meaning in the fact of the church, and thus of Christians who love and obey God in response to grace, even while living within the time of the fallen creation. This claim of Barth's is significant, as he is often accused of showing little interest in the human in relation to God and of over-emphasising the divine. Unpacking Barth's view of the church as the meaning of the entire age will not suffice to silence this claim, but it may help open up the possibility of a different reading, just as Webster's 'developing redescription' of Barth's ethics is doing.[2]

Significantly, Barth calls the foundational concepts of his theology of the church 'christologico-ecclesiology',[3] with the peculiar being, life, action, and history of Jesus Christ forming the determinative framework for the being of the community that He takes to Himself as His body. It is upon this foundation that all his ecclesiology is built. The theology of the church is second order, in that it derives from the primary work of Christology. A significant contrast may be made with the claims of Farrow at this point, who claims that ecclesiology is determinative of Christian theology. Barth's approach is clearly very different.[4] Beginning with the relationship between Jesus' as present and absent and the being of the church as His body, we will then move to explore the relationship between Jesus, holy scripture and the being of the church, and then church proclamation as witness to Jesus. Finally we will examine the nature of the 'time between' as specifically the time of the

---

[2] See Chapter 1.

[3] *CD* IV/2, p.680. Barth uses this phrase to sum up his description of the foundation of the being of the church in the agency of Jesus Christ. Thus it means 'that the Christian community is the human fellowship in which Jesus as the head is the primary Subject ...' *Ibid.*

[4] This contrast will be explored more fully in Chapter 7.

church – that is, as the time given for human response to God in Jesus Christ, and for action in Christ's service.

Once again, therefore, we will seek to examine material that explicitly, but also implicitly, relates to Jesus as ascended. The shape of Jesus' agency in the present age has already been outlined, especially in relation to His presence in the Spirit, and that outline allows for further development of our understanding of Jesus' ascended work in relation to His self-witness, lordship over, and mission in the church.

Note on the Materials Examined

There is no shortage of ecclesiological material available in *Church Dogmatics*, especially in the threefold treatment of the church in volume IV parts 1 to 3. For the most part, however, this chapter is shaped by ecclesiological passages from volume I/2, with numerous glances at material drawn from volume IV. The material from I/2 is in fundamental agreement with that in volume IV, with the advantage in this is that is briefer and more easily treated in limited space. Moreover, the focus of the present investigation is much more upon the presence and absence of Jesus as ascended, rather than upon the matter of His heavenly session *per se*. The treatment of ecclesiological issues in volume I/2 offers particular help in understanding the way presence and absence influence ecclesiology, while that in volume IV is more reliant upon Barth's treatment of Jesus' heavenly session in itself. Moreover, volume IV offers a significant emphasis upon Jesus as *exalted*, but, as earlier, Jesus' ascension and exaltation are not to be confused in Barth, and so the lack of treatment of material related to Jesus' exaltation should not be understood to mean that material on Jesus' ascension is being overlooked. By focusing at key points upon volume I/2 we may expose many of the significant moves Barth makes in ecclesiology and the relationship that these bear to Jesus' being as the ascended one, without becoming lost in detail, or being forced into violent leaps from section to section and idea to idea.

The Church in Service of the Ascended One

The first statement we must make is that, for Barth, the church simply *is* the community of Jesus Christ. 'The community is the earthly-historical form of the existence of Jesus Christ Himself'.[5] This is the community which hears His voice, and in which His (*de jure*) act of reconciliation is realised *de facto* in the world. The church is a community that is inescapably a part of the world, but which the Word of Jesus Christ also separates from the world.

---

[5] *CD* IV/1, p.661.

What is heard by it distinguishes its hearing from that of the other peoples around. The One who precedes it and whom it follows, who is present and acts among it as its Head in the power of His Holy Spirit, is seated 'on the right hand of God the Father Almighty'.[6]

As the ascended Lord Jesus is present to and in the church, but also absent, and His absence calls out and separates the church, even as it exists as a genuinely historical community within world history. Moreover, Jesus' availability to the church as the sender of the Spirit, arises from His being 'seated with the Father Almighty', and thus He remains Lord and Head of the church. Barth does call the church united with Christ ascended the *totus Christus*, (the complete Christ), and does see the church as the current form of Jesus' earthly-historical existence, but he also maintains a sharp distinction between the Head and the body. The dialectic of Jesus' presence and absence exercises a level of control over Barth's conception of the relationship between Jesus ascended and the church as His body in the 'time between'.

In Barth's view the church exists as a peculiar creature of this 'time between': the church is created by Jesus Christ in the gift of His Spirit, and created for His purpose. That purpose is the service of revelation, firstly simply in existing as the body belonging to Jesus, as the communion of those granted to have faith in Him, and secondly in the proclamation of that faith.

> In the time between the ascension and the second coming, the Church as the communion of those who have been summoned by the Word and who have believed the Word, is the sign of God's revelation, the sign of the incarnation of the Son of God and the sign of the new humanity redeemed by the Son of God in His coming kingdom.[7]

Thus the church must work to serve the Lord in whom it trusts and undertake the mission for which it is created. 'But it must not, and cannot, do this in its own strength. It is not the case that the time between the ascension and the second coming is to some extent the kingdom of the believing man autonomous in and by virtue of His faith'.[8]

The particular character of the 'time between' is the determinative context for the nature of the church, and the core of this context is the relation of Jesus' presence and absence. As explored in more detail below, the manner of Jesus' presence – always in the Spirit – is manifold and complex, but nonetheless the *authoritative* witness of His presence is holy scripture. It is through holy scripture, in the agency of the Spirit, that Jesus rules as Head over the church.

A significant aspect of Barth's ascension theology is perhaps a key here. If we ask where Jesus is, bearing in mind a bodily resurrection and ascension,

---

[6] *CD* IV/3.ii, p.686.

[7] *CD* I/2, p.692.

[8] *CD* I/2, p.692. Thus Barth criticises Neo-Protestantism for failing to recognise this truth, and for exalting both believing humans and their faith as their special capacity for the divine.

then Barth's answer is 'with the Father in heaven'. But what does this mean? Heaven, Barth says, is the dwelling place of God *within* creation. Jesus goes 'to the sphere within the created world which is hidden from that which is earthly, to its ἄδυτον, to the cosmic holy of holies'.[9] In other words, Jesus in ascending has not abandoned the *creaturely* sphere of His existence, even as He continues in full humanity. This being so, we can in no way see the church as the sum total of Jesus' current creaturely existence – in fact the being of the church as His body is placed in quite another light. Jesus Christ's primary existence *within the created world* – although not the earthly-historical world – is as the risen and *ascended* Son, and this is the basis of His life in the church.[10]

> Jesus Christ also lives as the Crucified and Risen in a heavenly-historical form of existence; at the right hand of the Father, before whom He is the advocate and intercessor for all men ... But He does not live only and exclusively in this form, enclosed within it.[11]

His earthly historical-existence in His community can only be secondary, and indeed *derivative* upon His being as the Son of Man in the presence of God the Father. Jesus does not depart in such a fashion that His action among humans ceases – as we have seen in the previous chapter – and neither does His absence imply that the church simply fills up the gap that He leaves.[12]

It is thus that the Spirit acts to create Jesus' body on the earth, in uniting a particular community of humans with their ascended, living, Lord.

> The Holy Spirit is the power, and His action the work, of the co-ordination of the being of Jesus Christ and that of His community as distinct from and yet enclosed within it. ... He is the One who constitutes and guarantees the unity in which [Jesus Christ] is at one and the same time the heavenly Head with God and the earthly body with His community.[13]

This means that the church is a community in which the subjective pole of reconciliation – the process of redemption – occurs. What God has achieved and reveals in Jesus Christ 'has its counterpart here and now in human faith and love and hope and knowledge, its echo in human confession at this specific time and place ...'[14] In a qualified fashion, as a genuine human community that remains dogged by sin and rebellion, the church marches with Jesus Christ as He moves through this time – the time specifically of the church. Jesus Himself is 'on the way' from ascension to *eschaton*, and the church is that

---

[9] *CD* IV/2, p.153. 'ἄδυτον' means 'holy of holies' or 'inner sanctuary'.

[10] We may note that Barth has no particular interest at this point in spatial designations – what concerns him is a spiritual/theological distinction between the being of God in aseity and the realm of creation.

[11] *CD* IV/1, p.661.

[12] *Dogmatics in Outline*, p.127.

[13] *CD* IV/3.ii, p.760.

[14] *CD* IV/3.ii, p.761.

community which hears His Word, and to a greater and lesser degree responds in obedience, and so is on the way with Him.

Two important points regarding the presence and absence of Jesus Christ must be maintained. Firstly, Jesus *is* present to the church, He does speak and He does exercise His authority. The church cannot allow some form of overt doubt or agnosticism to overcome its faith in the Saviour who is its Lord, because His promise is to be present and never to abandon it. But at the same time the mode of Jesus' presence challenges an overblown confidence in the church as human institution.

Such an excessive confidence may arise in two ways. On the one hand, too great an emphasis on Christ's spiritual presence in the church, combined with a clear sense of His own localisation in heaven, may see the church identified directly and without remainder as the creaturely being of Jesus. The church is then not seen as the limited body of a heavenly and eternal Head who is not only absent but also present to the church in concrete self-witness. Rather the church represents the complete and eternal presence of Jesus in immediate proximity and availability. The church is then seen as more or less self-governing – as the institution that in one way or another possesses the truth of God as a deposit. Such an understanding, according to Barth, may well involve serious claims that Jesus rules the church. But in reality Jesus is not permitted to rule in and through the form in which He is actually present and reveals Himself in the 'time between' – that is, in holy scripture.

> [The] rule of Jesus Christ may be seriously acknowledged in form, but it is represented as a direct leadership of the Spirit, and it is only a secondary question whether the point at which this leadership of the Spirit touches and seizes the Church is supposed to be an infallible Pope or Council, or the office of an authoritarian bishop, or that of a hypostatised pastor, or a free leadership or inspired individuals in the community, or finally the whole community as such. The false thing in all these types of Church government is the ambiguity with which the rule of Jesus Christ is (perhaps very seriously) asserted, but Scripture is ignored as though it were not the normative form of this government for this intervening period.[15]

Barth's concern is to emphasise the nature of scripture as an *external* authority over the church, but only as it mediates the presence of the ascended Christ. If Jesus is seen as only in heaven and not mediated in the creaturely form of the word of prophets and apostles, then the church is left to see itself as the supreme authority, and Jesus' *external* authority as somewhat distant and finally without practical import. Some aspect or other of the church's life and function (for instance; the Pope, Councils, the church as a whole) will become a hypostatised spiritual authority, the bearer of the authority of Christ Himself. As Barth continues from above: 'If we speak of a purely heavenly lordship of Jesus Christ, and then of one of these earthly manifestations of His

---

[15] *CD* I/2, p.693-4.

sovereignty, we may speak 'enthusiastically' but in the last resort we are still speaking of the autonomy of human faith, and therefore not of the church of Jesus Christ'.[16]

The second form of excessive confidence in the self-government of the church, and in the immediate presence of Jesus to the believer, represents a lack of faith in Christ ascended at all. The lordship of Christ is subsumed into the believer's experience of faith, whose religiosity becomes the mainspring of life in the Spirit. The present age is not seen as the 'time between', awaiting the immediate presence of the Lord in the *eschaton*, but rather as the age of faith triumphant, progressing into eternity without rupture or judgement.

> We can only say that this is the mistake especially of Neo-Protestantism. For it sets man on a plane which dispenses with the horizons of accomplished atonement and the coming redemption. The former has become a dim historical memory and the latter the equally vague goal of a gradual progress in the direction of this memory; neither of them has any real significance for those who exist in the interval. All that is left to them is faith. But without this twofold reference to the Lord as its proper object, and deprived of the power of the 'Glory alone to God on high', this faith can only be a special mode of human capacity, will and activity, and therefore, in comparison with Christian faith, only a false faith.[17]

This error is a function of the failure to recognise the boundaries of the 'time between', to look back to the event of the revelation of the glory of Jesus Christ in resurrection and ascension, and to look forward to the return of this same glorious One. 'It consists in the optical illusion that the plane on which the believer exists is unbounded, and without horizons; he does not notice the direct proximity of the hills before and behind him, whence comes his help'.[18]

The limitations that apply to the church's relationship with Jesus within earthly history are, as above, a function of the tension in which the church finds itself – the tension between the *de jure* of justification and the *de facto* of sanctification. But this tension is itself created by the very fact that the church's Head is Himself, at least in one sense, 'on the way'. As the One who has achieved the union of God and humanity, and the reconciliation of all creation, the ascended Lord is proceeding to reveal this reality, and thus is 'on the way' toward the *fulfilment* of His work in the redemption of all things. In walking with its Lord on this way the church functions as a firstfruit of the calling of all created things. This calling has taken place, fully and perfectly, in Jesus' resurrection, but will also take place, definitively, in the *eschaton*. The church is therefore called to obey this call as it has occurred in the resurrection, but also to precede and anticipate this call as it will take place at the end.[19] As the community of the Lord who is moving toward His own *eschaton* the church

---

[16] *CD* I/2, p.694.
[17] *CD* I/2, p.692.
[18] *CD* I/2, p.692.
[19] *CD* I/2, p.793.

is a manifestation of the true, genuine and practical presence of the Saviour. As the body of an 'absent' Head, the church reflects the dialectic of His presence and absence, of His lordship *and* its hidden nature.

In describing the relationship between the church and its Head, or the church and the Holy Spirit, we must therefore be both exceedingly bold and rather careful. Positively, the church *is* the body of the ascended Lord – its Spirit is His Holy Spirit, present in the power of His resurrection and ascension. Negatively, the fullness of the reconciliation of God with humanity is present in Jesus the Risen One, and He is ascended into heaven – we must not lose sight of the provisional nature of the church's representation of the Lord. To quote at some length:

> For all its weak and doubtful character, therefore, there takes place in [the Church] a subsequent and provisional fulfilment of the prophecy of Jesus Christ which takes up the Easter message and anticipates the 'Behold, I make all things new' (Rev. 21^5) of the last day, not with the perfection with which Jesus Christ Himself, risen from the dead, was once its fulfilment, nor with the perfection with which He will be at His coming again to judgement, but, in virtue of His presence and action in the Holy Spirit by which it is constituted in this time between the times, as a reflection and replica of the glory which is His alone, in participation in it, and therefore with its own glory as the representation, indication and likeness of His prophecy.[20]

In this way also Barth discovers the task of the community of Christ: just as Jesus is active as the True Witness in His being as Priest and King, so the community which is His body finds its primary role in witness, or mission. It is as hearer of this Lord that this community has its being and this task. The community cannot exist apart from this task, and cannot have this task without being this community. Jesus Christ is present in His office as Prophet, and thus His body is a prophetic community, which witnesses to the world of the reconciliation accomplished in Christ, and the redemption He is bringing. The activity of the ascended Lord needs must be the activity and being of His people.

The nature of the church with its mission, and of church government by the Lord through scripture, is thereby linked inextricably to the character of the 'time between'. Only in the witness of scripture is Jesus Christ present to confront the church in the manifestation of His Lordship, and the revelation of His rule. Any other way in which the church may be ruled must simply return the church to the autonomy of human beings, and thus lead back into false faith. This would be a denial of the very character of reality: 'It can consist only in a denial of the character of our time as the time between the ascension and the second coming'.[21]

---

[20] *CD* I/2, p.794.
[21] *CD* I/2, p.693.

Here again we may justly claim that the entire nature of the dogmatic task, as Barth seeks to explicate it, relies upon His particular understanding of the 'time between' – the time initiated by Jesus Christ's ascension. The very being of the church, which it is the task of dogmatics to serve and protect, is revealed as a function of the character of this age as the age in which Jesus is ascended and awaited. Moreover (as explored later in this chapter) the being and servanthood of the church supply the very meaning and goal of the 'time between' itself. This means that, while the nature of the present age informs a description of the being and action of the church, the being and task of the church also explains the purpose of the time between ascension and *eschaton*. Before turning to Barth's comments upon this we will unpack more of the nature of church as created by attending to the nature of Jesus' Word in the witness of holy scripture, and of church proclamation as the servant of Jesus' self-proclamation.

The Church under the Living Word

Holy Scripture and the Presence of the True Witness

The Doctrine of the Word of God, in Barth's thought, is first and foremost a matter of Christology. Jesus Christ is the one Word of God – the Eternal Son. However, the reality of Jesus Christ's presence as the True Witness, His self-revelation, brings the Doctrine of the Word of God to bear upon holy scripture. Barth finds that in a strictly derivative sense is also the Word of God. What is the meaning of this 'also'?

There is no sense in which Barth wishes to set up scripture alongside Jesus Christ as another or a different Word of God. Holy Scripture has no authority in and of itself, and the human writers of the Bible do not have an authority that they might pass on to their writings. Rather the writers of scripture encounter revelation in such a fashion that revelation masters them and they become its servants. They do not possess revelation as a deposit which may then be passed on, but rather they become obedient to it as a living and active Word.[22] In this relation of obedience the writers of the Bible are witnesses to revelation, and their words can become the vehicle of the living Word. The relation of revelation to the Bible is not strictly accidental; the authority of scripture is related to the divine appointment of certain people to be witnesses in this particular medium, and in this way Jesus manifests His objective authority, standing outside, or beyond, the subjectivity of the church's immediate experience of the Spirit. In contrast to a view which sees the Bible the earliest example of the church's continuing tradition, Barth understands scripture as the authority through which Jesus Christ, risen and ascended, speaks in ever new power as He confronts His church, with its tradition, and

---

[22] *CD* I/2, p.542-3.

makes it His own. It is thus that Jesus' authority in the church is a 'concrete authority', differentiated from the subjective life of the church itself.[23]

Once again, Barth's description is based upon his desire to be faithful to what he perceives to be the realities of the situation. The church simply must obey holy scripture as the present form of the Word of God because that is how Jesus makes Himself present. It is only in this form of obedience that the church is found to be 'subordinating itself to Jesus Christ and the Holy Spirit in the form in which Jesus Christ and the Holy Spirit is actually present to it …'.[24] Scripture is the *witness to revelation* of the prophets and apostles, and it is this word that Jesus takes up in order to enact His own *concrete* self-witness – which is to say, Jesus makes Himself *present* in and through the word of the biblical witnesses. 'Their existence is the concrete form of the existence of Jesus Christ Himself in which the Church has the foundation of its being'.[25]

> Accepting the word of the apostles, [the church] allows Him to speak. Being led by them, it is led by Him. His Holy Spirit acts and works in the concrete form of the power and truth of their word.[26]

However, Barth is not claiming an ontologically based authority for holy scripture – it is not that scripture is simply or straightforwardly God's Word, the deposit of revelation. Scripture is not Jesus Christ, but in His lordship Jesus chooses to make Himself present in and through holy scripture. Like any other human proclamation, the Bible becomes the Word of God in the event of God's speaking through it, as God takes up human recollection of revelation in order to enact fresh revelation. 'The Bible is God's Word to the extent that God causes it to be His Word, to the extent that He speaks through it'.[27] On this basis, that the Word of God is always an event, the event of God's own speaking, we cannot merely identify revelation and the Bible.

This event of God's speaking through the Bible is closely tied to the agency of Jesus ascended to the Father's side. The church listening to scripture hears the voice of her heavenly Head. The church does not simply listen to itself in listening to scripture, nor can the church listen to itself and ignore scripture. The being of the church is indeed Jesus Christ Himself, but the church does not therein capture or possess Jesus – in His grace He remains transcendent, and overrules the church from Heaven.

> One thing is clear, that [the church's attention to the apostolic witness] belongs together with its character as the body, the earthly-historical form of the existence of Jesus Christ in this interim period. If, apart from His hidden being at the right hand of the Father, in which He is the head of His body, He also exists in this

---

[23] *CD* I/2, p.579.
[24] *CD* I/2, p.586.
[25] *CD* I/2, p.580.
[26] *CD* IV/1, p.718.
[27] *CD* I/1, p.109.

interim period in earthly-historical form in His community in the world, then it belongs to this that He gives Himself to be known in this earthly-historical form [of apostolic witness in Holy Scripture] ...[28]

The church seeks its being in seeking Jesus, and it is only thus that the church is itself and can fulfil the commission to proclaim Jesus until He comes. Jesus is the life of the body – but only as He remains transcendent to it. Jesus has the church within Himself, but the church does not capture Him: He is the heavenly Head, and the earthly body remains here on earth. Nevertheless, as the heavenly Lord in His transcendence He is able to become immanent in the church, and does so![29] What is more, it is holy scripture that stands as the tangible reminder of the transcendence of the Head over the body, of the dependence of the church upon His constant grace. The concrete presence of scripture expresses the distinction between the Head and the body – the church's proclamation answers to another, superior, proclamation, which is holy scripture.[30] Once again, the impression that ascension creates the transcendence of the heavenly Head over the body must be avoided. Jesus Christ simply *is* transcendent, and His transcendence will become even clearer in the coming *eschaton*, which will itself dissolve the conditions of the ascension. Nonetheless, the ascension does regulate the current form in which Jesus' transcendence is expressed, the manner of His presence and absence in the 'time between', and holy scripture is at the heart of the relation between Jesus ascended and His people yet on the earth.

God's speech through the Bible is an event of the Word of God – of Jesus Christ who has ascended to the Father. The non-identity, as well as the identity, of scripture with God's Word is a function of both the presence and absence of the ascended Lord. Because He is ascended He is neither to be identified with scripture, nor with the current active proclamation of the church, but in both cases He is transcendent, the ascended Lord seated at the right hand of the Father.[31] But equally, it is as the One who is ascended that He comes in the Spirit and speaks through these human words. Jesus' speech in and to His church, His presence, is predicated upon His absence in His being as the heavenly Head of the church. The Bible is truly and absolutely the Word of God because Jesus, the eternal Word, is ascended and in His complete freedom and authority He brings Himself to us in it.

---

[28] *CD* IV/1, p.718.

[29] *CD* I/1, p.100-101.

[30] *CD* I/1, p.101.

[31] Once again, it is *not* that the ascension or even Jesus' absence creates this transcendence – Jesus simply is transcendent, as the only Son of the Father, but it is true that Jesus' ascension and His non-identity with the human word of Scripture do protect His transcendence and constantly reveal His transcendence to His body the Church.

> There is only one Word of God and that is the eternal Word of the Father which for our reconciliation became flesh like us and has now returned to the Father, to be present to His Church by the Holy Spirit. In Holy Scripture too, in the human word of His witnesses, it is a matter of this Word and its presence.[32]

Thus we can regard the absence of Jesus in His glory and His presence in the weak human instruments of scripture and proclamation as a continuation of His incognito, of His being veiled in the likeness of sinful flesh. To any ears but those of faith the proclamation of the church is simply the sound and speech of a human group much like any other, to any eyes but those of faith the Bible appears as a religious book much like any other, perhaps more doubtful than some as to its provenance and divine reference.

> The Bible is not the Word of God on earth in the same way as Jesus Christ, very God and very man, is that Word in heaven. ... But in His eternal presence as the Word of God He is concealed from us who now live on earth and in time. He is revealed only in the sign of His humanity, and especially in the witness of His prophets and apostles. But by nature these signs are not heavenly-human, but earthly- and temporal-human. ... For if they are to act as signs, if the eternal presence of Christ is to be revealed to us in time, there is a constant need of that continuing work of the Holy Spirit in the Church and to its members which is always taking place in new acts.[33]

Here we turn once again to the presence of the ascended Lord in the promise of the Spirit. As scripture attests the revelation of God in Jesus Christ it does so in the power of its object – Jesus Himself. This means that the witness of scripture must always be the witness of the Spirit of Jesus, the Holy Spirit of God.[34] In the hands of the Spirit the Bible is the powerful and objective truth of God over and against all human subjectivity. This is the meaning of the 'inspiration' of the Bible. This being so, inspiration must mean a continual work (or 'decision') on God's part to speak in this concrete form, and through such speaking to bring about and maintain our fellowship with Christ in the Spirit.[35]

To return to a point made above, the church can never become a rival authority to holy scripture as God's Word, even and although the church is Christ's body. The dialectic of Christ's presence and absence in this 'time between' applies particularly strongly to the being of the church as Christ's body. Barth affirms Jesus Christ's presence in and to the church, but in rejection of both Roman Catholic and Neo-Protestant opinions he refuses any assimilation of Jesus' authority to the church, and any assimilation of Jesus' Word to the word of the church. Jesus is genuinely present to and in the

---

[32] *CD* I/2, p.512.
[33] *CD* I/2, p.513.
[34] *CD* I/2, p.538.
[35] *CD* I/2, p.534-5.

church, but only as He is other than the church, only as He continues to transcend the church in His very immanence in it.

> [The] Christian Church cannot reflect on its own being, or live by it, without seeing itself confronted by the Lord, who is present to it but as its real Lord, with a real authority which transcends its own authority. Its Lord is Jesus Christ. ... The relation between Jesus Christ and His Church is, therefore, an irreversible relation. ... The glory and authority of Jesus cannot, therefore, be assumed or subsumed, but will always be fulfilled and maintained in a contradistinction between the disciples and the Master, the body and its members and their mutual Head. The basis of the Church, its commission and authorisation, even the personal presence of Jesus Christ in His Church, does not remove the possibility and necessity of this differentiation between its authority and His.[36]

As above, this differentiation between the authority of the body and the supreme authority of the Head finds its expression in the authority of holy scripture within the church. Thus the church is required to recognise the absence as well as the presence of the Saviour, in a particular and important relation. It is this recognition of the authority of Jesus Christ expressed in holy scripture that lies at the heart of the dogmatic task itself, as the church attempts to maintain faithfulness in proclaiming Jesus, and indeed lies at the heart of the reality of the church as Jesus' community in the time between.

The Presence of the Ascended Lord in Church Proclamation

The description of Jesus' presence to the church in holy scripture, and the limitations thereby imposed, are not finally negative in their implication, but rather are a part of God's resounding 'Yes' to humanity in Jesus Christ. To recognise the particular and in a certain sense limited way in which Christ rules the church and makes it His church is precisely to affirm that He *does* rule it, and that in this particular form He *is* present to it in the power of His resurrection and the authority of the eternal Son of the Father.[37] In this presence there is the grace and therefore the encouragement and faith in which the church is enabled to proclaim Jesus Christ and have that proclamation taken up and made an event of the Word of God. Moreover, proclamation is the work the church must do – or better, mission is the task the church

---

[36] *CD* I/2, p.576.

[37] Although it is appropriate to speak of Jesus' rule of the church as to some degree limited – that is, limited in this 'time between' by the lack of His immediacy and by the gracious manner in which He allows a church of sinners to exist as *His* church – nonetheless it must also be stringently maintained that Jesus rules the church absolutely and completely, and that by definition the church is the church of Jesus Christ to the degree that He is its absolute Head. These two truths are simply expressions of the one reality of Jesus' ascended Lordship of this particular body.

embodies. 'Its mission is not additional to its being. It is, as it is sent and active in its mission'.[38]

Clearly there is no sense in which we can see here, anymore than elsewhere, an innate human capacity for such activity. Humans are no more able to make themselves proclaimers of the Word of God than they are able to bring themselves to redemption. The Word of God altogether transcends them. Yet, in humility the Word of God condescends to become enfleshed and to inhabit the feeble words of human creatures. We cannot exalt the fallibility of our creaturely speech to the same level as the grace of God – there is in fact no competition between them, and human sinfulness does not possess the same eternal and autonomous reality as the reconciliation of humanity with God in Jesus Christ. It is the freedom and lordship of Jesus Christ that underlies the reality of church proclamation. The Lord, Jesus Himself, takes weak and even ambiguous human speech and makes it His own speech. Thus church proclamation operates in a freedom which is secondary and derivative upon the freedom of Jesus Himself – the 'omnipotent Word of the grace of God'.[39] In omnipotent freedom God can and does do more than human words can do, even in and through those very human words.

A Christian preacher is indeed a sinner and a liar, but that truth is not finally determinative of the reality of Christian proclamation, rather the final reality is the power of the risen and ascended Lord to reveal Himself in such frail vessels. Certainly there can be no thought of whitewashing human frailty in the matter of church proclamation. 'We can identify the church with its Lord only indirectly, in the unity of the body with its Head'.[40] But equally we cannot exalt our fallenness to the place of God over us. 'It is a self-contradiction, which is only possible as we deny Jesus Christ, to interpret the relativity of our situation, its human fallibility and sinfulness, as something absolute and final, or, as it were, to let ourselves go down in the assault'.[41]

Church proclamation is therefore truly the presence of Jesus Christ the Word of God, indirectly, but nonetheless genuinely preached. The church exists as a creation of the Word and in submission to the Word. It does not create or possess the Word – that is not the meaning of church proclamation as a form of the presence of Jesus Christ. 'But this does not alter in the very least the fact that in this case, too, it is really and truly the one integral Word of God to be believed as such by those who speak and those who hear it'.[42] The entire basis of this confidence is the promised presence of Jesus Himself – it is the risen and ascended Lord who speaks, and who overrules the proclamation of the church through the authoritative word of the Bible. Jesus Himself is

---

[38] *CD* IV/1, p.725 (small print).
[39] *CD* IV/3.ii pp.736-7.
[40] *CD* I/2, p.755.
[41] *CD* I/2, p.755.
[42] *CD* I/2, p.744.

present in the church, and thus it serves Him in proclamation as He proclaims Himself.[43]

The presence of the ascended Lord, in the Bible's testimony to His self-revelation, summons the church to be a teaching body, a missionary people. Jesus' very identity, His being, requires that He be proclaimed – He is after all the Word of God. Jesus' presence demands that proclamation take place, and at the same time that presence enables the demand to be fulfilled.[44]

Therefore the church is the body of the ascended Lord, and the means of His self-revelation, only to the extent that it listens to Him. 'The redemption of church proclamation consists in the fact that it is proclamation of what has been heard afresh. It takes place as the church which teaches Jesus Christ turns from teaching to hearing Him'.[45] That this is so in no way relies upon Jesus' ascension – His being as the exalted One is neither a function nor an effect of His ascension. But the *manner* in which He is present is a function of His ascension, in that once again, as ascended Lord He chooses to be heard in the word of scripture, and it is to this word that the church must always attend. Thus the presence of Jesus is profoundly eschatological – it is limited and always points forward to the fullness in which it will be consummated when He returns in direct and immediate glory. All of the reality of justification and regeneration only exist in the being of Christ, and that being is as the *coming* Redeemer; these things are therefore always eschatological realities.[46]

The dynamic of the existence of the teaching church is profoundly shaped by the reality of Christ's ascension, for as the ascended One, in His absence, He gives space for the existence of the church, and for faith. It is thus that the church exists to teach, to proclaim, for where the Lord is immediately present there is no need for teaching or proclamation – 'every eye will see and every tongue confess'. Barth's emphasis upon the presence of Jesus Christ in the church is predicated upon his understanding of Jesus' absence, his hiddenness. Apart from the in-breaking of the Word of God, speaking into the place of His own absence, humans are lost and quite unable to know the Lord who has reconciled them.

> The Word of God exists and the human vacuum exists. This vacuum is revealed as such by the Word of God itself, so that it can no longer be overlooked. But the Church has the Word of God in virtue of the promise given to it. According to this promise the Church lives in the presence of Jesus Christ. Just because it is the bearer of the Word of God, and in face of this vacuum, it must always teach.[47]

This incognito and revelation, absence and in-breaking presence, is characteristic of the current age, the 'time between'. The ascension of Jesus to

---

[43] *CD* I/2, p.749.
[44] *CD* I/2, p.848.
[45] *CD* I/2, p.804.
[46] *CD* I/2, p.876.
[47] *CD* I/2, p.849.

the Father's side is at once His revelation as the One to whom all authority is given, the one to whom the place at the Father's right hand belongs. But at the same time it is also the veiling of this reality, and the creation of the situation in which Jesus comes to the church mediated in the word of scripture, and in His Spirit. In this time the mission of the church is simply to witness to the gracious presence of her otherwise hidden and veiled Lord.

This presence of the Lord of the church is even so not a donation, or the possession of an autonomous church. Jesus is always and forever the transcendent Lord – ascension can add nothing to the glory of His transcendence – but apart from the event of revelation even the church does not see His glory, it is hidden at the Father's side. Once again we are confronted by the conditions that create the need for dogmatics – that is, the church does not possess knowledge of God in Christ, but must ever receive it afresh, and this imposes upon the church the need to critique its proclamation against God's Word heard through holy scripture. We may see the role that Jesus' ascension and heavenly session play in generating those conditions. On that note we turn now to the significance of the church for the creation of the 'time between' itself, and the stress which Barth places upon the being of the church as Jesus' earthly-historical form and, as we have seen, upon the task of the church as the present *locus* of Jesus' mission.

The *Time Between* as the Time of the Church

In a significant section of *Church Dogmatics* volume IV/1 Barth describes 'The Time of the Community' (section 62.3) and places considerable weight upon the notion that the 'time between' is created specifically for the church and the church's mission. This is the time of Jesus' 'absence', of His *invisible* presence in the church, and of His continued veiling, as we have seen.

> The time of the community is the time between the first *parousia* of Jesus Christ and the second. '*Parousia*' means the immediate visible presence and action of the living Jesus Christ Himself. ... The community exists between His coming then [at Easter] as the risen One and this final coming [in the *eschaton*]. Its time is, therefore, this time between. Its movement is from direct vision to direct vision; and in this movement by His Holy Spirit He Himself is invisibly present as the living Head in the midst of His body.[48]

It is not that the church itself is the most important thing in this age – in one sense the reverse is true, for the church itself exists to serve the world, even as Jesus exists to serve. Rather the church's *mission*, having its end in service of Christ and of those to whom the church is called to witness, is at the centre of this time. Thus the church's limited but genuine witness to Jesus Christ is the meaning of current history. The church's witness is the purpose for which it is

---

[48] *CD* IV/1, p.725.

given time, indeed this is the reason for the 'time between' itself. The task and work of the community of Jesus Christ in representing Him is the meaning and content of this time.[49]

It is in this reality of the 'time between' that both the strength and the weakness of the church reside – as we have already seen. The church's strength resides in the absolute reality of all that Jesus has accomplished, and in the revelation of this in the resurrection. The church, as above, moves from direct sight of Jesus in the resurrection to direct sight of Jesus in His *eschaton*, and it is thus that the church is strong.

> It is strong because for it Easter stands behind every yesterday, the first *parousia* of the One who is its Lord, but who as the great Servant of God is also the Lord of the whole world, of all men. It is strong because for it His coming in glory is proclaimed and present beyond every morning – His second and final *parousia*. It knows what time it is because it knows that it is this time between, and because in this knowledge it is held and impelled and directed both behind and before.[50]

But the church's weakness resides in the absence of her Head, and the fact that He is known in faith and not by sight. Jesus is present, but in such a way that the church moving from Easter to *eschaton* sees Him only as through a veil. 'The community moves from the one point to the other like a ship – a recurring picture – sailing over an ocean a thousand fathoms deep'.[51] At the root of this lies the being of Jesus as ascended to the right hand of the Father. The outcome of the forty days was Jesus' ascension, and the result of this event is that the apostles were caused to fall back upon the Spirit of the Lord, and faith in His living presence in that Spirit.[52] Thus the community exists in this 'time between' as an all-too frail human community, but nonetheless, in the grace of God as the body of Jesus Christ. The humanity of Jesus in heaven is the church's anchor and goal, but in the meantime it remains unseen and a matter of hope and faith. 'To Him in this [heavenly] form of His existence it can only look and move as, "absent from the Lord" (2 Cor. 5[6]), it waits with all creation for His appearance from heaven, for His coming forth from the hiddenness of God'.[53]

Barth places considerable emphasis upon this reality of the church as Jesus' body – His earthly-historical form of existence – and at the same time as a fully human and frail society. In fact the two sides of this cohere entirely, for it is only as Jesus' ascension creates the time between, and therefore the conditions in which He can take to Himself the community of those whom He is sanctifying, that Jesus takes an earthly-historical body of this kind. Given the conditions of the 'time between' – the continuation of fallen time, and the

---

[49] *CD* IV/2, p.621.

[50] *CD* IV/1, pp.727-8.

[51] *CD* IV/1, p.728.

[52] *CD* IV/1, p.728.

[53] *CD* IV/3.ii, p.755.

continued existence of fallen humanity – the genuine and indeed fallen humanity of the church is necessary if it is to be Jesus' *earthly-historical* body (as opposed to His *heavenly-historical* body). The identity between Jesus ascended and His earthly body is therefore strongly posited. 'For the Jesus Christ who rules the world *ad dexteram Patris omnipotentis* is identical with the King of this people of His which on earth finds itself on this way and in this movement'.[54]

At the heart of this is Barth's determination to avoid ecclesiological doceticism – there is no church but the earthly, weak, and even sinful church, just as Jesus took no other flesh than earthly, weak, sinful flesh. It is for *this* community that the 'time between' exists. Indeed, just as Jesus has not divested Himself of His human nature in ascending, so the church at the *eschaton* will receive the fullness of eternal life precisely as this human society, which currently exists within and for the world.

> As surely as its Lord was elected from all eternity, not as the λόγος ἄσαρκος, but as the *Verbum incarnandum*, in his concrete humanity and visibility as the man Jesus of Nazareth; as surely as He came and lived and suffered and died 'in the flesh' (1 Jn. 4²); as surely as He did not lay aside His concretely human nature but in it rose again from the dead, and ascended into heaven, and, clothed in it, sits at the right hand of God ... so surely in the same Jesus Christ God has also elected His community in its very being *ad extra*, in its visibility and worldliness, in its likeness to other peoples, and so surely it will not be divested of this being, but will be manifested in its visibility and worldliness at the fulfilment of His return, when it will ... share eternal life in fellowship with God.[55]

Thus, in that the 'time between' is given for the life of the church and for its work of service, this time involves the giving of space for further human history. The present age is the affirmation of the importance of human history before God. Jesus' death and resurrection mark the end of all time – and yet, as we have seen, the old time of the world is not immediately wound up, space is created for additional history.

> A history which is a postscript, but a real history, and therefore more generations, more opportunities for human existence from God and before God and to God, more opportunities of fellowship, of psycho-physical life, more spans of life – and all within the great and astonishing span which has still been allotted to the world as a whole.[56]

And at the heart of this gift of time and history is God's desire for genuine human response to and participation within the economy of God's grace. Jesus ascended is very much still at work saving His people. '[Salvation] is a living redemptive happening which takes place. Or, more concretely, it is the saving operation of the living Lord Jesus which did not conclude but began in

---

[54] *CD* IV/2, p.622.

[55] *CD* IV/3.ii, p.724.

[56] *CD* IV/1, pp.736-7.

His revelation on Easter Day'.[57] Strikingly – especially in light of the criticism Barth receives for devaluing humanity and human action – the purpose of the Jesus' ascension and heavenly session, as a delay of the *eschaton*, is human participation in the work of God through human response to God's grace. The 'time between' is the time given for humanity and human history within the realm of Jesus' victory. God intends that the final Word spoken should not be completely uttered without a human response also being spoken – God intends and demands that there be a response, a human response from within the reality of a fallen human world. God will receive praise from within the old creation, before the final dawn of the new creation.[58]

It is thus that the church is the secret meaning of the 'time between' and thus of Jesus' ascension and session! As above, not only is the church a peculiar creature of the present age, but as God's workplace in this age, and as the earthly-historical form of Jesus' existence, she is at the centre of God's purpose for this age.

> The community is and has the answer which has to be given to the question of the good and gracious purpose of God in the puzzling distance between the first *parousia* of Jesus Christ and the second, the question of the time between, in which the world is held, as it were suspended between the provisional and transitory and particular revelation of its reconciliation with God in Jesus Christ and the perfect and definitive and universal revelation of it in His final coming.[59]

Even though the church is weak, and fragile, and seemingly powerless against the great currents and powers which roll through the age, God works in it and wills its being as Jesus' body. It is for the sake of God's purpose in and through this community, the people who acknowledge and worship God in Jesus Christ, that the second coming is delayed.[60]

Concluding Comments

What then characterises Barth's ecclesiology, particularly in the light of the ascension and the 'time between' which it inaugurates? It is very clear that the church is a creature of this 'time between', peculiar to and existing within the tensions and limitations of the present age – the age of penultimate realities. Barth is certain that the church is a profoundly limited, and yet a profoundly rich creature. A large degree of the church's limitation is derived from the absence of her ascended Lord, and moreover, from the fact that in His ascension He still occupies a place within the creation. Thus, although the church is Jesus' earthly-historical form in the time between, she is not His

---

[57] *CD* IV/2, pp.621-2.
[58] *CD* IV/1, p.737.
[59] *CD* IV/1, pp.733-4.
[60] *CD* IV/1, p.739.

primary form of embodiment within the creaturely world – Jesus exists as the risen man of Nazareth ascended to the Father's side. The church can never be said to possess Jesus, but rather exists in derivation from Him, and as His creation in the Spirit – the church always exists in eschatological tension, and must not attempt to overcome that tension by arrogating to herself powers and authority which remain Jesus' alone. Nonetheless, the church does belong to Jesus, and does hear His voice – particularly in the dual words of scripture and proclamation. The church is the place where Jesus is made known, and wherein the work of redemption takes place. Paradoxically perhaps, the wealth of the church is therefore also a function of Jesus' ascension, for as the heavenly head He is the source of its life. Jesus has ascended to the place of all authority and power – 'the right hand of the Father almighty' – and although this does not mean that He is now *exalted* in a manner He was not before, it does mean that He exercises His lordship in a new fashion, and exercises the authority that is His as the ascended One.

For Jesus the 'time between' is not a period of inactivity, or passivity, but of active self-witness in which His being as King and Priest is manifested in His work as Prophet. The Son of God united with the Son of Man continues the humility, and intercedes for His own in such a way that they are made to know Him and share His life. It is the dynamic of presence and absence – allied to Jesus' lordship and transcendence – that underpins Barth's doctrine of holy scripture, and shapes the way in which scripture is described as Jesus' concrete presence. That scripture both is and is not God's Word is strongly related to the presence and absence of the ascended Lord who makes it His own. It is thus that the church has her mission to make Christ known – again, on the basis of His lack of immediacy to the earthly historical world – and to preach Jesus even as she listens to Him.

Very much in Reformation tradition, Barth conceives of the church as *creatura verbi* (creature of the Word), and although he is not disparaging of the eucharist, it is quite plain from his lack of comment that he does not see the eucharist as constitutive of the being of the church. He often enough mentions the Lord's supper as an event of Christ's presence, but not in any way to rival the presence of the Lord in self-witness via the witness of apostles and prophets. Positively, the church is that community which hears and obeys the Word in and through the word, negatively, the church may not claim to possess that Word, or to control it. The living Lord remains beyond the church, and beyond the scripture through which He rules the church. This means that the church is called ever to be a listening, and a humble, body. The church's mission – the event and act in which the church exists – is primarily the act of hearing, and it is this work of listening that must occupy us.

Nonetheless, as a listening body the church is called to speak and to itself proclaim what it hears. This is not a secondary move, separate from the listening that is the church's life, rather, the form of listening obedience in which the church lives and moves *is* mission. The church cannot choose whether or not to be a missionary body – the church's existence is also the act of its mission. The ascended Lord has not ceased to reach out in mission to the world He died for, and so His body is that group of people whom He takes to Himself as a witness. As the earthly-historical form of Jesus' life the church *is* His self-witness to the world, and this is incontrovertible.

As Jesus marches inexorably toward His *eschaton* the church is moved with Him. It is essential that alongside Barth's awareness of the church as limited, and as penultimate in character, we place the Christological emphasis upon Jesus' achievement on the cross. Barth is certain that Jesus' victory – the victory of God as Tom Wright has it[61] – is already achieved, and is objectively realised. But in the 'time between' the subjective realisation of that victory is limited, partial, and penultimate. The church endures that penultimacy, but the church also possesses an anchor and foundation in the victory of God – in fact, to put it better, the church possesses a foundation and anchor in the Victor, seated upon the throne of God. If we may extrapolate from the discussion for a moment, this means that there is an appropriate Christian confidence which clings to the mercy of God and hopes for all things in the One who lives and reigns, and who will return. In enduring the difficulties of the present age as the age of 'not-yet', of the continued absence of the saviour, and of the seeming triumph of sin and evil, the church suffers, and yet also knows that nothing can take away from what has already been achieved, and from the One who is seated in the heavenlies. The church must 'seek things that are above, where Christ is, seated at the right hand of God', remembering that all that its 'life is hidden with Christ in God'.[62]

All this belongs to the fact that the present age is the 'time between', and as such the time of the church – the space and time of grace and mission. Jesus' work and life as the heavenly Head of the earthly body determines the shape of the church and of its tasks. Indeed, the very existence of the age of Jesus as ascended and awaited is for the purpose embodied within the church – the church is the secret meaning of the 'time between'. God wills that there be a further history and a further time in which human may respond to Him and act in accordance with His grace. Far from being unimportant Barth sees in human action and obedience the very reason for the creation of the present age, even as the nature of the age conditions the manner and form of that obedience. As we turn to the being of individuals as Christians in the present age, a similar set of dynamics will apply, as the ascended Lord works to redeem those who belong to Him, and as they obey the commands He gives them.

---

[61] *Jesus and the Victory of God: Christian Origins and the Question of God* vol. 2, N.T. Wright, Fortress Press, Augsberg, Minneapolis, 1996.

[62] Colossians 3$^{1\&3}$ (NRSV).

Chapter 4

Ascension and the Christian

(*Church Dogmatics* I/2, section 18)

Christians are God's children as they live 'between the times', and so the life of the children of God is shaped by the theological reality of the 'time between'. That is to say, Jesus' ascension, as it inaugurates the present age and introduces the absent presence of Jesus Christ, places the children of God within time and space as it awaits the fullness of redemption, and as Christians they themselves stand within the tension of belonging wholly to Jesus while remaining sinners who live still within fallen time. So, reflection on Christian existence, and particularly upon ethics – the form that life as God's children must take – involves reflection upon the nature of the 'time between' and upon God's work among Christians in that time. Two things follow as we move into an examination of Barth's treatment of ethics (an area of his thought which is much criticised, or simply ignored): Firstly, we may gain genuine insight into what it is to be those who belong to Jesus 'between the times', and in particularly the theme of 'seeking' as the primary mode of Christian existence – seeking the life that is hid with Christ above, seeking the being that is ours in Christ and in the future God is bringing but that is only partially realised this side of the *eschaton* – will provide a *locus* of thought regarding our being as God's children. Secondly we may be enabled to better understand what drives Barth's thinking about ethics. It is not the aim of this chapter to directly engage the debate about Barth's ethical material. But by exposing the way in which Barth's treatment of the command to love God and to love the neighbour is characterised by his attention to the conditions of the present age we may open up some important avenues for further investigation, and help to make clearer sense of Barth's key moves within ethics.

In what follows we will focus on one section of the *Church Dogmatics*, section 18 'The Life of the Children of God', found in volume I/2. This will allow a close reading of significant piece of Barth's ethics, and in particular we will be able to identify a clear reliance upon ascension theology within the section. Barth focuses on the dual command of Jesus, to love God and to love the neighbour. In doing so he claims that he is simply doing ethics, but ethics within the proper mode of Christian discourse – that is, within reflection upon the Word of God.[1] As those who hear the Word of God Christians exist and act accordingly - - they cannot help but do so. The question is therefore: 'What have we to do who know that we have heard and believed the Word of God?'[2] Reflection upon the Word of God itself, with all the christological focus involved, in its awareness of humans as the recipients of revelation, anticipates and already involves examination of the Christian life and 'it takes ethics into itself, thus making special theological ethics superfluous. For without ceasing to be dogmatics, reflection upon the Word of God, it is itself ethics'.[3] All this is to say, for Barth, to do ethics is a specifically *theological* task – a task that is totally a part of the dogmatic task of listening to the gospel of Jesus Christ in such a way as to bring every thought into submission to it. It is reflection upon Jesus and what it means that He is the Saviour, now seated at the right hand of the Father, and that in Him we are now made God's children, that drives ethics. Nothing else can provide the basis for reflection on human reality in the 'time between' than attending to the life, reality, and absent presence of the Lord whose ascension inaugurates that time, and whose being at the Father's side reveals His Lordship and rule over all creation.

The Life of the Children of God

As ethics, section 18 represents the practical outworking of all that has gone before. 'The structure of *Church Dogmatics* makes its method clear: to move *from* dogmatics *to* ethics'.[4] Barth has earlier treated the being and work of the Holy Spirit, following upon sections relating to the Father and Son, and within this trinitarian structure section 18 involves a practical application of the preceding material, especially in relation to the Spirit of the ascended Lord. The practical matter of Christian life is worked out from its basis in the being and act of the eternal God who is present in the saving action of the Son and Spirit.

Christological matters are therefore crucial in reflecting upon the being and action of Christians. A whole complex of significant christological affirmations hold sway over Barth's thought, in particular the central truths of the incarnation, of Jesus Christ's being as the mediator between God and fallen humanity, and as the bearer of human flesh in union with the eternal Word of God. The identity of Jesus Christ, and the nature of the salvation He brings in the activity He undertakes on behalf of His own, is supremely important to Barth. We may therefore argue that the doctrine of the ascension has a

---

[1] For a brief analysis of Barth's ethical thought that takes his method seriously and avoids simplistic criticisms, while describing Barth as a limited ethicist, see Nigel Biggar's 'Barth's trinitarian ethic' in Webster, John B. ed. *The Cambridge Companion to Karl Barth* Cambridge: Cambridge University Press, 2000, pp.212-27.

[2] *CD* I/2, p.371.

[3] *CD* I/2, p.371.

[4] Biggar, Nigel, 'Barth's trinitarian ethic', p.223.

particular and significant role to play at this point. That Jesus is ascended forms part of the complex of christological material that controls and shapes Barth's discussion, particularly as we look to the implications of the nature and shape of the present age. We may perhaps see that in affirming and utilising the doctrine of the ascension Barth is able to offer a worthy and faithful account of the life of the children of God in all the tensions inherent in the age 'between'.

Barth describes the being of Christians as in 'two times and worlds', due to the partial presence and absence of Jesus Christ, and all that he has achieved. Christians are those who 'seek' God in Jesus Christ, and who live in futurity as Jesus enables their participation in the time and world which He is bringing and which will appear with Him in His coming again. As Biggar has it:

> We, accordingly, stand 'between the times' in an ambiguous mixture of light and darkness, encouraged by the manifestation of God's reconciling grace in the past, but still radically dependent upon the final manifestation of his redemptive grace yet to come.[5]

Barth's treatment of Jesus' dual commandments is explicitly founded upon the distinction between the present age, as the penultimate age, and the eternal time of God which is breaking in upon it. In seeing God's children living in the crossover between these 'two times and worlds', as Barth puts it, he moves to see the two commandments as tailored to this dual nature of Christian existence, and as comprehensible only upon presupposition of it. The purpose of this chapter is to draw attention to the role of Jesus' ascended being in shaping, sometimes at a distance, but genuinely, the fundamental presuppositions Barth works with.

The Ascended Christ and the Being of the Christian

As above, Christian existence is defined by Barth in terms of existence in *two* times: the time of Jesus, in which we stand before God in the fullness of redemption; and yet also still within our own time in which we are sinners and in which we await the redemption which is ever coming. Nonetheless, within the tension of these two times, Christians are recipients of the Spirit, and as such hearers and doers of the Word. The time of Jesus, of redemption, is greater than the time of the old world – the old world is passing, but in the Lordship of God the time of Jesus Christ comes and remains.

In line with his constant emphasis on the incapacity of humans to achieve salvation or any of the reality of redeemed life for themselves, Barth is insistent that the character of a human as a 'doer of the Word' is utterly and totally God's gift. While the free self-determination of the Christian is clearly affirmed, the character of Christian life is not strictly identified with the things that a person does or does not do – instead it is about the acquiring of that

---

[5] 'Barth's trinitarian ethic', p.219.

character from outside, from God in the agency of the Holy Spirit. The character of the Christian is the fruit of revelation.

> The free decision of man, the act and work of man, the life of real men, is revealed in the fulfilment of revelation as the outpouring of the Holy Spirit. But it does not have its character as the life of the children of God from itself, but from the light in which it is placed. No positive – and we must add at once, no negative – description of what man does or does not do can clearly reproduce, in the strict sense, the 'Christian' character of his life and activity and suffering. It acquires this character only 'from outside', that is, from God.[6]

Barth defines the actual tension in the shape of Christian existence eschatologically, but in doing so he relies explicitly upon the fact that Jesus is ascended and as the heavenly Lord He exists eternally. Jesus is God, and He is the true reality. We must be made anew by Him, as He is the reality and we are only 'real' insomuch as we are found in Him. It is Jesus who has eternal life in Himself, while we are mere earthly creatures, and there remains an 'eschatological frontier between Him and us'.[7] Christians exist in this state of tension – between what we are as creatures of the time between and what we have already been made in Jesus Christ who has ascended and presents us before the Father in Himself. So we are called into a constant seeking after God. In Christ God has put to death, taken away from us, the life we have in and of ourselves, and we must instead seek the life that is 'hid with God in Christ'.

> [The Christian] cannot exist without seeking God in Jesus Christ. He is denied any other being than that which consists in the specific act of seeking. ... He is saved in Christ. He is a sinner pardoned, a *peccator justus*. He lives in his activity as a seeker after God.[8]

The only being the Christian has is as a seeker after and hearer of the Word, as both occur in the power of the Spirit, but it must be remembered that the Word whom we seek is Jesus Christ who has ascended to the Father's side. Those who belong to Jesus have life only as they seek Him. 'They can have it only as they have the Word, and therefore only as they seek the Word, only as they seek God in Christ, only as they 'seek that which is above' (Col.3[1f])'.[9]

Barth calls the character of the Christian 'the love of God' – that is, the love of the Christian toward God in the power of God's original and initiating love for her. This being is the only possible being for the human person in relation to God, because in Jesus Christ God has brought to an end all human existence that is not existence in Christ Himself. In being incorporated into Jesus Christ the Christian is made to share in His resurrection, with the

---

[6] *CD* I/2, p.368.

[7] *CD* I/2, p.368.

[8] *CD* I/2, p.370.

[9] *CD* I/2, p.370.

implication that he is a sharer also in His death and ascension – a sharer in the whole complex of His being as the crucified, risen and ascended One. '[Love for God] is the only being which remains when his other being is taken away from him, because he has risen again with Christ'.[10] Christian life exists in love and praise to God, but as Barth explicates the nature of this existence in greater depth we will find that his treatment is very much shaped around his notion of two times, and of the eschatological tension between them created by Jesus' ascension into heaven.

Loving God

The capacity to love God is not something that Barth's considers to be innate in humans, or to be in any way abstractable from the redemptive activity of the Holy Spirit. God Himself, in the priority of His love for us, creates our ability to love Him. However, this is not to imply that we are not genuinely, humanly, involved in the act of loving God – in fact, quite the reverse. True humanity is the creation of God, and exists only in the reality of His action upon us redeeming and recreating. Indeed we 'must insist that the love of the children of God does become an event in an act or acts of human self-determination: it is a creaturely reality'. [11]   It is a creaturely reality which certainly is recreated by God in grace and predetermined favour – but it does not on that account cease to be genuinely human.

The tension present here, the sense in which love toward God is simultaneously the Christian's being and failure to be, is a function of the current form of the Christian's relationship to the source of the power which creates the new being. Jesus Christ, the incarnate Word of God, is in Himself the reconciliation of God with humanity, and in His presence we are reconciled to the Father. But, once again, Jesus in this age 'between' is both present and absent, precisely because He is ascended. As the ascended One He presents us in accomplished reconciliation before the throne of the Father – in union with his heavenly being we simply *are* reconciled creatures existing in love to God. But we do not exist with Him purely in His ascended reality – rather we continue to exist in the 'time between', and in that time Jesus ascended is also absent and only mediate in the Spirit. Nonetheless, it is Jesus' very ascension *in His adopted humanity* which is the source of the new being of the Christian, even as it is the source of longing for the fullness of that new being.

> In strict analogy with the incarnation of the Word in Jesus Christ, what takes place in man by the revelation of God is this: his humanity is not impaired, but in the Word of God heard and believed by him he finds the Lord, indeed in a strict and

---

[10] *CD* I/2, p.370.
[11] *CD* I/2, p.373.

proper sense he finds the subject of his humanity, for on his behalf Jesus Christ stands and rightly stands in His humanity at the right hand of the Father. [12]

It is thus that the Christian must ever seek God in Jesus, and in seeking God, love God. This is what it means to be part of the earthly body which seeks its heavenly Head.

In his recital of the 'bare bones' of Jesus Christ's history as the history of salvation of the children of God Barth gives particular place to the role of Jesus as ascended – that is in His heavenly session. The history of Jesus Christ is in fact the love of God for us, and that love culminates in Jesus' presence at the Father's side as our mediator and advocate.

> The self-sacrifice of God in His Son is in fact the love of God to us. 'He gave Him', which means that He gave Him into our existence. Having been given into our existence He is present with us. Present with us, He falls heir to the shame and curse which lie upon us. As the bearer of our shame and curse, He bears them away from us. Taking them away, He presents us as pure and spotless children in the presence of the Father. [13]

Having then explored in some detail the orientation of the Christian toward loving God as a function of election, Barth returns to the theme of 'seeking' as a summation of Christian being in love. Obedience to God is, again, a grasping of the future that we have in the form of promise, the future that is already present, and indeed ultimately real, in Jesus Christ. Love for God is the form that this obedience takes.

> To love means to become what we already are, those who are loved by [God]. To love means to choose God as the Lord, the One who is our Lord because He is our Advocate and Representative. To love means to be obedient to the commandment of this God. In every case, therefore, love is an accepting, confirming, and grasping of our future. In it this future is identical with the reality of God, who in the most pregnant sense of the word is 'for us'. [14]

Jesus Christ is this God 'for us', [15] and He is the future of the children of God. Yet plainly our being in and of ourselves remains profoundly at odds with this future. In the space and time of grace our sin is ever before us, even and especially as those who do in fact love God.

---

[12] *CD* I/2, p.374.

[13] *CD* I/2, p.378.

[14] *CD* I/2, pp.389-90.

[15] Of course not in any sense which excludes the being of the Father and Spirit as 'for us', but rather in such a wise as to reveal the inclusive nature of the gracious determination of the Trinity toward us.

The man who loves God will let himself be told and will himself confess that he is not in any sense righteous as one who loves and in his loving before and over against God. On the contrary, he is a sinner who even in his love has nothing to bring and offer to God.[16]

Yet, in this age between, as those who do indeed love God, Christians realise their future in God simply in seeking God – in seeking Jesus who is above. 'Strictly speaking, our being and activity as such can only be this seeking'.[17] Certainly this need to seek is tied to several key doctrinal sources, and not to Jesus' absence via ascension alone. So, for instance, our need to seek Jesus is just as much a function of our sinful being and our inability simply to have Jesus, or to even maintain relationship with Him. Equally we must seek Jesus because of His transcendence as the Son of God, and because we are limited creatures who are not able to overcome the barrier of His transcendence, or to simply exist in His presence.[18] Yet Barth's emphasis on the being of the Christian as member of the earthly body of the heavenly Head remains an important part of the complex. Moreover, the character of Christian existence as seeking *is* thoroughly grounded in the fact that the present age involves a 'space', a 'lack' as well as a 'fullness' in regard to redemption. Christians exist now as seekers after their future being in God because that being remains future as long as they await the *eschaton*. As we shall see, the explication of loving God as love for the neighbour (below) turns upon Barth's understanding of the 'time between'.

To pick up upon the motif of time, as explored earlier, the fact that the Christian seeks the future in God is an expression of the fact that the time of Jesus is the only genuine time – it is the time of God which will be all in all – and yet that Jesus' time remains the coming time. The grace of God reveals the poverty of those whom He loves; the patience of God reveals the desperate straits of those who although condemned are nevertheless redeemed. Grace cannot but point sinners away from any self reliance, and must result in a

---

[16] *CD* I/2, p.390. The German original is:

> Gerade der Gott Liebende wird es sich gesagt sein lassen und wird es auch bekennen, daß er ganz und gar auch als Libender und seinem Lieben vor Gott und Gott gegenüber nicht gerecht, sondern ein Sünder ist, der auch mit seinem Lieben Gott nichts darzubringen und zu bieten hat. (*Kirchliche Dogmatik* I/2, p.429.)

> 'Indeed, the lover of God will allow himself to be told, and also will [himself] confess, that he is entirely unrighteous – even as one who loves, and in his love for God, and over and against God – and is rather a sinner, who even in his love has nothing to bring and nothing to offer to God.' (Author's translation).

[17] *CD* I/2, p.391.

[18] We might draw attention once again to Barth's affirmation of the *extra Calvinisticum* as a key plank in his Christological structure – Jesus Christ is ever the transcendent Son of God, the irreducible and eternal Logos, and events such as His resurrection, ascension, and eschaton can never add or subtract anything from this, His being.

turning to the external source of life. There is no home in the self, no place to stand, no strength or health. All boasting can only be boasting in the grace which meets sinners and saves them.[19] The presence of the time of Jesus is the end of all other time – Jesus is the only future and in Him the being of Christians is taken up in such a fashion that apart from Him they are destroyed. Yet because the fullness of redemption is only present in Jesus, who is at the Father's side, Christians exist as those who are only invisibly redeemed, and who are visibly sinners worthy of judgement.

Barth makes strong use of the language of visibility and invisibility in arguing that the hidden form of existence in Christ can in no way be allowed to drive a wedge between future redemption and the actuality of being and activity in the present time.

> There can be no division between the man I am visibly in myself and the man I am invisibly in Jesus Christ .... It is as the man I am visibly in myself that I am invisibly in Jesus Christ. And it is the fact that I am invisible in Jesus Christ that imposes upon me as the man I am visibly in myself the duty to love.[20]

Thus within the dynamic of 'visible' and 'invisible' Barth turns to a discussion of love for the neighbour as the particular form of obedience commanded and therefore appropriate in the time between as the time of cross-over between two times – the residual time of the fallen creation and the in-breaking time of Jesus Christ.

Praise of God in Love for the Neighbour

Barth's treatment of the life of the children of God follows Jesus' teaching that 'You shall love the Lord your God with all your heart, with all your soul, with all your mind and with all your strength. This is the first commandment, and a second is like, namely: You shall love your neighbour as yourself'. (Mark 12[29-31]). Having examined the command to love God, Barth turns to the question of loving the neighbour, and discovers the meaning of this love in that it forms an activity of praise to God – its practical expression. The meaning and content of the command to love the neighbour is found in the task of praising God, as those who love God with every part of our whole being.[21]

As Barth turns to explore the nature of this command, the very fact that Jesus calls it 'second' causes some pause, for he is not willing to see two entirely separate commands here. Yet, because Jesus names them as two commands, with one second and 'like' the first, Barth will also not claim that there is really only one command. Having, then, rejected the notion of two broadly independent commands, and examined the arguments for seeing love for the neighbour as simply identical with love for God, Barth asks whether we

---

[19] *CD* I/2, p.393.
[20] *CD* I/2, p.395.
[21] *CD* I/2, p.401.

may see the second command as derivative and relative in relation to the absolute command to love God Himself. Yet this too cannot be maintained, for this command is not given lesser status but remains absolute – indeed we 'must also ask the radical question whether it is even possible to conceive of a commandment of God which is subordinate, derived and relative? Is not the commandment of God always and whatever it says an absolute commandment?'[22]

How is the relation between the first and second commandments finally to be resolved? The answer for Barth lies in the nature of the activity involved in obedience to the second commandment: 'It is praise of God which breaks out in love to the neighbour. And in Holy Scripture the command to praise God rings out with the same note of central and absolutely decisive urgency as that of love to God'.[23] The specific character of this activity of praise, and its relation to the command to love is worked out in relation to the nature of the present age as the time of Jesus ascended and of the *eschaton* as future event.

Initially Barth's claim is very straightforward – the being of Christians as those who are called by God to belong to Him in the present age is the key to the puzzle of understanding the relation between the first and second commandments.

> The connexion and the difference between the two commandments are plain when we remember that the children of God, the Church, now live, as it were, in the space between the resurrection and ascension of Jesus, and in the time of the forbearance of God and their own watching and waiting. In effect they live in two times and worlds.[24]

Christians live in two times, and in two worlds, because they live in the 'time between', this age in which God expresses His mercy and forbearance by tolerating the continuing presence of sin and evil while at the same time having

---

[22] *CD* I/2, p.407.

[23] *CD* I/2, p.406.

[24] *CD* I/2, p.408.

> Der Zusammenhang und die Verschiedenheit der beiden Gebote werden sichtbar, wenn wir uns vor Augen halten, daß die Kinder Gottes, daß die Kirche in dem Raum zwischen der Auferstehung und Himmelfahrt Jesu in der uns gelassenen Zeit der Geduld Gottes und des uns auferlegten Wachens und Wartens in Wirklichkeit in zwei Zeiten und Welten leben ...
> (*Kirchliche Dogmatik* I/2, p.450).

Two different typological errors might provide an explanation for this strange saying: firstly, 'zwischen' may simply be an error, and the original word intended might be 'nach'. Alternatively, Barth may have intended to say 'in dem Raum zwischen der Auferstehung und Himmelfahrt Jesu und das *Eschaton* ...' but 'und das *Eschaton*' never eventuated. This latter notion might be encouraged by the lack of a separate article before 'Himmelfahrt', effectively pairing it with 'Auferstehung', which would fit with Barth's usual treatment of the two as poles of a single event.

accomplished the destruction of all sin and the institution of His kingdom in the person of His Son.

However, as it stands the above quotation also clearly creates some difficulties for the thesis that the *ascension* of Jesus and His *ascended* state are key to this understanding. Barth seems to claim that it is as if the ascension has not happened – as if Christians exist between resurrection and ascension. This statement is not mirrored or repeated elsewhere, and therefore in its brevity provides some difficulties for interpretation. Perhaps Barth means that like the Apostles, and because the church exists solely in reliance upon the testimony of the Apostles, Christians exist in the time of the resurrection appearances, of the forty days. Farrow has called Barth a 'theologian of the forty days', and perhaps this is what he has in mind.

But what are we to make of this somewhat isolated saying of Barth's? If we look further into even the same paragraph we find that Barth redescribes this being 'between the times' in more familiar language. The two commands, to love God and neighbour, are in fact both about unrivalled love and obedience toward God. But the two different aspects commanded correspond to the reality of the two times. It is therefore not a question of two different objects requiring our love, but rather of the love of God's children being shaped by their parallel existence in two times or ages.[25] Love for God is the reality of eternity, of redeemed human existence. As those who belong with Jesus in His resurrection and ascension, Christians are simply those who love God, and who will love God into eternity.

> The resurrection and ascension of Jesus Christ have taken place. On this basis they are already members and participants of the new world created by Him. ... They are in Christ; and it is in the totality of this their hidden being, which is none other than their actual human and creaturely existence here and now, that in the way described they are put under the commandment to love God ...[26]

On this account, the resurrection and ascension of Jesus provide one pole of the tension within which the current age exists, and in particular which characterises the being of Christians as 'in two times and worlds'. The other pole, familiarly enough is the second coming of Jesus Christ, the *eschaton*, the full revelation of the kingdom of God. Christians also *await* their redemption – as above, their being in Christ is a *hidden* being, 'hid with Christ in God'. It is as *iusti peccatores* that Christians exist, waiting for the resolution of all things – including themselves! – and so they are call to serve Christ within the matrix of relationships and circumstances that belong to the fallen age which continues. All this has, of course, already been overtaken by Christ resurrection from the dead, and the new reality is not yet visible as we await Jesus' return, when all

---

[25] *CD* I/2, p.408.
[26] *CD* I/2, p.408.

shall be transformed.[27] Thus the tension within which Christians exist is the tension between Jesus' resurrection, including as it does His ascension, and His return in all the authority that is His as the risen and ascended One.[28]

This particular description of the current being of Christians, as earlier, provides the framework which Barth now uses to unpack the nature of the second commandment in relation to the first. Each of the three rejected descriptions of the relation of the first and second commandments is taken up and re-examined for whatever truth it may be seen to possess *in the all-important light of the description of the two times which Barth has now established.*

So, having earlier rejected the notion that we have two separate and distinct commands, Barth now affirms the sense in which this is actually true – on the basis of the distinction between the two times attendant within the present age. In these commands we have the single claim to our obedience made by the one absolute Lord on His children.

> And yet because of the twofoldness in which [Christians] exist before God and for God, they are not one but two commandments. The first one, the commandment to love God, is intended for the child of God in his completed existence in Jesus Christ as the heavenly Head of His earthly members. The second commandment, to love the neighbour, is intended for the child of God in his not yet completed walk and activity as an earthly member of this heavenly Head. It is the same God speaking to the same man. He speaks in two ways, because he exists in two ways.[29]

Just as the disjunction involved in the tension between the two times implies the dual nature of the commandments, so also the fact that Jesus Christ's revelation is the source of the movement from one age to the other implies the unity of the commandments. This is the truth which Barth finds residing in the claim that the two commandments are in reality one, the second of the ideas he earlier rejected.

> It is His revelation which underlies the twofold reality and aspect of human existence. It is by means of this revelation and in the light of it that there is the transition, the movement of the one time into the other, and therefore the twofoldness of the demand upon man.[30]

---

[27] *CD* I/2, p.409 This lends weight to the thesis that the initial troubling quotation above is the result of a error, possibly typological. See footnote 24 above.

[28] We may recall that Barth regards the resurrection, ascension, and eschaton as three moments of one event – the event which is the revelation of the glory of the Mediator, and which is also the establishment of the kingdom in all fullness. Thus in this treatment we discover a sense of an almost 'unnatural' delay of the eschaton while Jesus remains 'absent' via His ascension, and it is in the space created by this delay that the children of God live on earth and seek that which is above.

[29] *CD* I/2, p.409.

[30] *CD* I/2, p.409.

Although, as Barth continues, there is no sense in which we should see the neighbour as one with God in the time that is passing away, or finally unite the two commands into one. We must simply acknowledge their single source, and the single claim upon our allegiance that they involve.

So also Barth examines the third rejected idea, that the command to love the neighbour is only a secondary and derivative command, and finds that in the light of the twofold nature of our present there is some truth to it. The commandment to love God has a forward reference to the coming world, while the commandment to love the neighbour refers to the passing age, and to that extent we do after all have a first and second commandment – the one superior to the other, and the one derivative upon the eternal priority of the first. Indeed, this is straightforwardly related to the lack of equality between the two times – the time of God has overcome, and overcomes, the time of the fallen creation.[31] Thus love of the neighbour is acknowledged as an absolute claim upon Christians living 'between the times' because it is a manifestation of love toward God: obedience to this commandment is an expression of obedience to the commandment to love God.

> Love to God is in fact the real cause and expository principle of love to the neighbour. Love to the neighbour is in fact the token of love to God. To that extent, as something commanded in respect of our existence which now is and passes, by its very nature it can be the erecting of a sign, and not of a completed and eternal work.[32]

To what extent can we claim that Jesus' ascended state is genuinely important in all this? Once again, the significance of Jesus' ascension and heavenly session lie in their shaping, and even creating, the present age. Thus they also determine the shape of Christian existence within the parameters of that age. This is very much to the fore in Barth's exposition of the relation between the first and second commandments, and exercises considerable influence on his discussion of the precise nature of the second commandment. Barth describes the second commandment with tools shaped by his insistence that this command is specifically related to the present age alone, and that it therefore depends for its reality upon the particular conditions of this age. In the second commandment the 'totality and absoluteness of the [first] commandment acquires the concrete shape which corresponds to the world which now is and passes'.[33] In two ways the reality of Jesus' resurrection and ascension impose the present conditions. Firstly, in the ascension as revelation we see that Jesus is at the Father's side and has made a place for our humanity there also – He has achieved all reconciliation and we see the present age as the age of redemption – we see that Christians exist as those who are reconciled to God and belong with Him as His children. Yet at the same time the ascension

---

[31] *CD* I/2, p.410.
[32] *CD* I/2, p.410.
[33] *CD* I/2, p.411.

involves the (temporary) absence of the fullness of redemption, the time of
Jesus' ascended state is the time of the patience of God, of the residual
presence of the old age, of Christian's continued existence as sinners. The
present age is therefore very much the age of waiting and watching, of the
coming kingdom present in limited eschatological forms.

Barth ties this insight into the present age as the age of Jesus' absence as
well as presence. God's commands invoke the future which God is bringing –
the future as yet only present at the Father's side in Jesus Christ, and which the
earth yet awaits. In obeying the temporal command to love the neighbour
Christians bear witness that in eternity they already belong to God. 'It is
actually the case that in the midst of the world which now is and passes, they
cannot cease to attest that God has found them'.[34] God's command requires
obedience in which Christians are made to be what they already are. Existing
in the tension between the world which passes and the world which is coming,
Christians live in both, but live toward and in obedience to the future which is
God's – they have no choice, Jesus alone is Lord. This future defines also the
command to love the neighbour, in all its temporality.

What it is to be a child of God in this present age is altogether a function
of the tension we have outlined – the tension, at least to a significant degree,
created by the ascension of Jesus Christ.[35] Existing still within this world, the
children of God belong to Jesus Christ and their true existence is defined by
His existence at the Father's side. While still bound to fleshly and earthly
existence faith Jesus introduces the command of God which acts upon them as
people who belong to the world which is coming. In obeying the command of
God they therefore seek God and God's coming kingdom.[36] The theme of
seeking, so strong in this section of Barth's work, lies at the heart of his
understanding of the existence of Christians – because Jesus Christ is risen and
ascended and salvation is complete in Him they seek God in Him, they seek
their life in Him. But even so, because He is yet absent, because His kingdom
is yet the *coming* kingdom, Christians *seek* and do not simply possess life in
Him. Thus the children of God live by faith, and in faith, hope, and love, they
obey.

> By the very fact that Jesus is risen and ascended, we are compelled and constrained
> in our simple sphere, which has not to be confused with His, which is the very
> sphere in which we can and must be the children of God, to let our walk and
> activity be the walk and activity of those who are thankful. Not to do this, not to
> desire it, to hold back is to deny the position in which we are put, to deny our love

---

[34] *CD* I/2, p.411.

[35] As earlier, the ascension belongs with the *extra Calvinisticum* and other significant
factors that shape the relation of likeness and difference, belonging to Jesus and
hoping to belonging to Him, which is the reality of the being of the children of God.
However, in the context of this discussion, the influence of the ascension seems
peculiarly plain, as it is the ascension in particular which lends the present age its
character as the age of the *coming* of the Lord, rather than of His full presence.

[36] *CD* I/2, p.413.

to God and therefore the fact that we are loved by Him, to deny in fact our very status as children.[37]

Therefore, as Barth moves to explicate the particular *content* of the command to love the neighbour, he does so with reference to the particular conditions of the present age. The neighbour may be this or that person in any given situation, and Barth gives considerable space to discussion of the question of the identity of the neighbour. But in the final analysis the neighbour exists because God sets her before God's children in a particular form, 'as the instrument of that order which is so necessary and indispensable for us in this time and world, in which God wills to be praised by us for His goodness'.[38]

The Neighbour as Christ's Witness 'Between the Times'

In his singular treatment of Jesus' second commandment, Barth, perhaps counter-intuitively, sees the neighbour as one who offers the Christian a service. The neighbour is the person in whom the children of God are given occasion to obey and therefore to praise God, and in the encounter with the neighbour opportunity arises to be who they are as the children of God. 'The primary and true form of the neighbour is that he faces us as the bearer and representative of the divine compassion'.[39] The children of God need to express the heavenly reality of their being in Christ in the earthly and often mundane reality in which they also exist, for without the reality of obedience and praise toward God in this passing world where would be the Christian's citizenship of heaven? Their whole being, visible and earthly as well as invisible and heavenly must be shaped by the ultimate truth of redemption in Christ – there can be no separation between the two poles of Christian existence, or else one pole must simply disappear.

In this way the children of God rely wholly upon God's mercy both in providing the commandment and its occasion in the person of the neighbour, and moreover in the mercy which enables true obedience to occur – the mercy which flows from Jesus Christ who is at the Father's right hand. As those who live in two worlds and times Christians cannot live a bifurcated existence. They must be, and therefore act as, the children of God not only in the eternal reality which comes, but also in the age which passes. Thus, without Jesus' presence enabling their obedience, the children of God cannot and do not exist.

They would simply cease to be what they are. They can only be what they are as the children of God if in respect of their twofold existence they are surrounded and borne along by the mercy of God. In their existence in the world which comes and

---

[37] *CD* I/2, p.413.

[38] *CD* I/2, p.416.

[39] *CD* I/2, p.416.

remains they are surrounded and borne along by virtue of the high priestly advocacy and intercession of Jesus Christ.[40]

We need to take careful note of the decisions Barth makes about the relation between the eternal time of Jesus Christ, ascended, and the passing age in which those who belong to Him still live, and in particular the place of the neighbour within this reality.   For, although Barth at this point is straightforwardly calling upon the high priesthood of (the ascended) Jesus Christ as the source of obedience in the Christian, he is also turning to the existence of the neighbour as the peculiar and appropriate expression of Jesus' provision.   In eternity Jesus Christ lives to make intercession for His own, but in the world which passes that intercession is *mediate*.   Clearly Barth would affirm the mediacy of God the Holy Spirit at this point, but in God's economy Jesus' intercession is also concretely mediate in the person of the neighbour, who is granted to proclaim Jesus Christ to those who belong to Him.

> The bearer and representative of this temporal as well as eternal mercy of God is simply my neighbour, i.e., the fellow man who emerges from amongst all others as my benefactor. To what extent my benefactor? To the extent that, in virtue of a special commission and authority here and now, he proclaims and shows forth Jesus Christ within this world, thus giving my praise of God direction and character: ... enabling me as I offer it really to live in this world really by faith.[41]

Two things are to be described here: firstly, as above, the neighbour serves the children of God simply in offering the occasion for obedience within the constraints of the world which passes – an opportunity to realise the truth of the coming world within the passing world. But secondly Barth is in some way wishing to make the neighbour a representative of Jesus Christ Himself within the passing world. What is involved within this latter move?

The core claim is that the humanity of the neighbour – her frailty and affliction, in whatever form it is encountered, even behind a mask of strength – can become a sign of the humanity of the Son of God united with the Son of Man. Barth is willing to say at this point that any human being can become the neighbour, and therefore that any human being can be a witness to Jesus Christ, a representative of His mercy. Indeed, humans can and even must now become a summons to praise of God because they point us to the suffering and humiliation of the incarnate One. 'Man himself now becomes a sign'.[42] But, not surprisingly, Barth does not in any sense want to say that human beings by virtue of common humanity become a source of the *primary* material of the gospel, or that shared suffering may become the starting point for some sort of 'natural theology'. Rather, the witness of the neighbour is second order and derivative – derivative upon knowledge of God in His self-revelation in Jesus

---

[40] *CD* I/2, p.421.

[41] *CD* I/2, p.421.

[42] *CD* I/2, p.424.

Christ. Humans, as 'neighbours' may offer a testimony to God's child that 'is a confirmatory and not a basic witness. But granted that there are apostles and prophets, granted there is a people of God and a church, granted that God is already loved, they have the authority and power to summon those who love God to the praise of God which is meet and acceptable to Him'.[43]

Thus the work of the neighbour is in the first instance aligned to the work of the church, for in the crossover between the two times and worlds it is the church which first and foremost has this task of proclaiming Jesus Christ – the purest service humans can offer to each other. How can a fellow human being emerge as a bearer of God's mercy?

> To the extent that there is within the world a Church, created by the Word and Spirit of God to be the earthly body of the heavenly Head, Jesus Christ, the great sign of revelation in the time between the ascension and the second coming of Jesus.[44]

But the service of bearing witness to Jesus cannot be restricted to the church *per se*, although it is dependent upon the existence of the church. As above, any human can, in the light of the gospel of which the church is made the bearer, become witness to the weak and broken humanity adopted by the Son of God, and therefore become an occasion for the praise of God, which is the very life of the children of God. Due to the incarnation, we may be confronted by any other human in such a way that they become for us a bearer of this mission in revealing the humanity of the Son.[45]

Once again this is true because the overwhelming and determinative reality of the present age is that it is the time of Jesus Christ ascended, the time between ascension and *eschaton*. It is this fact which relates every human to the church, whether they will or no, because God is at work in this age bearing witness to Himself.

> It is impossible to be absolutely outside the Church, to have absolutely no part in it. ... Whatever a man does or does not make of it ... every man is actually related to the Church by the fact that he exists with it in the space between the ascension and the parousia of Jesus Christ. To that extent he is actually involved in the calling to that service which is offered in its true and explicit form in the Church: the service of proclaiming Jesus Christ.[46]

This activity of God's self-witness through humans takes place primarily, but *therefore* not exclusively in the church. Jesus Christ in taking our flesh has become our neighbour – He is the archetype of the neighbour, for He is the source of all witness to God, the source of God's mercy – and for this reason

---

[43] *CD* I/2, p.426.
[44] *CD* I/2, p.421.
[45] *CD* I/2, p.426.
[46] *CD* I/2, p.423.

humans can be made bearers of His self-witness. This witness is the task of the church, but because of the fact that the church bears this task those outside the church may become witnesses also.

> [The] Church and all that takes place in it exists only representatively for the world, just as it has its own life only representatively in its heavenly Head. It is not the churchman in particular, but man generally, every man, who comes to light in the promise: 'Ye shall be my witnesses' (Acts I[8]). For that reason we must expect to find the witness of Jesus Christ, and therefore our neighbour, not only in the Church, but, because in the Church, in every man.[47]

The reality of this situation is that as those who have heard the gospel, the children of God can recognise in the suffering and weak humanity of any other person the very flesh which Jesus Christ has taken to Himself, and therefore praise God. This is not a capacity of humanity as such but a matter of reconciliation and revelation – as Jesus reveals Himself in the person of the neighbour He reveals Himself as the broken and humiliated servant of God who took our sinful flesh and perished with it. 'Our fellow-man in his oppression, shame and torment confronts us with the poverty, the homelessness, the scars, the corpse, at the grave of Jesus Christ'.[48]

Reminded thus of Jesus Christ, indeed genuinely meeting Him in the form of the neighbour – for 'this is how we have to do with Jesus Christ Himself in this world, in the time of waiting and watching'[49] – the children of God offer praise to God *in and by* loving the neighbour. But what form does this love take? Perceiving afresh in the neighbour the truth of the gospel, Christians are called themselves to bear witness to the neighbour – for how can the neighbour not be another for whom also Christ has suffered, seeing as they bear the flesh which Christ Himself yet bears? 'To love the neighbour, therefore, is plainly and simply to be to him a witness of Jesus Christ'.[50]

There are three clear aspects to this task, or better, two forms of activity and thirdly an attitude, which is their common origin in the worship of the Christian toward God. Firstly, there is verbal witness to Jesus Christ, 'the name of Jesus Christ as the essence and existence of the loving kindness in which God has taken to Himself sinful man, in order that he should not be lost but saved by Him'.[51] Secondarily there is the witness in deed, the help offered to the neighbour's need, as a sign of the promised help of God. Thirdly Barth speaks of the attitude to God which is involved in and inseparable from the activity of God's children.

In all this it is the power of God to witness to Himself, to reveal Himself, that lies at the centre – neither in word nor deed can the children of God

---

[47] *CD* I/2, pp.424-5.
[48] *CD* I/2, p.428.
[49] *CD* I/2, p.430.
[50] *CD* I/2, p.440.
[51] *CD* I/2, p.443.

communicate the gospel of God, or persuade another into faith in the resurrection. Yet Jesus Christ remains the gracious Lord, who takes up the efforts and failures of His people and makes them His own. 'The crucified Jesus does not contract out of the mediatorial position He adopted in His resurrection and ascension'.[52] Once again, the interplay of presence and absence in the relation of Jesus Christ to the present age is to the fore. Jesus is in one sense absent, yet He encounters His people in the form of the neighbour, and in so doing commands their obedience – an obedience which also takes particular shape within the conditions of the present age – but Jesus does not abandon them in this obedience, rather He is the One in whom it is possible. What Jesus has made His people – that they are truly the children of God – is hidden in the present age, but the invisible reality of reconciliation and the visible reality of human frailty and sin are not utterly divorced. As earlier, the two times and worlds are not equal, and the time which is coming is the overcoming of the time which is passing away – redemption in Jesus Christ penetrates sinful human existence in such a fashion that even sinners live as the children of God, in obedience and praise of God. In eternity I am perfected by the love of God, and may be a perfect witness: here and now I cannot be, but the two must not be radically split.

> Of course, we can and must differentiate between our petty attitude, as well as our petty word and deed, and our existence before God: for the one is only our activity as the children of God in this present, passing world, whereas our being before God is our being in Jesus Christ and in membership of the age which comes and remains. But this differentiation can only be made within the unity of our existence as the children of God. It is we who are involved either way.[53]

In relation to the commandment to love others as ourselves Barth acknowledges that, once again due to the reality of the present as the age 'between the times', self-love and sin are unavoidable parts of the being of God's children – yet for this very reason the current time remains the time of grace, of gospel. 'This reality of self-love and therefore of sin is the reality of the life of the children of God in this present, passing world and therefore in relation to this activity [of loving the neighbour]'.[54]

Thus, examining Barth's treatment of the life of the children of God – which he acknowledges to be 'ethics' – we have seen the strongly christological determination he employs. The life of the children of God is the life of the Son of God, with whom they are united and in whom they stand before the Father as those who are objects of grace and are forgiven. Yet at the same time the nature of Jesus Christ's present being as ascended and awaited means that Barth sees this relationship of the earthly members of the body to the heavenly Head as in tension and not without difficulties of its own. As living in two

---

[52] *CD* I/2, p.433.

[53] *CD* I/2, pp.449-50.

[54] *CD* I/2, p.451.

times and two worlds, Christians are described as those who 'seek' God in Jesus Christ, and who do not yet possess the fullness of the life granted them in Him.

These factors exercise a profound influence on Barth's treatment of the central matter of the two commandments, as he explicitly aligns them to the dual nature of the worlds in which God's children live and act.   He differentiates between the two commands by orientating the thrust of each toward one pole of the tension between the two worlds of the 'time between'. The first command relates specifically to the eternal time of redemption, the coming time of the kingdom of God, and therefore also applies to the passing age – for the coming age has already invaded and overcome the passing age in the person and work of Jesus Christ. However, the second command forms a particular application of the first within the temporal and passing reality which Christians yet inhabit.   The second command is a gift of God's grace that enables God's children to become obedient, to encounter Jesus Christ in the form of the neighbour, and therefore as those who praise God to be who they are in all eternity – that is, those who love God.

The shape of this work is clearly dependent upon Barth's christology in the broadest sense, and not upon any single doctrinal affirmation. Yet, as above, we may still note the particular role Jesus' ascension and heavenly session play in determining the shape of the current time – as the 'time between', the age of two times and two worlds – and therefore in shaping Barth's treatment of issues relating to this age, in this case specifically the life of God's children.

The Strengths of Barth's Ascension-based Approach

The strength of Barth's approach lies primarily in his refusal to pursue anything other than a specifically *theological* ethics of the Christian life. Although the results are hardly likely to satisfy professional ethicists, they are nonetheless noteworthy for their thorough-going Christological emphasis. Barth refuses to downplay the utter reality of Jesus Christ as the measure of all other reality – even when faced with the ambiguities of life in this world and indeed the ambiguities of Christians as justified sinners.

Barth's analysis of the present age as the 'time between' – predicated on Jesus' ascension – allows him to affirm the absolute nature of God's claim upon God's children, and yet to recognise the manner in which we encounter that claim within the limited and even fraught conditions of the present age. Barth does not subscribe to an abstract absolutism, which takes no account of eschatological tension, nor a liberal enthusiasm for human capacities, which equally lacks genuine eschatological limitation. Rather, drawing upon his description of the present age as the time of Jesus' ascended absence, Barth is able to avoid simplistic representation of the ethical life of Christians.

On the other hand, as noted early in this work, Barth's attention to the ascension is significant in avoiding a disinterest in ethics altogether – a failure of which Barth is often accused. Rather than avoiding any ethical claim upon Christians, or reducing everything to a command of God without any anchor in human agency, Barth's description of the 'time between' involves a tremendous practical requirement upon Christians to live as children of God – which is to say, to live as children of the coming kingdom present in the life and work of Jesus Christ.

One significant outcome of this is an avoidance of any bifurcation between God's agency and human agency – Barth does not see the two as competitive. Rather, genuine human agency – an expression of true freedom – is once again seen in terms of creatureliness and dependence, but without thereby downplaying the human component. For humans to act is simply for them to *act as conditioned by the creative Word and Spirit of God.* Thus Barth finds a way to talk about God and humanity together, even as we have claimed that he wished to, while maintaining the absolute priority and initiative of God.

Chapter 5

Conclusion to Part I

'The Significance of the Ascension in Barth'

At the beginning of this book we claimed that to attend to Jesus' ascension, and even more so, to His ascended life is extremely significant for a theology of the present age. Our intention has been to demonstrate this claim by examining the influence of Jesus' ascension within the theology of Karl Barth. It should by now be very clear that Barth's work does involve the ascension as a significant event, and its result in Jesus' heavenly session is a key influence on Barth's theology of the age. The aim of this chapter is to draw together the conclusions reached in the previous chapters, and to offer an overall assessment of Barth's ascension theology.

One of the goals of this work thus far has been to engage Barth's work as an example of ascension theology operating within an entire theological programme, rather than in abstraction. This should have helped readers who are not Barth specialists to gain more from the work, by allowing them to gain insight into the function of the doctrine of the ascension within the complex of Barth's work as a whole. In this way some understanding of Barth may have been gained at the same time as an investigation of ascension theology undertaken. At the heart of all of this is the dialectic of presence and absence, to which we will turn in a moment, which influences key moves within Barth's treatment of key aspects of theology relating to the present age. The claims made at the beginning of this work – that the doctrine of Jesus Christ's ascension is influential within Barth's entire programme – have been borne out by analysis of the part the ascension and Jesus' ascended state play in that programme. The entire understanding of the present age as the 'time between' ascension and *eschaton* is self-evidently predicated upon the event of Jesus' ascension and its outcome in Jesus' ascended state. Barth works out the all important relationship between humanity and the transcendent Word of reconciliation and redemption with specific reference to the presence and absence of the ascended Lord, so that the ascension determines the particular *form* that Jesus' transcendence takes in the present age. So we find that knowledge of God and the existence of the church in this 'time between' are both penultimate, as they are simply anticipations of the future that is awaited while Jesus remains at the Father's 'right hand'.

It is within these conditions that the church exists, and indeed, it is for the being and work of the church that Jesus' second coming is delayed. God wills for there to be a human response to, and human thanksgiving for, all that He has done and continues to do in Jesus. It is for this purpose that the 'time between', the age of penultimate knowledge of God, is created. The ethical existence of Christians and their obedience are shaped by this penultimate reality, and as God meets them 'between the times' in the witness of the neighbour. Thus this present age is the age of grace, in which human creatures are granted space for faith and hope in obedience, as Christ is present in the mediation of the Spirit, and in the concrete forms of Holy Scripture and church proclamation.

The Present Age as that of Jesus' Presence and Absence

Johnson observes that Barth seeks to pay due heed to both the presence and the absence of God. His interest is in the possibility of crossover between Barth's thought and the concerns of theology in a post-modern era, and he focuses on the post-modern philosophical rejection of 'pure presence'.[1] Johnson describes Barth's bold claim that humans have been reconciled so that they may be in God's presence, but he also notes that this claim is always worked out eschatologically. Christian theology that is not 'wholly and utterly and irreducibly eschatology has nothing whatsoever to do with Jesus Christ'.[2] Thus God's presence in the Spirit is never a simple presence, or a given (as noted earlier), on the contrary, the Spirit's presence 'impinges upon us, but for now it is available only in the mode of "promise"'.[3]

Johnson is at pains to note Barth's refusal to allow God to be captured in human theological statements, or Christian life to seen as straightforwardly, or triumphantly, redeemed life. Rather, redemption as the work of the Spirit is an ever coming, eschatological work, which looks forward to its consummation at the end of the age, but which has its presence among us now primarily in the form of promise. Thus the Christian life is first and foremost based upon faith and hope. Christians exist in the Spirit's own eschatological tension, looking toward the day of consummation and crying 'Come Lord Jesus'.

Drawing on our earlier investigations of the work of the Spirit and the relation between Jesus' time and our own, we may recognise that this dialectic of presence and absence, which Johnson speaks of pneumatologically, is at base christological. The One who is present and yet absent is none other than Jesus Christ, the completed reconciliation of humanity with God. Precisely because He is both present and absent, redemption takes on this extended form while history and individual Christian lives await fulfilment in Christ's return at the end. Christ's *eschaton* will be His simple presence – the full, complete

---

[1] It is necessary to note that Barth's concern is a *theological* one, i.e. the freedom and Lordship of God, even in reconciliation and revelation, while Johnson's is *philosophical* and specifically *epistemological*.

[2] Barth, Karl *The Epistle to the Romans* trans. E.C. Hoskyns, London: Oxford University Press, 1933, p.314, (cited by Johnson, *The Mystery of God* p.130).

[3] Johnson, *The Mystery of God* p.131.

and undeniable revelation of His being and majesty. The shape of Christian existence, and of all history, in the time between ascension and *eschaton* is controlled by the relationship between this time and Jesus Christ. He is the Lord, and He is the truth of all reality – the future that exists in Him is the only future, and it is the future of all creatures, whether they know it or not. Jesus' presence and absence are based upon the event of His ascension, and so it is this event which forms the basis of the present age. In fact the transcendent reality of Jesus' life and work guarantee the immanent power and reality of that life and work. Thus Barth can comment, with regard to the present 'time between' and the Word of judgement and grace in Christ, that '… what is involved and meant by that Word is … woe and salvation which are eternal and *thus also* temporal, heavenly and *for this reason also* earthly, coming and *therefore* already present'.[4]

The most cursory glance at the event of the ascension will reveal that it creates an absence – sometimes the ascension scene is described simply as 'Jesus' farewell', implying that from henceforth He will be quite absent. However, such pure absence does not fit Barth's reading of the New Testament. During the forty days Jesus has been immediately (although not constantly) present with His disciples *cum* apostles, and now He leaves them. He is no longer available in the localised form which they have seen, heard, and even eaten alongside. Nevertheless His departure and absence make possible a new form of presence that will achieve what even His previous immediacy cannot – the *parousia* in the Spirit creates the subjective realisation of the revelation of Jesus as the God-man. The ascension cannot be seen as a simple absence – rather it creates the possibility of an altogether different form of presence. It is true; Jesus is to be found in heaven – above (Col. 3[1]) – and not in physical immediacy.

> This does not mean, however, that He is imprisoned there (for we remember that this is indeed the mystery of the living God). It does not mean that He is prevented from being and working and revealing Himself here too.[5]

In fact, salvation as event, while accomplished on the cross, may be said to begin with Easter. '[Salvation] is a living redemptive happening which takes place. Or, more concretely, it is the saving operation of the living Lord Jesus which did not conclude but began in His revelation on Easter Day'.[6]

Yet the nature of ascension as absence remains. We might expect that Jesus' ascension would immediately resolve into His final *parousia* in the *eschaton* – the ultimate form of presence. But instead God creates, even 'unnaturally' extends, the 'time between', and so creates the time of the church – the community of Christ – and therefore of mission and of grace. Jesus'

---

[4] Barth, Karl *Evangelical Theology: An Introduction* Grand Rapids, Michigan: Eerdmans, 1963, p.79.

[5] *CD* IV/3.i, p.357.

[6] *CD* IV/1, pp.621-2. Cited in Chapter 3 above.

extended absence establishes the possibility of faith, and of a community of the Spirit that lives the life of the Reconciler in a world ignorant of its reconciliation. The church appears as the 'earthly historical form of Jesus' in this time, and a form of His agency in the power of the Spirit.[7]

Significantly, Jesus' absence represents a continuation of His incognito – His identity remains veiled, only visible now in the weak flesh of the community of His people, and their witness to Him. He continues to be misunderstood, and rejected. Barth notes that in this way – rather surprisingly – Jesus continues to suffer the same passion He suffered in His earthly life. He is not crucified again and again, but He undoubtedly continues as the Crucified and as the Rejected. Contrary to theological descriptions of Christ's ascension which emphasise glorification erasing suffering and rejection, or deification swamping humiliation, Barth sees this 'time between' as an extension of humiliation and rejection. 'The crucified Jesus Christ does not contract out of the mediatorial position which He adopted in His resurrection and ascension'.[8] Christ *is* glorious, but in a parallel of His life and death among us, while He is absent His glory is hidden and the possibility of His rejection remains, even as He offers the possibility of faith, hope, and love in the gift of His Spirit. Jesus is Lord, yet as we await the *eschaton* His Lordship continues to be proclaimed in weakness and in 'absence' as well as power and presence. A profound tension and ambiguity mark out the time of the church, and even Christ's own history in this time.

At the same moment, Jesus' absence guards and enforces His lordship. He remains other, and even in the gift of His Spirit the peculiar form of 'absent presence' allows for no notion of capture or givenness in human relationship with Him. Jesus Christ is the supreme agent, and His agency in the promise of the Spirit is the agency of the Lord – He is present among us as He comes to us, and in His coming He takes hold of us and transforms us into His image, and not *vice versa*.

Thus, we are confronted with a real presence of the ascended Lord. 'Barth turns to the Holy Spirit as the one in whom the Reconciler, Jesus Christ, continues to exist among the many who believe in Him'.[9] Jesus Christ is the supreme, indeed the only, sacrament of God with humanity,[10] and He is present in the promise of His Spirit. All that we can say in description of the agency and Lordship of God in self-revelation hangs upon the genuine

---

[7] As earlier, it is important to note that while Barth describes the Church as the current earthly-historical form of Jesus' availability, he in no way is prepared to countenance a reduction of Jesus' post-crucifixion existence to the life of the Christian community. For another example of this see, *Knowledge of God in the Service of God,* trans. J. Haire and I. Henderson, London: Hodder and Stoughton, 1938, p.161ff.

[8] *CD* I/2, p.433. Quoted earlier. Barth is referring to the way that Jesus can meet His people in the form of the neighbour, suffering, sinful and afflicted, with whom Jesus remains in solidarity.

[9] Rosato, *The Spirit as Lord*, p.109.

[10] See *CD* IV/2, p.55.

presence of the Word in the gift of the Spirit. As Gorringe notes, revelation is the power of God transforming humans, and creating new *human* acts.

> 'Revelation', an account of the significance of Jesus Christ for human history, is not esoteric knowledge, nor is it a 'controlling concept' which can feed philosophical debates about how we might or might not know God, but issues at every point in 'ethics' – the behaviour of human beings which corresponds with the liberating God.[11]

The Spirit does not merely point to the objective reality of reconciliation in Jesus Christ, but as the real presence of Jesus – who *is* Reconciliation – the Spirit realises reconciliation in the realm of the human subject. Yet, again, it is only the ascension as a form of absence that creates this possibility. The 'time between' is created for the being of the church, and thus for a further history in which humans may and will respond to and participate with the movement of God's grace. Barth sees Schleiermacher and Bultmann as failed pneumatologists because in attempting to describe the subjective realisation of salvation in Christ they lose sight of the objective pole – the otherness of the fact of Christ Himself – and allow the human pole to become the centre of theology. To return to Rosato's descriptive image, Barth sees theology as an ellipse, held in shape by the tension between its two foci – the subjective reality of reconciliation, and the objective reality of Jesus Christ the Reconciler.

For Barth *both* foci, or poles, are established and maintained by the Lordship of God in reconciliation and revelation. The subjective reality of reconciliation is created by the redemptive power of the Spirit, who brings the effective presence of objective reconciliation to bear in the subjective realm. It is impossible that these two foci should collapse into one, and theology become a simple circle centred upon human possibilities, because of the *absence* of Jesus Christ (even as He is present). Theology can never be simply a matter of the human – even the earthly human before God – because its subject matter is the *humanity of Jesus Christ* in unity with His divinity, and the truth of that reality is not simply present, but hidden in Christ with God. Thus Barth's already noted emphasis on the eschatological character of Christianity – he is fond of either quoting or referring to Colossians 3^1 (or 3^{1-3}) '... seek the things that are above,

---

[11] Gorringe, Timothy *Karl Barth: against hegemony* Oxford: Oxford University Press, 1999, p.274.

where Christ is, seated at the right hand of God' (NRSV).[12] The presence of Jesus Christ in the promise of the Holy Spirit is inescapably eschatological, because His *parousia* in the Spirit is the middle term of His *parousia* as a whole, and as such it points forward to, and indeed presses toward, its own fulfilment in the *eschaton*.

> In the New Testament sense everything that is to be said about the man who receives the Holy Spirit and is constrained and filled by the Holy Spirit is an eschatological statement. Eschatological does not mean in an inexact or unreal sense but in relation to the ἔσχατον i.e., to that which from our standpoint and for our experience and thought has still to come, to the eternal reality of the divine fulfilment and consummation.[13]

Christian (churchly) confidence in God, in this time between, is therefore based upon Christ's absence as the ground of His particular form of presence. To receive the Holy Spirit, the presence of Jesus Christ, is not to lose our creaturely nature, or even to experience the fullness of redemption as it will be: neither do we ourselves become the basis of any confidence, or of our own salvation.

> [The] creature to whom the Holy Spirit is imparted in revelation by no means loses its nature and kind as a creature so as to become itself, as it were, the Holy Spirit. ... The statements about the operations of the Holy Ghost are statements whose subject is God and not man, and in no circumstances can they be transformed into statements about man.[14]

Any failure to maintain the otherness of God, and even of salvation will see theology dissolve into anthropology, or at the other end of the spectrum, lose all ability to talk about humanity with God at all. If we ask what enables Barth to maintain the integrity of the two foci, then we may argue that it is the doctrine of the ascension. It is precisely because Jesus Christ continues to have an embodied (human) existence that He cannot be reduced to the being of the Christian community, or to the subjective experience of Christian believers. In

---

[12] The index to *CD* lists approximately eighteen quotations of, and references to, either Col.3[1] or 3[1-3], spread through the work as a whole (although IV/2 contains more than any other volume and parts of volume III lack any references). It might be possible to undertake brief but useful study of Barth's thought about Jesus' ascended location and the meaning of His session, especially for the being and life of Christians, simply by tracing His references to this set of verses. See for example IV/2, p.375, where Col.3[1-3] underpins the 'not-yet' of Christian's redemption and their seeking of the life that is 'above' with Christ. Alternatively, in II/1 (p.475) Col.3[1] is referenced in relation to the location of God's space, and the fact that in Jesus Christ creaturely space has been taken up by God, so that in Him God may be said to be enthroned in a space (heaven) which He both occupies and transcends.

[13] *CD* I/1, p.464. Cited earlier.

[14] *CD* I/1, p.462.

His heavenly session Jesus lives in separation from, as well as in relationship to and even unity with, His body and the people who are members of it. It is because He is in this sense absent that neither anthropology, nor religious studies, nor psychology are able to become the centre from which the circle of theology takes its shape.

Yet, as we turn toward the other focus, we see that only as Jesus' absence and Lordship are expressed in the gift of the Spirit – the supra-human form of His presence – that theology is able to speak of Jesus' reconciliation of actual, historical, human creatures at all. 'In allowing the community of redeemed men to exist as their Reconciler exists, and thus to share in His being, the Spirit neither blurs the distinction between Christ and Christians nor exaggerates it'.[15] An absent Christ who did not come in the Spirit would yield a Christianity that is wholly transcendent, and marked with an otherness that makes it effectively meaningless.

This acknowledgement of a genuinely human existence before God has been explored via a steady intensification of exposition, concentrating finally upon the being and integrity of the Christian as an agent in the 'time between'. Moving through the presence of Jesus to the church in the concrete forms of Scripture and proclamation, deriving their reality from His being in heaven as the God-ward side of creation, and thence into the life of God's children we have been able to trace the tremendous influence of Barth's understanding of the present age. Jesus' ascended state provides the basis for Barth's ecclesiology and also his ethics. The present age of the world is the age created by Jesus' ascension and His heavenly session – the age of the delayed *eschaton* – and this age is specifically the age of the church and earthly human subjectivity before God. God wills that there be a human response to His grace – a response of thanksgiving and worship which works itself out in obedient participation in God's mission to the world. Thus the heavenly session is focussed upon the being of the church and the Christian as a member of the church. The church *is* to be understood as Jesus' earthly-historical body, and His work is to be understood in relation to this body.

Thus, attention to Jesus' ascended state allows an explication of the subjective realisation of salvation in the love and praise of God. Jesus as ascended mediates Himself, even in the person of the neighbour, in such a way that those who belong to Him are transformed and enabled to become those who obey. The particular forms of obedience – love and praise – are entirely predicated upon the nature of the current age, and therefore upon the being of Christians as those who live in the tension of two times and worlds. It is Jesus ascended state, and the fact that we await His *eschaton*, that shapes Barth's reading of the dual command that stands at the centre of Christian life. Because His humanity is in heaven and not therefore immediate itself, Jesus mediates Himself, with the dual outcome that His people are caused to remember His suffering humanity and praise God for it, and that they therein

---

[15] Rosato, *The Spirit as Lord*, p.116.

become those who obey. The presence and absence of Jesus inform a reading of human being before God that, as above, seeks to maintain both the absolute objectivity of justification in Jesus – who is hidden with the Father while we await His return at the End – while also giving real space and weight to the penultimate reality of subjective realisation of that salvation. As we have seen, the form of *absence* proper to the ascended Christ is the 'coming' form of His lordship in and for those whom He has reconciled. His absence maintains His incognito, His suffering and rejection, but always in such a fashion that He creates the space in which to come to human beings and in the promise of the Spirit to create faith, and yield transformation.

Perhaps because the main targets in his sights were often those protestant theologians whom he viewed as tending toward anthropology, Barth himself can be read as tending in the opposite direction – the reality of the human subject reconciled and receiving redemption can appear to be missing. But not if we read well: Christ's presence is if anything more heavily treated than issues involved in His absence, and thus Jesus Himself is understood as the agent of human transformation, rather than fallen humans themselves, and so the absolute reality of objective justification stands as the guarantee of the reality of subjective sanctification.

The Significance of the Ascension for Barth

At the heart of all of this is Barth's peculiar understanding of the nature of revelation, as worked out in His prolegomena, based upon his resounding affirmation that 'God reveals Himself as the Lord'. This revelation, the particular lordship of the triune God, is present in Jesus Christ, and thus, once again, is characterised in this age by the ascension of this same Jesus Christ. All salvation was accomplished in the life and death of Jesus Christ, but the presence of that salvation in the 'time between' is shaped by the ascended reality of the Saviour who is Himself salvation. The ascension in many ways can therefore be seen as a continuation of the incognito of the Son of God veiled in human form. The glory of the Mediator is immediate only in heaven, where He is seated at the Father's right hand, while on earth Jesus' presence and glory are hidden in human forms such as Scripture, the church, and church proclamation. Thus also, the being of the church and of Christians is eschatologically focussed, as they look toward the fulfilment of revelation in the final *parousia* of the ascended Lord.

We have claimed that the influence and role that the ascended being of the Saviour has within Barth's thought is highly significant in his controversy with other theologians and theological points of view. His doctrine of revelation provides a key weapon in his breach with Neo-protestantism, and rejection of both an older Protestant Scholastic view of Scripture and of Roman Catholic ecclesiological inspiration, and his doctrine of revelation has strong links into the doctrine of Christ's ascension. Barth's disagreement with both Roman

Catholic and Neo-protestant ecclesiology turns in part upon the particular form of Jesus' Lordship envisaged in the 'time between'. In differing ways Barth sees both of these opponents investing too much in the earthly church, and in the case of Neo-protestantism too much in the faith of the believer. In Barth's opinion, both mistake the nature of the 'time between', in the case of Roman Catholic ecclesiology, and indeed of other forms of 'enthusiasm', by reducing the freedom in which the 'absent' Lord acts toward His church. By identifying Jesus Christ's Spirit too strongly with a particular aspect of the church institution the Word of God is made to appear as a donation the church has received, and Jesus Himself appears to become somewhat of a possession of the church, rather than the other way around. In the case of Neo-protestantism, Barth berates a lack of faith in the agency of the ascended Lord, with the resultant emphasis on the faith of the church and of the individual believer as the power to save. Jesus' absence is recognised, but not His ascended agency and power to make Himself known. Barth's view of the presence and free Lordship of Jesus Christ expressed in the rule of Scripture over the church has been shown to have strong ties to His particular affirmation of Jesus as ascended, and as present and absent in certain ways.

In opposition to much comment to the contrary, we hold that Barth is ever concerned to do justice to the authenticity of human redemption. Human subjectivity before God is affirmed and strongly developed – the entire 'time between' is created as a space for human response to God in Christ – but human subjectivity is therefore described in a thoroughly christocentric fashion, and the appropriate limits are maintained. It is the ascension and heavenly session of Jesus which give Barth's argument for authentic subjectivity its particular shape. The presence and absence of Jesus Christ are *both* determinative as humans find themselves genuinely confronted with the presence of the living God, in the outpouring of the Spirit of the Father and the Son. Jesus' absence – His being at the Father's side, and His Lordship of all things – will not permit a theology in which the church or the Christian becomes the ruling idea. 'Seek things above, where Christ is ... Set your minds on things that are above, not on things that are on earth' (Colossians 3^{1-2}). In Barth's thought however, this emphasis on the otherness of Jesus will in no way permit a disengagement of Christian and world. As the risen and ascended One, all authority is His, and on the basis of the full and complete reconciliation He achieved on the way from Bethlehem to Golgotha He has and is the power of God to make humans new, and to bring to bear the redemption which is His. Jesus as both present and absent acts with power within the history of this present age, and calls humans into radical discipleship with Him.

In affirming the ascended Lordship of Jesus Christ Barth is able to maintain the elliptical shape he believes theology must have – he is able to keep the two foci in necessary tension, and allow each to assist in drawing an appropriate theology. The ascension of the Reconciler to the right hand of the Father allows Barth to insist upon the absolute Lordship of God in reconciliation and revelation, while the description of the coming of the Spirit as a mode of Christ's *parousia* gives full weight to the reality of subjective human response in the face of God's self-revelation. We have noted Barth's claim that Schleiermacher's theology fails to maintain an elliptical shape – the human pole which provides one focus of the ellipse over powers the divine pole, and the ellipse becomes a circle centred upon humanity. It might well be argued that the twin doctrines of resurrection and ascension are precisely the theological 'tools' which enable Barth to find an alternative to both Schleiermacher and Bultmann.

At this point we must ask how well the metaphor of an ellipse suits the theological work Barth attempts himself. Clearly the image has strength in the way it demands a necessary duality. This is exactly the way in which Barth uses it to describe Schleiermacher's failed attempt to theologise beginning with the human subject. But Barth does not himself use the image of his own theology, (at least to the knowledge of this author). Apart from its strength as a description of a field circumscribed from dual centres, the image of an ellipse has a significant weakness as a description of Barth's thought.

The two foci of an ellipse are equally weighted, and (presumably) originate in independence. Not so the divine and human poles of theology. For Barth the human pole is always, and absolutely dependent upon the divine. The reconciling work of God stands ever prior to the being of the creatures reconciled, and thus to every genuine response they make. (Witness, for example, Barth's description of creation upon the basis of reconciliation.) The subjective human pole of reconciliation – redemption in the Spirit – is utterly and genuinely human, but it is derivative upon the initiative of God, and finds its reality in the humanity of the God-Man Jesus Christ. In this light the image of an ellipse – or a theology that fits this image – may even become the cause of difficulty, for as soon as we give the two foci independent status the likelihood is that one will overtake and swallow the other. For Schleiermacher the human pole must swallow the divine.

If the image of an ellipse is in any way to be applied to Barth's thought, then both foci must represent humanity united with divinity in Jesus Christ, and thus the absolute priority of His objective achievement. The form in which this is achieved is the agency of the Spirit in uniting subjective humanity with the objectivity of the Reconciler. Thus the dependence of the second pole (reconciled humanity) on the first (God the Reconciler) is maintained because the agent is none other than God the Spirit, while the authenticity of the human pole is protected by the fact that it is with genuine humans that the Spirit deals in the power of the exaltation of the Son of Man. The Spirit's work is in fact to create genuine *human* knowledge of God and obedience towards God.

So it is that Barth finds his solution in the christocentric pneumatology of which Rosato speaks. Barth *is* thoroughly pneumatological – against those interpreters who consider the Spirit to be missing from his thought – but it is a definitively *christological* pneumatology. It is the doctrine of Christ ascended and seated with the Father which enables Barth to develop this sort of pneumatology.[16] Jesus Christ is the agent in all the Spirit's work, and His Lordship dominates both foci, reconciliation and redemption, as above. Jesus Christ's absence enables the form of presence which is His *parousia* in the Spirit, and which unites humans with Him as He pursues His way from resurrection to *eschaton*. On the basis of the ascension theology cannot be *christianocentric* for the Lordship, and otherness, of Christ remain irreducible. Jesus is with the Father, in the place of all power and authority, and from there He reaches out in love and forgiveness, making people His own, but He also remains absent and awaited.

Equally, the church as the community of the Lord cannot take centre stage, or be promoted in a simple identity with its Head. The church is extremely important – the 'time between' is created specifically as the time of the church. Jesus Christ as Lord of the church is genuinely present as the Spirit of the church, but He is *more* than the church. In His ascension He is also at a remove from the community of His own – existing as the Incarnate One, within the realm of creation, and as the supreme agent – and yet in His agency He truly makes the church His own, but as *Lord* of the church.

The ascension gives the current age of the world an identity as 'eschatological time', and the being of both Christians and the church are shaped by the *telos* toward which Christ moves them. This age is the 'last time', and with Jesus Himself it hastens toward the *eschaton* – the third moment of His *parousia*. Eschatological time is the time of Jesus' absence – the time 'between' – which follows the immediacy of His presence in the forty days of resurrection appearances, and which looks forward to the immediacy of His presence at the end. Once again, the ascension and the balance of presence and absence involved in the ascension, provides the key to Barth's thought. The eschatological hope of Christian faith does not need to break down into either an empty longing for an unimaginable and infinitely distant future, nor into an affirmation of this age or this world as the fullness of redemption. Rather, Jesus ascended stands as the True Witness to the future already created in Him, and as the guarantor of that future, and yet at the same time, Jesus comes in the Spirit and interrupts world history with the foretaste of His *eschaton*. His presence is the deposit which seals faith and hope, and orients them toward the fullness of redemption which He is, which He brings, and which He will bring. Jesus Christ's *parousia* in the Spirit as the middle term of His threefold *parousia* gives space for this age of faith, grace, and hope, and for the mission of the people of God.

In examining Barth's view of Jesus as ascended we can see the significant role this view plays in his thought. In this way we can see grounds for

---

[16] Once again, the claim is not that the ascension alone causes Barth to think of Jesus as transcendent or as the Lord present in the Spirit, nor do we claim that Barth could not have developed a christological pneumatology without reference to the ascension. The reality is, however, that this *is* what Barth wrote, and that the doctrine of Jesus' ascension significantly informs the pneumatology that he developed.

somewhat of a retrieval, or the creation, of theological room for this aspect of Christian doctrine to do its work. Douglas Farrow has made a notable contribution at this point in raising the profile of the ascension, and arguing for its importance, although we disagree with his reading of Barth. The profound effect that Jesus as ascended has upon Barth's thought simply emphasises further the importance of attending to Jesus' ascension as a key aspect of the continued work of theology that seeks to serve this same ascended Lord and His mission in this world. The task of the second part of this work will therefore be to interact with other views of the ascension, and of Barth's thought, in such a way as to further develop both an understanding of Barth and of the issues raised by examination of the ascended Christ within the complex of his thought.

Finally we may therefore conclude that Jesus Christ ascended is without doubt significant within Barth's thought and programme. The undertaking of *Church Dogmatics* I/1 and I/2, as prolegomena to dogmatics proper, is to explicate the task of dogmatics as the church's critique of its own proclamation in the light of Holy Scripture as witness to revelation. The specific form of Jesus' transcendent lordship and agency in the 'time between' – including His witness to Himself in Scripture, and the very character of the age as that time flanked by the ascension and the eschaton – is to be understood as shaped by the ascension itself. Jesus Christ ascended is present and absent in particular ways which relate directly to the nature of this 'time between' as the age of grace, of faith and not of sight, and which therefore also relate directly to the penultimate quality of church proclamation and of dogmatic work itself. The ascension as precursor to the *eschaton*, indeed as the event without which – as a form of absence – Jesus *coming* presence would be hard to imagine, informs the understanding of this age as entirely eschatological, and all knowledge of God as eschatologically conditioned and directed. For all the ambiguity that necessarily surrounds it, Jesus' ascension, and His resulting ascended life, is in fact an important element in understanding all that Barth is about.

In Part II we turn to dialogue with other theologians, both those who comment directly on aspects of Barth's thought that are crucial to our own investigation, and thinkers who address the matter of Christ's ascension. As we do so many of the points involved in the argument so far will become further clarified, especially where conflict over interpretation arises, or large scale differences between Barth and others is evident.

PART II

DIALOGUES

Chapter 6

Thomas F. Torrance

'Between Barth and Farrow'

Introduction

Thomas Torrance has provided one of the few significant twentieth century treatments of Jesus' ascension. The second half of his book *Space, Time and Resurrection* is an explicit treatment of Jesus' ascension, and its implications for Christian understandings of salvation in Christ.[1] In particular Torrance is concerned to elucidate an understanding of Jesus' ascension in relation to cosmology and eschatology. In doing so, he aims to discover what impact Jesus' bodily resurrection and ascension should have upon Christian cosmology.

Torrance is usually regarded as very similar to Barth in his theological determinations – R. D. Williams has called him 'one of Barth's foremost disciples in the English-speaking world'[2] – and in the preface to *Space, Time and Resurrection* he attributes a certain influence to Barth as he introduces the work before him.[3] Yet Torrance does diverge from Barth in the way he views the ascension and session. In fact, it is on matters related to Jesus' ascension and heavenly session that Torrance offers some of his strongest critique of Barth, suggesting that Barth's failures in this area of his thought leave him open to a charge of dualism and doceticism. The heart of the criticism is that Barth's reading of ascension and session emphasises the presence and work of the Spirit in such a way that the risen humanity of Christ becomes somewhat lost.

These criticisms are important in their own right, but they are also particularly interesting because they introduce a critique of Barth which is also present in other thinkers. In particular, Torrance's work identfies a number of issues that will appear in more acute form in the work of Douglas Farrow, who provides a major dialogue partner within this work. Farrow offers a significant treatment of Barth's ascension thought, and in that treatment he takes up some of Torrance's worries and develops them in some depth. He acknowledges a

---

[1] Torrance, Thomas F. *Space, Time and Resurrection* Edinburgh: Handsel Press, 1976. (Subsequent references are to the T&T Clark edition of the same work, Edinburgh, 1998.)

[2] R. D. Williams 'Barth on the Triune God' in S. W. Sykes ed. *Karl Barth: Studies of his Theological Method* Oxford: Clarendon Press, 1979.

[3] See the Introduction.

significant debt to Torrance, whom he sees as largely overcoming the weakness he perceives in Barth's work – in particular Barth's refusal of a sequential reading of humiliation and exaltation. Nonetheless Farrow is not finally satisfied that Torrance is altogether successful or consistent.[4] After briefly examining significant aspects of Torrance's thought we will return to Farrow's comments in the context of our own critical interaction with Torrance. To a large extent Farrow highlights difficulties which will be noted in our own examination of Torrance's work. At the same time, the influence of Torrance upon Farrow's work – and also the differences between them, particularly as Torrance is closer to Barth at certain points, and operates in some ways within Barth's framework – sheds further light upon Farrow's position, the discussion of which occupies the next chapter.

Although he criticises Barth's work on the ascension, a great deal of Torrance's treatment of Jesus' ascension is not dissimilar to Barth's work, and we will not devote a great deal of space to exploring his position in detail. We will note the general shape of his ascension thought and especially the significant aspects of it, but our interest is mainly focused upon areas of difference from Barth – linked to his criticism of Barth – and also areas of interest in relation to the subsequent discussion of Farrow.

The Shape of Jesus' Ascension and Heavenly Session

Like Barth, Torrance reads Jesus' ascension in terms of His presence and absence, and in a thoroughly eschatological fashion – that is, Jesus' ascension and the absence it introduces always directs us forward toward His *eschaton*. The key difference from Barth's treatment lies in Torrance's adoption of the view that it is in the ascension that Christ's new humanity is taken up into the communion of Father, Son, and Holy Spirit. Jesus' ascent to the Father therefore correlates to the descent of His incarnation.[5] Moreover, this view of the ascension involves seeing in it the final step of the work of salvation – ascension is a work of Jesus, in which He offers Himself in the Father's presence. The ascension begins Jesus' ministry before the Father, from which flows the continuous grace of His endless self-offering and the advocacy it yields. As the key difference between Barth and Torrance, and the point at which Farrow takes up Torrance's account in order to further it, this issue will receive considerable attention below. Torrance also places a greater emphasis than Barth upon the eucharist as a fundamental place of Jesus' presence to the church during the age of His heavenly session, but although he attends to it in various places, the eucharist does not appear to wield any significant influence over Torrance's ascension theology, and is therefore not central to our concerns. In the following chapter we will argue that Farrow places a strong

---

[4] For Farrow's acknowledgement of a debt to Torrance see *Ascension* p.263, note 24. For his judgement of inconsistency in overturning Barth's failings see pp.263 and 266.

[5] See *Space, Time and Resurrection* pp.115, 123, 132-4, 135.

emphasis on the eucharist, and indeed, a much greater emphasis than Torrance, so that in many respects his eucharistic thought appears to drive his theology as a whole. Given this claim and the attention that we will pay to it in Chapter 7, and especially taking into account the fact that Torrance's ascension theology does not seem to be in any way driven by his eucharistic claims, we will not attend so closely to this matter in his thought.

Christ's Risen Absence and Presence as the Historical Jesus

Like Barth, Torrance sees the ascension as establishing a particular form of Jesus' absence. Thus he also writes about the existence of the church and Christians in 'two times', and 'between the times', awaiting the eschaton in the return of Jesus:

> Until then the Church and all its members live *between the times*, between the time of the resurrection and Pentecost and the time of the final advent; they participate in the time of this on-going world, yet already participate in the time of the new creation through the Spirit of the risen Christ. If Christ holds back the final unveiling, and keeps us within the overlap of the two ages, still engaged in the humble mission of the servant under the Cross, it is in his compassion and patience, for he waits to be merciful, and wills to rule over history solely by the Word of the Cross.[6]

Thus the ascension, as for Barth, determines the *form* of Jesus' presence 'between the times' – that is, in the Spirit – and the gap between ascension and eschaton is an expression of the mercy of God, characterising the age as that of the church's service of Christ in mission. In the present age Jesus wills to be present still in the form of the servant, so that once again the veiling of the Risen One in His ascension serves a mission in which He is unveiled through the Spirit, and believed upon in grace by faith.

For Torrance the absence of Jesus via His ascension is therefore specifically the absence of His *risen humanity*. The result of this is that our space-time, creaturely, encounter with Jesus is encounter with Him in his *historical* form. In His absence Jesus causes us to turn back to His previous earthly history as the place in which we still are to meet Him. It is in the God-man Jesus of Nazareth that God and humanity are *hypostatically* united, and Jesus' ascension simply throws us back upon that truth – for the one who is ascended and 'absent' is none other that this same Jesus. God will never speak a different word, or an additional word, for Jesus *is* the unity of God with humans.[7] The gospels therefore remain the source of our knowledge of Jesus Christ. The implications of this, as Torrance unpacks them in the latter half of the statement above, require some detailed attention. We must ask what, if any, distinction is being drawn between Jesus' historical being and His

---

[6] *Space, Time and Resurrection* pp.103-4. Emphasis original.
[7] *Space, Time and Resurrection* p.133.

ascended being, and whether Torrance sees the ascension as instrumental in *establishing* Jesus as the eternal Word of God, or whether he simply means that Jesus' ascension reveals the being of Jesus as the eternal Word.

Torrance's affirmation that the Gospels' witness to Jesus of Nazareth is the medium through which the Spirit realises Jesus' presence initially looks similar to Barth's treatment of Holy Scripture as the authoritative mode of Jesus' self-witness to the church and world. Similarly the claim that the historical man Jesus is the eternal Word of God, to whom we turn to meet God, is at least very similar to Barth's description of the same reality. However the questions introduced above raise at least the possibility of a divergence of thought between Barth and Torrance at this point.

The implication of a general distinction between the being of the man Jesus in history, and His being as the ascended One will be more fully explored below, in a discussion of Torrance's sequential reading of exaltation and humiliation. At this point, however, we are confronted with the question of Torrance's understanding of *human access* to Jesus through His historical being rather than His ascended humanity. Having stated that Jesus' ascension removes His risen humanity from our sphere of space-time, why does Torrance need to distinguish between Jesus' risen humanity and His historical being by claiming that, through the agency of the Spirit, Jesus is made present through His historical being and not His ascended humanity?

Although this way of putting things is clearly troubling – in that it implies some sort of bifurcation between Jesus' earthly-historical life and being, and that He now has in heaven, thus throwing doubt over the strict continuity of His being – perhaps clarification of Torrance's meaning lies in his use of the word 'through' rather than 'as'. Torrance does not say Jesus is present 'as' the historical man and not the risen man, but that He is made present 'through' the historical Jesus. We may see this as something like Barth's description of Holy Scripture as the concrete self-witness of the ascended Lord. Thus Torrance wants to maintain the absolute identity of the historical man and the ascended man – as is clear from his claim that (because He is ascended) Jesus of Nazareth is to be understood as the eternal Word of God – but in doing so his language does tend to suggest some bifurcation occurring in the ascension.

The description of the historical Jesus as 'the *one locus* within our human and creaturely existence where God and man are hypostatically united'[8] is perhaps a key at this point. As we will see, Farrow speaks of Jesus' history diverging from general human histories in His ascension, and perhaps something similar is being suggested here. In contrast, Barth's description of heaven as the God-ward side of creation involves thinking of Jesus ascended existing in creaturely space and time. Revelation and justification are therefore the in-breaking of redeemed space and time into the old space and time of the *fallen* creation. Thus the *hypostatic* union of Jesus' two natures functions in His resurrection in the same way it did during His historical existence. For Barth

---

[8] See above.

Jesus' heavenly existence is the place within our 'human and creaturely existence where God and man are hypostatically united' because Jesus *makes* heaven the place of human union with God simply in that heaven is where He now is. The difference here is that Torrance seems concerned with revelation as the presence of the *hypostatic* union within *fallen* space-time. Barth sees the presence of Jesus' ascended humanity as mediated in the Spirit in such a fashion that it breaks into the old space-time and *transforms* it, so that those who hear His voice are in that event sharers in His existence in the new age, the new space-time.

This would appear to cohere with Torrance's critique of Barth's ascension theology.[9] He was concerned about Barth's 'account of the ascended Jesus Christ in *CD* IV.3, in which Christ seemed to be swallowed up in the transcendent Light and Spirit of God, so that the humanity of the risen Jesus appeared to be displaced by what [Barth] called "the humanity of God" in his turning toward us'.[10] Torrance believed that Barth should have given more attention to the role of Jesus, ascended, as the heavenly high priest – something 'which would have been fully consonant with Barth's anticipatory references to the high-priestly ministry of Christ in *CD* IV.1 ... and with his persistent emphasis on the vicarious humanity of Christ'.[11] We will explore Torrance's own description of Jesus' ascended high priesthood below, in an attempt to penetrate his critique. For the moment, the key issue is the way in which Jesus' continued in-breaking into the fallen world is worked out in relation to the agency of the Spirit, so that Torrance regards Barth's description of Jesus' ascended being as carrying a 'suspicion of docetism'. However, at least one way in which Barth works out the agency of the ascended Lord in the work of the Spirit is, as above, in terms of the in-breaking of the new 'time' of Jesus – that is of the in-breaking of the ascended *incarnate* One, in whom God has redeemed time, and in whose presence that time becomes ours. This is what is involved in the whole notion of two ages and two times – which Torrance himself describes in a fashion reminiscent of Barth.[12] At the centre of Barth's affirmations at this point is the belief that Jesus Christ as present in the Spirit is present in His being as the God-*man* and not otherwise, so that His presence is in no way merely as Spirit nor His being in any sense 'docetic'.

A question arises from all this: is Torrance in some way concerned to 'do justice' to *our* space and time – that is to *fallen* space-time, and the creaturely realities that go with it – so that he differentiates the historical Jesus from the ascended Jesus because the latter no longer occupies our fallen space-time? This might help to explain the emphasis on Jesus' presence in the eucharist,

---

[9] Torrance does not take up the question of Barth's ascension theology in his own work on the ascension, but he offers a brief critique in his book on Barth's mature thought. See *Karl Barth, Biblical and Evangelical Theologian* Edinburgh: T&T Clark, 1990, pp.132ff.

[10] *Karl Barth* ... p.134.

[11] *Karl Barth* ... p.134.

[12] See *Space, Time and Resurrection* pp.143-58.

which although more moderate than Farrow's, is still a feature of his ascension work.

The Eucharist as the Primary Locus of Christ's Presence?

In many places Torrance emphasises both word and sacrament as the vehicles of Jesus' presence and work – as He comes in the Spirit. So Torrance can speak of the ministry of the Word involving Christ's presence.[13] Moreover, the above discussion of Jesus' risen presence 'through the historical Jesus' would seem to privilege the Gospel accounts of Jesus as the mode of His self-witness over any other form.   However, at times the eucharist seems to assume primacy as the 'place' of God's work and presence in the church.[14]

So, for instance, as Torrance explores the eschatological participation of the church in the new time of Jesus Christ he notes the way in which the Kingdom of Christ 'already knocks at the door' of the church:

> That happens above all at the Holy Supper, where the risen Lord is present, in *Eucharistic Parousia*, and where we taste already the powers of the age to come and are given an antepast of the great banquet of the kingdom that is to come. ... Thus as often as the Church partakes of Holy Communion in the *real presence* or *parousia* of Christ it becomes ever anew the Body of the risen Lord.[15]

Or when speaking of the healing and forgiveness of sins, he recognises that Jesus has freedom to do this in His church as and how He pleases, but nonetheless still says that:

> ... now in on-going history [as opposed to the years of his earthly life] his healing and forgiving work is normally mediated through the Holy Sacraments which are given to the historical Church to accompany the proclamation of the Gospel and to seal its enactment in the lives of the faithful.[16]

In fact, Torrance claims that due to the ascension as Jesus' veiling He is now only mediate in *sacramental* communion.[17] Thus the individual Christian lives by both Word and Sacrament, but where the Word tells her that she is forgiven, it is baptism that involves participation in Christ, and where the Word commands the abandonment of all sources of life other than Jesus, it is in the eucharist that Jesus feeds her. Christians are said to be nourished from

---

[13] See *Space, Time and Resurrection* p.122.

[14] As explicated earlier, Torrance's eucharistic claims will not receive a great deal of attention, due to the moderate nature of his treatment, and the emphasis on the eucharist we will find in Farrow's thought. In this section we will simply document Torrance's comments on the eucharist.

[15] *Space, Time and Resurrection* pp.101-2. Emphasis original.

[16] *Space, Time and Resurrection* p.149.

[17] See *Space, Time and Resurrection* p153. This is a claim that takes a much stronger form in Farrow, and will receive considerable attention in the following chapter.

week to week by the supper, and it is the strength supplied in this way that is to enable believers to live between the times. Sharing in the eucharist is sharing in Jesus' self-consecration, His self-offering, and it is thus a consecration in Christ before the Father.[18]

Getting Beyond Barth: The Heavenly High Priest

Various aspects of Torrance's treatment of the ascension combine above with his critique of Barth in such a way that a number of questions remain outstanding. The complaint that Barth's notion of Jesus' ascended humanity is too weak, and the question of whether Torrance wants to in some way 'to do justice' to the fallen world in which we exist in a way which Barth does not, both remain unanswered. Perhaps they may be gathered up, and located with other aspects of our discussion in the following question: *What is it that Torrance wants to find in Barth's ascension theology, but considers to be lacking?*

Torrance traces three steps in his brief critique of Barth regarding the ascension. The initial complaint is that Jesus' risen humanity appears to be swallowed up by 'the humanity of God', which is then focussed into a concern that not enough attention is paid to Jesus' ascended intercession as high priest, and these together finally point to a 'suspicion of docetism'. These concerns over Barth's ascension material are traced back to the fact that Torrance himself 'had taken the incarnation of God in space and time in the fully realist way taught by Barth himself'.[19] Therefore he was striving 'to think out more carefully the relation between our fundamental concepts in theological and natural science', which in turn required 'profounder thinking about the relation of the incarnation to creation'.[20]

What might this mean? Torrance's adoption of Irenaeus' scheme of descent and ascent involves a particular way of thinking about Jesus' history as the history of salvation. The emphasis falls on the step-by-step recovery of the creation and creature through the obedience of Jesus, so that recapitulation is understood to mean that humanity is somewhat gradually redeemed and perfected through His life-acts. Thus Torrance speaks of the ascension as the presentation of perfect humanity to the Father, since that perfection is only present after the sequence of obedient acts is completed at the cross. If Jesus' role as ascended high priest is worked out with an emphasis on his humanity, then the outcome might be that Jesus' ascension brings about the offering of the redeemed cosmos before the Father – in His own person – and the mediation of the new being as God's children to humanity as it still lives between the times.

Before exploring the question of the shape of Jesus' ascension as His exaltation – that is, of Torrance's sequential approach to humiliation and

---

[18] *Space, Time and Resurrection* p158.

[19] *Karl Barth* ... p.135.

[20] *Karl Barth* ... p.135.

exaltation – we shall attempt to explicate the matter of Jesus' ascended high priesthood. Torrance's treatment of Jesus' high priestly ministry is developed around three loci: Jesus' endless self-oblation, His eternal intercession and advocacy, and His eternal benediction. The passages to which we turn are themselves remarkably brief, and so therefore is our examination of them.

Jesus Christ's Endless Self-oblation

In Torrance's work, Jesus' ascended role as priest involves His ceaseless offering of Himself as the one perfect sacrifice or offering on behalf of all humanity. Jesus' obedience, especially in His cross, is now taken up into the life of God, via resurrection and ascension, in such a way that in His ascended humanity the life of the one man Jesus' is offered for all. [21] 'Here we think of the ascension as the act of Christ's self-offering to the Father in which his self-sacrifice is backed up by his own resurrection and endless Life, and made an offering to God through the Eternal Spirit'.[22] As this is the aspect of Jesus' high priesthood that Torrance's links most strongly to Jesus' ascended humanity, which is of course the locus of his complaint against Barth, we will focus in more detail upon this area than upon the two that follow.

What does Torrance mean here when he says that Jesus' cross is 'backed up' by His resurrection and endless life? Does this indicate that something is added to the cross? If so, this would indicate a genuine point of difference from Barth. Certainly we can see that were Jesus not to have risen, and not to live now, then the work of the cross would remain dead with Him – and this is something that Barth would accept. Moreover, Barth is quite able himself to describe Jesus' continuing existence, and therefore *action*, as Mediator.[23] We may recall a statement from *Church Dogmatics* along these lines: 'The crucified Jesus does not contract out of the mediatorial position He adopted in His resurrection and ascension'.[24]

In Torrance's development of Jesus' office as priest he directs the reader to William Milligan's work,[25] and so we may seek insight into Torrance's thought via Milligan. It would be far too much to claim that Torrance is reliant on Milligan for the shape of his own programme. However, Torrance's move to offer Milligan's earlier treatment as a source of further insight into his own comments does demand that we see Milligan as a significant figure for Torrance. In particular we may investigate whether the cross is the final

---

[21] Although Torrance is concerned that Barth fails to focus enough on Jesus ascended humanity, particularly in relation to His high priesthood, it is a curious fact that this section in which he focuses most clearly on Jesus' ascended humanity is the shortest of the three.

[22] *Space, Time and Resurrection* p.115.

[23] Thus *CD* IV/3.i section 69, 'The Glory of the Mediator'.

[24] *CD* I/2, p.433.

[25] See, e.g. *Space, Time and Resurrection* p.111, note 5. Milligan, William *The Ascension of Our Lord* London: Macmillan, 1894.

offering of Jesus to the Father, or whether further self-offering may be said to take place in Jesus' ascension and heavenly session. Two steps are involved in Milligan's answer to this question. The first is to see that Jesus offers Himself before the Father in the event of the ascension itself. Jesus' ascension is the occasion of His entry into the Father's presence, as the obedient and *glorified* human, and in His entry He presents Himself in heaven for us – as it were, for the first time. Thus the cross is the *beginning* of the self-offering, but the cross results in Jesus' offering Himself also in Heaven – an offering which must be understood totally in the light of the cross. 'When our Lord died on Calvary He presents to us the idea of offering. When He entered heaven the same idea penetrates and pervades His first presentation of Himself to the Father there'.[26]

Jesus' self-offering, begun on the cross, is therefore realised *in the presence of the Father* only through His ascension. More than that, however, in Milligan's second step regarding Jesus' self-offering, the heavenly session itself takes on the character of an oblation, and thus, as Torrance has it, it is an eternal self-oblation. The question therefore becomes, what is it that Jesus offers? Does He endlessly repeat His sacrifice of the cross? To this Milligan responds in the negative, and develops the notion of offering around the oblation of a life rather than of a death. Thus, Jesus offers His life of service and obedience – which is to say, He offers *Himself*. This is the meaning also of the cross, not Jesus death for its own sake, but rather the offering of His life.

> When [Jesus' blood] was shed for us on Calvary it was His life given for us in another and deeper sense than that in which we use the expression 'to give one's life', that is, to die. His life was what He gave to God *as life*, although it was a life which then and there ... passed through death.[27]

So, the idea of offering is seen as able to gather up both cross, entry into heaven, and now also Jesus' heavenly session. 'The thought of 'offering' on the part of our Lord is not to be confined to His sacrificial death: it is so to be extended as to include in it a present and eternal offering to God of Himself in heaven'.[28] We can therefore see the sense in which ascended *humanity* is regarded as central to Jesus' offering – it is His human life which is offered to the Father, both in His crucifixion and in His risen existence. It is hard, however, to see how this really goes beyond Barth in achieving any insight into Jesus' ascended agency on our behalf. In fact, Barth's emphasis on the entirety of Jesus' life as self-offering might be argued to place *greater* weight on Jesus' obedient humanity in its union with His divine being, even though the ascension thereby ceases to function as the event that introduces Jesus' humanity into the Father's presence.

For Barth, as the union and reconciliation of God with humanity in His own Person, Jesus' whole life is His self-oblation – at Golgotha, and in His

---

[26] *The Ascension of Our Lord* p.125.

[27] *The Ascension of Our Lord* p.133. Emphasis original.

[28] *The Ascension of Our Lord* p.133.

resurrection and ascension, just as Milligan would have it – but also in His life even from birth. Milligan's own development of the idea that it is Jesus' life which is key in understanding His offering, which Torrance follows, may be used to argue for Jesus' life on the way to Calvary to also qualify as 'offering'. Milligan considers that it does not so qualify, presumably because death sets the seal upon the life, but that need not exclude the possibility of a different reading of the relation between Jesus' life and death, and therefore of the character of that life as also 'offering'. In fact, at least in some places, Torrance refuses to limit Jesus' high priesthood to cross and ascension. 'That is to say, the priestly self-consecration and self-offering of Christ *throughout the whole of his earthly life* are to be regarded as belonging to the innermost essence of the atoning mediation he fulfilled between God and mankind'.[29]   However, the weight of his treatment falls on the side of the ascension as the event in which Jesus becomes our priest in the Father's presence, as Milligan has it, which interpretation belongs with the sequential reading of humiliation and exaltation to which we have already referred, and which is treated below.

A significant point here is Milligan's (seeming) inclination to view Jesus' earthly ministry as strongly distinguished from His heavenly session, not least in terms of the *location* involved. There is an emphasis upon the heavenly nature of Jesus' saving work in Milligan's treatment, and although this is rightly opposed to any reduction of His being to the 'natural' or to His humanity alone, it turns upon the resurrection and ascension as the events which both glorify Jesus and *introduce* the heavenward aspect of His mission. It is this heavenly work that is our salvation, and although essential, Jesus' earthly life is merely preparatory.

> The most essential character of His work is not that he treads this earth of ours, engages its labours, bears its burdens, encounters its temptations, and drinks its cup of sorrows. He does all this, it is true, and it was necessary for Him to do it in order that He might be prepared for His work in heaven. But, these things done, His real work is heavenly.[30]

It is on this basis that we can understand Milligan's emphasis on Jesus' entry into heaven as the initiation of His priesthood.

It does not appear that Torrance follows Milligan whole-heartedly in this latter move – his willingness to describe the whole of Jesus' life in terms of priesthood clearly contradicts Milligan at this point – and yet he does not criticise Milligan for it, nor even note it. Indeed, there are indications that something similar does reside in Torrance's thought. Although Jesus' whole life is His true confession before God – both the Word of God directed to humanity (in this He acts as apostle) and the perfect human response to that

---

[29] *The Trinitarian Faith: The Evangelical Theology of the Ancient Catholic Church* Edinburgh: T & T Clark, 1988, p.167. Emphasis added.
[30] *The Ascension of Our Lord* p.102.

Word (in which He acts as high priest) – it is only in the ascension (once again) that this earthly reality becomes eternal reality.

> But this confession of Christ as Apostle and as High Priest is not in word only, for at the Cross it becomes the actual judgement of God, and the actual submission of Christ in perfect obedience to the point of death. It is actualised confession once and for all in historical event. ... But while this is concrete historical reality, it is also eternal spiritual reality, for Christ has opened up a new and living way to the Father. After His ascension He ever lives before the face of the Father as our *Leitourgos* and Intercessor, for there He confesses us before the face of God as those for whom He died, as those whose names He has entered as members of His body.[31]

Thus there is a strong distinction between the earthly reality of Jesus' human life, and the incorporation of that human life into the heavenly realms via Jesus' ascension.[32] Nonetheless, we maintain still that Torrance is not whole-hearted in adopting Milligan's moves at this point, and his refusal to deny any priestly function to Jesus' earthly life limits the effect of Milligan's emphasis within his theology.

Thus the difference between Barth and Torrance over Jesus' self-offering lies in the idea that Jesus' cross is *made* an offering to the Father in the ascension. It is hard, however to see how great this difference is in its outworking. Torrance's own treatment of this theme is very brief, and as we have seen, he is able to make statements that reflect both poles of our discussion – and so we will leave this to one side and continue with the remaining two descriptions of Jesus as heavenly priest.

The Eternal Intercession and Advocacy of Christ

Torrance develops a description of Jesus' entire existence and life as intercession and advocacy for us – as the God-man, the union of divine and human in one person, Jesus is both the perfect Word of God to humanity and the perfect human response to that Word, in His being He *is* intercession for

---

[31] Torrance, Thomas F. 'Royal Priesthood' *Scottish Journal of Theology Occasional Papers* No.3, 1955, p.13. Torrance refers the reader of *Space, Time and Resurrection* back to this work.

[32] It might be interesting to explore the notion of heaven that undergirds such a position. Torrance is highly critical of any 'receptacle' view of space, and it is thus that he rejects kenotic theory in favour of the *extra Calvinisticum* (see *Space, Time and Resurrection* p.124). But what idea of heaven is required for Jesus' earthly life to take on eternal import only in the ascension of His body? It may not be that this requires a 'receptacle' notion of space, but it certainly relies upon a strong distinction between earthly and heavenly, natural and spiritual. This is a distinction we find expressed in Milligan, who rejects any notion of Jesus' priesthood being like Aaron's, for Aaron's priesthood is earthly – the priesthood of Christ must be like that of Melchizedek because that is a heavenly priesthood. See *The Ascension of Our Lord* pp.72-83.

us, He *is* our advocate. 'It is with that ontological content of his Advocacy on our behalf that we are concerned here. It is an Advocacy in which his Word and Person and Act are one and indivisible'.[33]

On this basis Jesus ascended simply *is* our advocate before the Father – Jesus of Nazareth is God's intervention into and on behalf of fallen humanity, and Jesus ascended therefore intervenes on behalf of those whom He has already made His own. Jesus acts as both our representative and our substitute, not only taking up our prayers and worship, our poor obedience, and offering them to the Father, but substituting His own perfect worship as our own, and even causing our lives to reflect His being and activity. We worship the Father in Jesus' name, because Jesus makes His own prayer and worship to be our prayer and worship, and moreover, because Jesus takes up our poor efforts and instils into them His own truth.

In order to explicate something of this Torrance turns to the eucharist, together with the Lord's prayer, as an expression of Jesus' advocacy on our part. The eucharist is prayer, but prayer that includes and is furthered by the 'pledges' of Jesus' body and blood. Jesus Himself places these at our disposal with which to appear before the Father, so that they are the sacrifice we are to present – the sacrifice which Jesus Himself is.[34] Jesus thus 'stands in' for His people, while they in turn take refuge in His sacrifice. Yet even here, Torrance does not move to in any way embrace an idea of Jesus 'repeating' the sacrifice of the cross, nor of any addition to the work of the cross – there is one offering made once for all.

Once again Milligan may supply further explanation:

> We are to understand [Jesus' intercession in] every act by which the Son, in dependence on the Father, in the Father's name, and with the perfect concurrence of the Father, takes His own with Him into the Father's presence, in order that whatever He Himself enjoys in the communications of His Father's love may become also theirs.[35]

On this basis, Milligan sees Jesus' 'high priestly' prayer, in John 17, as a 'concentration of all the prayers of the heavenly Intercessor'.[36] We learn here how it is that Jesus intercedes for us, and what it is that He seeks for us. Once more an interesting point arises, however, in relation to Jesus' ascension as the necessary qualification for His high priestly work. How is it that Jesus is here found praying in such a fashion before His ascension – indeed, even before His death? As Milligan notes: 'At the moment when He utters this prayer He is less the humbled and dying than the exalted and glorified Redeemer'.[37]

---

[33] *Space, Time and Resurrection* p.116.

[34] *Space, Time and Resurrection* p.117.

[35] *The Ascension of Our Lord* p.152.

[36] *The Ascension of Our Lord* p.156.

[37] *The Ascension of Our Lord* pp.155-6.

Milligan's answer is to see Jesus as mentally projecting Himself forward into His heavenly session – he prays *as if* He were now in heaven. 'He has passed onward now in thought to the accomplishment of His work ...'[38] Milligan clearly envisages quite some difference in Jesus' being as the suffering servant and the exalted Lord. But might it be that Jesus can be both heavenly high priest and humbled unto death even at one and the same time – indeed in the very same event?

This question links back to the exposition of Jesus' self-offering, and the strong distinction between earthly and heavenly discovered there. Milligan is explicit that everything that may be said regarding Jesus' heavenly intercession and advocacy is predicated upon His continued self-offering, and so the link is not surprising.

> Finally it may be observed that the blessings of redemption thus applied to us through the Intercession of our Lord, in the wide sense in which we have been led to understand that word, are blessings that flow from His own continued offering. The Intercession and the Offering cannot be separated from each other.[39]

It is on this basis that the issues regarding the strong separation of heavenly and earthly, natural and spiritual flow over in the treatment of Jesus' intercession, and to the degree that Torrance follows Milligan's account of Jesus' self-offering he will need to wrestle with similar issues.

Jesus' Eternal Benediction

Finally, Torrance also discusses Jesus' heavenly benediction as a function of His high priesthood. In parallel to Melchizedek's blessing of Abraham, and of the Aaronic high priest's blessing of the people of Israel on the day of atonement, Jesus the great high priest is seen as blessing His people. The benediction that Torrance has in mind at this point is the gift of the Spirit – a gift directly flowing from the ascension.[40] 'In his ascension Jesus Christ blessed his people, and fulfilled that blessing in sending down upon us the presence of the Holy Spirit'.[41] If we recall Luke's account of Jesus lifting up His hands in benediction as He ascends and promises the Spirit,[42] then 'Pentecost is the content and actualisation of that high priestly blessing. He ascended in order to fill all things with his presence and to bestow gifts of the Spirit upon men'.[43]

---

[38] *The Ascension of Our Lord* p.156.

[39] *The Ascension of Our Lord* p.160.

[40] Torrace's own section on the Spirit as the content of Jesus' heavenly benediction is surprisingly brief. See *Space, Time and Resurrection* pp.117-18.

[41] *Space, Time and Resurrection* p.117.

[42] This is a reference to the account of Jesus' ascension at the end of Luke 24 – Jesus tells His disciples to remain in Jerusalem until they 'have been clothed with power from on high', and then, having gone to Bethany, He blesses them, 'while He was blessing them, He withdrew from them and was carried up into heaven' (NRSV).

[43] *Space, Time and Resurrection* p.118.

Again, the heart of this is the communion of the church with the heavenly Head of the body – something that Torrance speaks of in eucharistic terms once more. 'This is, again, an aspect of Christ's royal priestly ministry which is especially relevant to the Church's Communion in the body and blood of Christ through the Spirit'.[44] Thus, through the distribution of gifts of the Spirit, the church comes to share in Jesus' own ministry, and takes up a secondary and derivative priesthood – a priesthood that in no way competes with the one Priesthood of Christ, but rather reflects it. 'Through the Spirit Christ's own priestly ministry is at work in and through the Church which is his body'.[45]

Although he does not say so at this point, it would appear that all realisation of salvation 'between the times' is dependent on the presence of the Spirit in the church, and this gift is the heavenly benediction of the great high priest. So, for instance, in discussing Jesus' ascended role as *prophet*, and the church's prophetic task, Torrance turns to Christ's benediction and gift of the Spirit as the reality of His self-proclamation. The Word that Jesus *is* and His *act* of reconciliation are inseparable – Jesus is the eternal Word and thus the union of God and humanity – and this Word is made present in the Holy Spirit. 'That is the kind of Word that is mediated to us through the Blessing of Christ and the pouring out of his Spirit, a prophetic ministry in which Christ is himself its living, actual and full content, or in which Christ effectively ministers himself to us'.[46]

Jesus' Ascended Humanity: Torrance and Barth

To what extent does Torrance develop a better description – or even a different description – of Jesus' risen humanity in comparison to Barth? What does the adoption of a more explicit commentary upon Jesus as ascended priest achieve? These questions address Barth's own discussion of high priestly material. But they also raise the possibility that Barth may maintain Jesus' ascended and *human* agency, but developed through other means than discussion of ascended priesthood *per se*. In particular we will ask: What function and place does Torrance give to Jesus' ascended humanity, especially as compared to Barth? Of course, if Barth does not maintain some of the things Torrance does, we will need to decide why this is so.

As noted earlier, considering the nature of his criticism of Barth, Torrance's treatment of Jesus' ascended high priesthood is remarkably brief.[47] Two points stand out in that treatment. Firstly, Torrance locates Jesus' 'endless self-oblation' with particular reference to His ascended humanity – it is Jesus' human nature that enables Him to offer Himself on behalf of all humanity. Secondly the ontological reality of Jesus Christ, the God-man, is explicitly named at the centre Jesus' intercession and advocacy, and may also

---

[44] *Space, Time and Resurrection* p.118.

[45] *Space, Time and Resurrection* p.118.

[46] *Space, Time and Resurrection* p.120.

[47] It is for this reason that Milligan has occupied so much of our attention at times.

be argued to underlie His eternal benediction. Clearly, as one half of the ontological reality that is Jesus Christ, His human nature is key in any theology which relies upon it.

We have already asked how much Torrance's treatment of Jesus' endless self-offering opens up genuinely new territory for him – in comparison to Barth – and the answer appears to be that it achieves very little that is new. In as much as Jesus is seen as offering His life and death – the saving work that He undertook on our behalf in His human walk from Bethlehem to Golgotha – then it is hard to see that there is any advance here upon Barth. On the other hand, to describe the *ascension* as the peculiar act in which this offering takes place does indeed introduce something that is missing in Barth, and something that Barth specifically rejects. This aspect of Torrance's thought will receive considerable attention below. When applied to the issue of Jesus' ascended humanity *per se* it seems, however, to yield very little that is new. Torrance appears to emphasise that it is humanity as perfected through the step by step obedience of the Son that is offered. It is hard to see that Barth's refusal of the ascension as uniting Jesus to the Father *in any new way* necessarily interferes with such a view. What *is* different is the assumption that the life and death themselves do not also have the character of offering, and that Jesus' earthly career is some how cut off from the presence of the Father, so that it is only brought into His presence in the ascension. Barth's view does not necessarily deny that the *fulfilment* of Jesus' self-offering may be found in His presence at the Father's right hand – he says so himself – and neither does he deny that it is only through death that the movement of self-offering finds its completion, so that the history of Jesus of Nazareth remains all important.

For Torrance, Jesus' eternal intercession and advocacy on behalf of His people turns upon His perfect humanity as it is in union with the life of God Himself. This is exactly the central theme of Barth's Christology, which we have explored in relation to Jesus' ascension in some depth. The whole structure of objective and subjective justification, including the outpouring of the Spirit, turns upon the unity of God and humanity in Jesus Christ, not only in the life of the man Jesus of Nazareth, but very much in His continued life as the risen and ascended One. So Torrance's description of Jesus' sending of the Spirit as His priestly benediction does not appear to involve any relation to Jesus' risen humanity that we cannot also detect in Barth – the Spirit is the gift of Jesus in His ascended state, and in the Spirit we receive the presence of Jesus the God-*man*.

The question at this point is Torrance's claim that Jesus' ascended life is swallowed up in the Spirit, so that there is a danger in Barth of doceticism. In Barth's defence, he places considerable emphasis upon the Spirit as sent from Jesus – the risen God-man – and moreover as bringing Jesus' presence and undertaking Jesus' work. (So much so that this emphasis contributes, as we have seen, to the accusation that Barth has no pneumatology worth mentioning as such, and is 'Christomonist'.) The presence of the Spirit is therefore, as above, the presence of Jesus, not simply in His divinity – that is,

not simply a 'spiritual' presence – but also in His humanity.   Barth's
Chalcedonian Christology will not allow any separation of divine and human
in Jesus, whether before or after resurrection and ascension.

The 'Sequential' Interpretation of Descent and Ascent

To take up some of the issues of the preceding section, and to return to the key
matter of Torrance's reading of the ascension as the exaltation of the formerly
lowly One, we turn to Farrow's comments on Torrance.   Farrow reads
Torrance as attempting to overcome the deficiency in Barth's ascension
theology, and especially as endeavouring to make more of the function of
Jesus' ascended *humanity*, just as Farrow himself seeks to emphasise the
ascension of the *man* Jesus of Nazareth.   Incarnational issues are therefore very
much involved, so that what Farrow perceives in Torrance is a loosening of
Barth's 'chalcedonian clamp'.   Yet it is at this same point that Farrow criticises
Torrance, and we too will question Torrance's programme in respect of this
issue.   The key is found in the relationship between incarnation and
atonement, including the matter of the *hypostatic* union, and thus what Jesus'
ascension is taken to mean for His *humanity*.   In fact, the old theological
matters of *kenotic* theory and the *extra Calvinisticum* come to the fore.   Although
Torrance's treatment of Jesus' high priesthood *per se* has not yielded a great
deal of conflict with Barth, Torrance's claim that the ascension is to be
correlated with a descent in the incarnation provides a core point of
comparison.   At the same time this links back to Milligan's reading of the
heavenly and earthly poles of Jesus' ministry.

For Torrance, while the theology of the ascension belongs with that of the
cross and resurrection, and is to be developed in close relation to them, it is not
therefore to be denied a place which is distinctly its own.   The peculiar
function of Jesus' ascension involves a movement correlated to the movement
of incarnation: 'the ascension must be understood in correlation with the
incarnation, as the *anabasis* (ascent) of the Son of God corresponding to his
katabasis (descent)'.[48]   In no sense whatsoever is this a reversal of the Son's
taking flesh, but it is rather a reversal of God's entry into our 'place', as in
Jesus' ascension humanity now ascends to God's 'place'.   This difference from
Barth's approach to the ascension indicates a potential difference in thought
about the incarnation.   Earlier on the same page Torrance can speak of Jesus'
manifestation in the forty days as such that 'thoughts of suffering and glory, of
humiliation and exaltation, were bound together in his Person in indissoluble
union',[49] and this is something Barth himself might say.   It indicates the union
of humiliation and exaltation in the one person Jesus Christ *throughout* His life.

---

[48] *Space, Time and Resurrection* p.123.   Torrance attributes this thought to Irenaeus as a
'favourite theme'.

[49] *Space, Time and Resurrection* p.123.   Milligan, rather than Barth, is footnoted at this
point.

Indeed, previously in the same work Torrance has chosen to speak of the incarnation in a way that is strongly reminiscent of Barth's chalcedonian interpretation of humiliation and exaltation:

> It is because he who lives and acts in [the incarnation] is divine and human *in one Person*, that all he does in our fallen existence has a dark side and a light side, a side of humiliation and a side of exaltation – the one is the obverse of the other ...[50]

However, as we have seen, Barth's adoption of this view of exaltation and humiliation involves a refusal to correlate incarnation and ascension as descent and ascent in the way that Torrance does above.

How then does Torrance see this correlation? Perhaps surprisingly, given the above comments regarding the incarnation, the significant move is to see the ascension as the event in which Jesus' new humanity is united to God (and thus humanity's existence in time and space also). We have already encountered this in relation to Jesus' high priesthood. In the ascension the new humanity is exalted – with the 'place' for human life – into participation in and with the divine 'place'. That is, God makes space for the humans that God loves. In Jesus' ascension our humanity is taken up into the communion of Father, Son, and Spirit![51] Similarly the ascension is spoken of as the event in which Jesus' perfect priesthood is taken up into God,[52] the event in which Jesus ascends from 'man's "place" to God's "place" and thus establishes humanity in its proper "place" in space and time'.[53] It is thus, as above, the event of the ascension that unites humanity to God in Jesus Christ, and in this event humanity is given to participate in the divine nature. This is the final and great goal of the incarnation itself, as humans are taken up before the Father in Christ and share in His self-presentation there.[54]

Thus, although the outcomes of Torrance's treatment of Jesus' high priesthood do not appear to overturn Barth to any great degree, the manner in which that high priesthood is established does do so. Jesus becomes high priest in the event of His new humanity being presented to the Father, and that ultimately occurs in His ascension. Incarnation and ascension therefore correlate in that the descent of God in becoming human has its outcome in the ascent of humanity in Christ into the being of God. As Farrow too maintains, this is the sense of Irenaeus' doctrine of recapitulation – that Jesus Christ became human in order that humans may become what He is, in order that

---

[50] *Space, Time and Resurrection* pp.46-7. Emphasis original. See also pp.56-7 for a parallel argument relating to the hiddenness and revelation of God in Jesus of Nazareth.

[51] *Space, Time and Resurrection* p.133.

[52] *Space, Time and Resurrection* p.115.

[53] *Space, Time and Resurrection* p.130.

[54] *Space, Time and Resurrection* p.135.

humans may come to share God's life, not God or gods, but united with God in His divinity.[55]

When we examine these claims, with Barth's reading of the incarnation in the background, questions arise regarding the understanding of the incarnation involved. How is it that Jesus' humanity is only (fully) united to the life of God in His ascension? The reading of Jesus' history involved appears to require that some aspect of Jesus' being as the eternal Son is either given up or put aside in the incarnation, and then taken up again in ascension. Indeed it might imply that what Jesus gives up is the fullness of His relationship to the Father, as this would explain the claim that it is only the ascension that fully unites humanity to God in Christ. All this appears to cast a troubling light back upon Jesus' incarnate life prior to the ascension. To take this line of thought further, if our humanity is not united to God's life in the very fact of the incarnation, then what must we say of Jesus' being? Two options present themselves. Firstly it may be that Jesus' *kenosis* is such that His assumption of human being does not immediately unite that being with the Trinity – that is, Jesus must in some way give up the immediacy of His relationship to the Father and Spirit as it is in the eternal being of God. Or secondly it must be that the union of divine and human in Jesus Himself is somehow limited – that is, that the eternal Son continues to maintain the immediacy of His Trinitarian relationships, but somehow the human being He adopts is excluded from those relations until the ascension. But it appears most unlikely that Torrance adopts either of these approaches.

The solution to the difficulty initially appears to lie in Torrance's formulation of the matter in terms of *new* humanity in Christ – meaning thereby humanity as perfected through the life-acts of Jesus, and in particular His death. Thus the sense would be that Jesus takes up *fallen* humanity (as Barth would also insist) and through His life of obedience turns it back toward the Father at every point, and finally, in the ascension He takes that *now perfected* humanity to the Father's side and there presents it.[56] But it is still not clear that the distinction here between Jesus humanity as He adopts it in the incarnation and as He presents it to the Father in the ascension helps to overcome the difficulties indicated above. That Jesus only presents a new humanity before the Father in the ascension still appears to cast a shadow over the unity of God and humanity throughout the incarnation.

On the other hand, Barth's view involves the full presence of the new humanity, *because* in union with God in Jesus 'the Royal Man', *throughout* His incarnation, so that throughout the dynamic work of atonement Jesus presents the Father with perfect human obedience at every turn – obedience to the appointed will of the Father.

That the Word became 'flesh' means that the Son of God made His own the situation of man in the sense that with him He faced the impossible in all its power,

---

[55] We might call this a moderate doctrine of deification, such as also found in Jenson.

[56] Thus also the particular shape of the ideas of Jesus' high priesthood.

that He faced the dreadful possibility of ingratitude, disobedience, unfaithfulness, pride, cowardice and deceit, that He knew it as well as He did Himself, that He came to closer grips with it than any other man. He had to achieve His freedom and obedience as a link in the chain of an enslaved and disobedient humanity, the new thing in a strict and, for Him and Him alone, hampering connexion with the old. He had to wrestle with that which assaulted Him as one man with others, which for the first time brought all its force to bear against Him as the Son of God in the flesh. He was not immune from sin. He did not commit it, but He was not immune to it.[57]

Certainly this involves the fact that Jesus' work of perfecting humanity is not complete until the drama of atonement has been fully played out – that is, the perfection of humanity is not finalised until dramatic coherence is brought to Jesus' life by His obedient death – but that does not mean that Jesus' humanity prior to the ascension is not perfect. Rather, Barth simply holds that prior to the cross the story is not yet over, the journey not yet complete. As above, Jesus' being is sinless, due to the union of the Son of God with the Son of Man, but this perfect sinless being is expressed and indeed fulfilled in the dynamic movement of His obedient life. For Barth, therefore, the *cross* is the ultimate point at which Jesus offers His perfect humanity to the Father in atonement for the sins of the world, as it is upon the cross that His obedience is finalised in obedience even unto death.[58]

Jesus Christ was and is for us in that He suffered and was crucified and died. ...
The work of the Lord who became a servant, the way of the Son of God into the

---

[57] *CD* IV/1, pp.215-6. Note: the 'new' is already present in connexion with the 'old' – Jesus is the new humanity even as He assumes and reconciles the old. Note too, the obedience is not predicated of either Christ's humanity or divinity exclusively, but of the two in full union.

> For, according to the New Testament, it is the case that the humility of this man is an act of obedience, not a capricious choice of lowliness, suffering and dying, not an autonomous decision this way, not an accidental swing of the pendulum in this direction, but a free choice made in recognition of an appointed order, in execution of a will which imposed itself authoritatively upon Him, which was intended to be obeyed. If, then, God is in Christ, if what the man Jesus does is God's own work, this aspect of the self-emptying and self-humbling of Jesus Christ as an act of obedience cannot be alien to God. (*CD* IV/1, p.193.)

It is the case, however, that the obedience of the Son of God is the basis of Jesus' obedience *per se*, for the fallen humanity He assumes does not have it within it to obey. See *CD* IV/1 S.59, 'The Obedience of the Son of God', pp.157ff.

[58] G. Nicholson's work on the theme of ascent and departure in John's Gospel is interesting at this point. He describes the way in which John focuses Jesus' ascent, and departure to be with the Father, around the ascent of the *cross*. See G. C. Nicholson *Death as departure: the Johannine descent-ascent schema* Chicago: Scholars Press, 1983.

far country, His appearance in the flesh, His humiliation, all aims at that of which this statement speaks.[59]

The cross is therefore the absolute culmination of Jesus' entry into our place – 'the far country' – and on it He takes upon Himself the absolute negation that is proper to sinful humanity, so that He may overcome it. This is the *completion* of His work, in full continuity with every step of His career.

> The very character of the atonement is the overcoming of sin: sin in its character as the rebellion of man against God, and in its character as the ground of man's hopeless destiny in death. It was to fulfil this judgement on sin that the Son of God as man took our place as sinners. He fulfils it – as man in our place – by completing our work in the omnipotence of the divine Son, by treading the way of sinners to its bitter end in death, in destruction, in the limitless anguish of separation from God, by delivering up sinful man and sin in His own person to the non-being which is properly theirs, the non-being, the nothingness to which man has fallen victim as a sinner and towards which he relentlessly hastens.[60]

Thus, as we have seen, neither resurrection nor ascension can add to what is achieved on the way from Bethlehem to Golgotha, *except* as the revelation – the putting into effect – of the verdict of the Father in vindicating Jesus. This matter of the relation between cross and ascension will be taken up below. In the mean time, it seems that Torrance's language in his description of the results of ascension may lead to difficulties – even though at times he seems to say the same things as Barth regarding the union of God and humanity in Jesus Christ – and we will attend more closely to that possibility.

These are not new questions or issues regarding the manner in which the Son of God is to be regarded as present in the man Jesus of Nazareth, as Torrance himself notes. The controversies surrounding *kenotic* theory, and the *extra Calvinisticum*, turned on precisely the sorts of issues raised above. How is the eternal God to be thought of as 'contained' in the being of a man? How are the integrity of Jesus' human being and the importance of His history to be maintained without reducing His divinity to the vanishing point? Furthermore, a key matter in these debates was how Jesus' *ascended* human being was to be related to the elements of the eucharist, a matter which is of considerable importance in the following interaction with Farrow.

Because of the fundamental nature of these issues, both as they appear in our questioning above and in the historical debates to which they gravitate, we might expect that they are easily dealt with in regard to Torrance's thought. A single set of affirmations within Torrance's material on incarnation would seem to negate both the suspicions above. (That is, that if the new humanity is only joined to the life of God in Jesus' ascension, is Jesus' divinity in some way reduced so that His humanity is not to be regarded as united to the life of

---

[59] *CD* IV/1, p.244.
[60] *CD* IV/1, p.253.

God? Or, is the union of His two natures in some way imperfect until the ascension?) Torrance clearly sets himself against any limitation or undermining of the full *union* of God and humanity in Jesus Christ, therefore stands against any dilution of either nature. A strong theme running through Torrance's various works is his desire to remain true to, and indeed to further, what he sees as the orthodox theology of the church, grounded in the New Testament witness to Jesus and expressed in the ecumenical creeds.[61] One aspect of this 'orthodoxy' is Torrance's clear assent to the Nicene and Chalcedonian Creeds, with an emphasis on the maintenance of genuine and full humanity and utter divinity united in the person of Jesus Christ.[62] Thus, for instance, he can claim that the *homoousion* is the basis of the entire gospel, and that Jesus' Mediatorship rests upon 'the affirmation of oneness in being between the Son – and indeed the incarnate Son – and the Father'.[63]

> Throughout the apostolic tradition, in the Epistles as well as in the Gospels, Jesus is presented as acting out of an unbroken oneness between himself and the Father, which is the very ground of his significance.[64]

In his book on Barth's 'mature' theology Torrance is in fact complementary toward Barth's treatment of the hypostatic union, for the very reason that he sees in it a necessary return to patristic themes and an important correction of the Latin tradition.[65]

> It is entirely consistent ... that the incarnation and atonement should be understood in their mutual relations with each other. ... As the one Mediator between God and man, the man Christ Jesus is not only God with us, but God for us, God who has crossed the chasm of alienation between us and himself, God who has taken our rebellious and corrupt nature upon himself ... That is the doctrine of Jesus Christ as Mediator who is God of God and man of man in one Person, and who as such reconciles God to man and man to God in the hypostatic union of his divine and human natures.[66]

---

[61] The reader might be directed to many of Torrance's works. Nevertheless a particularly clear example is *The Trinitarian Faith*, with its exposition of an orthodoxy stemming from the patristic era of Christian theology, and emphasis on New Testament grounds for such an orthodoxy's claims.

[62] See, e.g., *Space, Time and Incarnation* London: Oxford University Press, 1969, pp.80-81.

[63] Torrance, Thomas F. 'Introduction', in *The Incarnation: Ecumenical Studies in the Nicene-Constantinopolitan Creed A.D. 381* Thomas F. Torrance ed. Edinburgh: The Handsel Press, 1981, p.xi.

[64] *The Incarnation*, p.xiii.

[65] This is the point of Farrow's complaint against Torrance – he feels Torrance should have sought to overturn Barth's thought at this point. See *Ascension* p.263, and Chapter 7 below.

[66] *Karl Barth* ... pp.229-30.

It is therefore unsurprising that in looking back to the Reformed-Lutheran eucharistic debates, Torrance, like Barth, upholds the Reformed *extra Calvinisticum*. He does so in order to protect the full humanity and divinity of Jesus – and moreover in direct opposition to any *kenotic* theory of the incarnation: '... it is clear that a rejection of the 'Calvinist extra' raises very great difficulties, as one can see in a kenotic theory of Christ's *self-emptying*'.[67] So, for instance, he can say: 'Jesus Christ is the place of contact and communication between God and man ...', and further on, that this 'is place that is filled with the energy of divine being and life, but place that is also filled with the energy of human being and life'.[68]

> [Thus,] this is to say that the transcendent God is present and immanent within this world in such a way that we encounter His transcendence in this-worldly form in Jesus Christ, and yet in such a way that we are aware of a majesty of transcendence in Him that reaches out beyond the whole created order.[69]

The difficulty that arises is how Torrance can maintain his avowal of the *extra Calvinisticum* – with all that it stands for – and maintain his sequential reading of humiliation and exaltation, (with the reading of Jesus' high priesthood as beginning with His ascension, as above), although many theologians before him have done so. As above, it is very plain that he is intent on maintaining both the full humanity and divinity of Jesus while at the same time upholding the utter unity of His person. But if this is right, how can Jesus' humanity not be seen as perfectly united to God throughout the incarnation? The answer lies in a further aspect of Torrance's reading of the relationship between incarnation and atonement – a view that he attributes to Barth – and the way in which he applies that view to the ascension. At issue is the conception of Jesus' history – the incarnate walk of obedience, including the cross, and His subsequent resurrection and ascension – as saving history. That is, given that the incarnation itself is atoning, and that Jesus achieves the union of God and humanity in His *person*, how is Torrance to give due weight to the life acts of the saviour as fully significant?

A solution appears in the continuation of an earlier quotation, as Torrance explicates his understanding of Barth's thought:

> [The] hypostatic union, however, was the atoning union in Christ between the Holy One of God and our sinful humanity which he made his own but which, while making it his own, he healed and sanctified in his own sinless life. ... Thus there took place in Christ as Mediator an agonising union between God the Judge and man under judgement in a continuous movement of atoning reconciliation running throughout all his obedient and sinless life and passion into the resurrection and ascension when he presented himself to the Father on our behalf

---

[67] *Space, Time and Resurrection* p.124. Emphasis original.
[68] *Space, Time and Incarnation* p.78.
[69] *Space, Time and Incarnation* pp.78-9.

and presented us in himself as those he had redeemed and consecrated to be his brethren.[70]

Thus the whole incarnation is 'one continuous and indivisible saving and sanctifying act of God'.[71] So the relationship between the fact that Jesus *exists as* the reconciliation of God with humanity, and the claim that he *acts* in order to reconcile humanity to God, is explicated in terms of an ontological (presumably 'static') pole and a dynamic pole.

> Regarded in this way the hypostatic union between the divine and human natures in Jesus Christ is the ontological aspect of atoning reconciliation and atoning reconciliation is the dynamic aspect of hypostatic union ... Hypostatic union and reconciliation inhere inseparably in one another and are, so to speak, the obverse and reverse of each other.[72]

As a reading of Barth, this would appear to be accurate enough, and provides a counterpoint to Farrow's claim that Barth's view of Jesus' history has a 'static quality' to it.[73] But, nonetheless a key difference emerges in Torrance's account of the ascension. Seeking to maintain the traditional view of ascension as the exaltation of Jesus' humanity into unity with God causes Torrance to diverge from Barth. Where for Barth, as we have seen, the high point and culmination of the 'dynamic' pole of the incarnation is the cross – the place where the obedience reaches its fulfilment – for Torrance it appears to be the ascension.

Farrow censures Torrance precisely in that he 'does not criticise Barth's treatment of the hypostatic union, and even seems to presuppose it at times, which may help to account for certain inconsistencies in his argument',[74] and this mirrors our own concern. We return to the same fundamental question: can Torrance maintain the *extra Calvinisticum* and hold the view of ascension that he does? He plainly does not opt for a dynamic view of the history of Jesus of Nazareth *over* a static reading, but rather seeks to hold them together, as can be seen in his treatment of the *hypostatic* union. But this very scheme appears to be disrupted by the notion that perfect humanity is only united to divinity in the ascension. It seems likely that Torrance would want to say that this only applies to the *dynamic* pole of the incarnation, and merely implies that the *completion* of the work of turning fallen humanity back to God occurs in the ascension, but it is not clear that this would overcome the difficulty. Surely his view still requires something more like *kenotic* theory?

---

[70] *Karl Barth* ... p.230.
[71] *Karl Barth* ... p.201.
[72] *Karl Barth* ... p.201.
[73] *Ascension* p.247.
[74] *Ascension* p.263.

This is what lies behind Barth's refusal of the traditional sequential reading of exaltation and humiliation.[75] It is because an alignment of human exaltation in Jesus with the *event* His ascension fails to sit well with his reading of the *hypostatic* union that Barth overturns it. This feature of Barth's thought may then be seen as a *locus* for a number of criticisms made against him by various commentators – many of which will appear in Farrow (unsurprisingly, given the link between Torrance's ascension theology and Farrow's subsequent programme).

The Cross or the Ascension as Highpoint of the Son's Self-offering?

At this point we shall simply comment on Barth's understanding of the cross as the peak of the movement of atonement, as a counterpoint to Torrance's emphasis on the ascension. Torrance's explication of Barth's reading of the *hypostatic* union makes it clear that this reading involves and to some degree turns upon his 'actualism'. The unity of Jesus' being and act is a function of His being as the God-man (for all other humans suffer disunity in their very selves) and this in turn informs Barth's interpenetrating exposition of incarnation and atonement.[76] Thus, Torrance's description of the *hypostatic* union as the ontological pole of incarnational atonement, and the obedient acts of the Incarnate One as the dynamic pole of the same reality, is simply another way of talking about Jesus Christ as the one Word-Act of God, who is what He does and who acts as He is.

Barth's refusal to compromise the *extra Calvinisticum* also belongs to fundamental decisions regarding both the nature of the incarnation, as above, and also the crucial matter of his doctrine of election. If Jesus Christ is the eternal Son of God in utter unity with the Son of Man, then He is elected as such from all eternity. Thus any question mark over the presence of the fullness of God in the incarnate Son – from beginning to end of His career – must be totally nullified. The cross must be seen as the high-point of the work of the Son, and everything that follows as an expression of the victory completed at the cross. If resurrection or ascension in some way add to that achievement something that was previously missing from it – especially in uniting Jesus' humanity to God as it was not before – then the full presence of God acting in our place and redeeming our humanity is perceived to be in danger.

Thus also the matters of objective and subjective justification, as explicated in the preceding chapters on Barth, involve the key matter of *what it is that is*

---

[75] Farrow criticises Barth for this move, as noted earlier and explicated in the following chapter. In reply to Farrow's criticism we may note that for Barth exaltation and humiliation should not be wholly aligned to descent and ascent, as Farrow assumes, and because of this Barth's move here does not necessarily imply that Jesus' ascension means nothing within His history, quite the reverse.

[76] See *Karl Barth* ... pp.200-201.

imputed to Christians, and therefore realised in them by the Holy Spirit. Given that the cross is the peak of Jesus' atoning work, it is the righteousness fulfilled on the cross that Barth sees as imputed to Christians and therefore realised in their sanctification in the Spirit. To receive a share in His risen and ascended humanity is therefore to receive a share in the Father's verdict upon Jesus' obedience – perfected upon the cross and summed up in the great cry 'It is finished' – not to receive a share in Jesus' relationship with the Father as *newly established* in the ascension, as Torrance would have it.

On the other hand, Barth's reading of Jesus' history does take in the ascension and even might be argued to see in the ascension the fulfilment of His incarnation. As the revelation of the fact that Jesus has always belonged at the right hand of the Father, *and of the perfect obedience completed in His death*, the ascension is indeed the proper fulfilment of His life of obedience. However, we might argue even more strongly that for Barth the *eschaton* is the goal of all Jesus' history – the full revelation of the Lordship of God in Christ and of the victory culminating upon the cross and revealed in Jesus' resurrection. It is on this basis that Barth understands Jesus' continuing agency in the 'time between' as He presses on toward the final stage of His *parousia* and the completion of His revelation as Lord.

Concluding Remarks

The issues uncovered in examining Torrance's critique of Barth largely point forward to the substantial criticism of Barth offered by Douglas Farrow. Torrance may be seen to have some difficulty with the matter of the *extra Calvinisticum* and to diverge from Barth in the way he reads the inter-relation of cross and ascension, but ultimately we hold that the difference between Barth and Torrance is not great. Torrance's theology of the ascension does not appear to have caused him actually to diverge from Barth in his description of the incarnation, nor even to any large degree in his vision of Jesus' ascended ministry.

This is not to claim that there are no differences, nor does it indicate that we simply consider Torrance to be in the right where he agrees with Barth and wrong where he does not. The most significant difference lies in the adoption of a sequential reading of humiliation and exaltation, and, *à la* Milligan, in the conception of Jesus' high priesthood that this involves, and it is here that Torrance appears to run into difficulty. It is, as Farrow observes, a difficulty in terms of *consistency*[77] – we might say that Torrance's overwhelming agreement with Barth appears to make this area of *dis*agreement difficult to maintain. In Farrow's theology, where the difference becomes full-blown, the issue is not one of consistency, and the discussion has more to do with a comparison of fully divergent programmes. Nonetheless, Farrow takes encouragement from

---

[77] See *Ascension* pp.263 and 266.

the line Torrance introduced, and the discussion of *extra Calvinisticum* and *kenosis* in relation to tendencies in Torrance's thought leads well into the strongly eucharistic flavour of Farrow's work, and the (arguably) eucharistic basis of his rejection of Barth.

Chapter 7

Douglas Farrow: Ascension, Church, and Karl Barth

Douglas Farrow has recently published a major work on the doctrine of Jesus' ascension, and in particular the impact of this doctrine on understandings of the church. As such Farrow's book is clearly of interest to the present work, even more so because within it he undertakes to expound and critique Barth's view and utilisation of the doctrine of the ascension.

Initially Farrow is complimentary toward Barth, and in an article that largely draws upon his book he says that *Church Dogmatics* volume IV 'stands as one of *the* major works of ascension theology'.[1] As Farrow treats the history of the doctrine of the ascension within Christian theology he sees that history as problematic and docetic. The docetic streak is traced back to Augustine, but more especially to Origen, while Barth, following Kierkegaard, is described as a 'step forward' and out of the problems. Jesus' ascension in the flesh, and a working out of the proper implications of this, are the matters of key concern for Farrow, and it is on this basis that Barth earns praise. However, reservations soon emerge, and Barth is finally found to have failed to live up to the legacy of Irenaeus, who is undoubtedly the hero of Farrow's book. 'Barth puts forward a position which represents only a partial recovery of that early father's vision'.[2]

In order to engage with Farrow's critique of Barth – a critique that is often highly technical, and in which the key moves sometimes remain obscure – we will begin with some of his own constructive proposals, before examining his comments on Barth in the light of these ideas. We have already noted, in the preceding chapter, that Farrow takes up Torrance's critique of Barth and seeks to apply it more rigorously. On this basis the issues surrounding Jesus' incarnation and the *extra Calvinisticum* that were raised in relation to Torrance's thought will be raised in relation to Farrow also. Given the treatment these matters have already received, and the other significant matters which involved in engagement with Farrow, this chapter will not do more than note similarities with Torrance's position, and therefore the possibility of a similar critique applying to Farrow.

---

[1] Farrow, Douglas 'Karl Barth on the Ascension: An Appreciation and Critique' *International Journal of Systematic Theology* 2 (2000) p.127, emphasis original.

[2] Farrow, Douglas *Ascension and Ecclesia: On the Significance of the Doctrine of the Ascension for Ecclesiology and Christian Cosmology* Edinburgh: T&T Clark, 1999, p.244.

Eucharistic Ecclesiology and the Ascension of Christ

In the first chapter of *Ascension and Ecclesia* Farrow makes his ecclesiological concern abundantly clear, as he intends to begin and end 'with talk about the church, a concern for the health of which is one reason for setting out'[3] to investigate Jesus' ascension. The 'church itself is a consequence of the ascension',[4] and investigation of the ascension will therefore yield important ecclesiological insight. At the heart of the project is his desire for a 'eucharistic ecclesiology' – a term which Farrow uses liberally, but not always with precise definition. 'Eucharistic ecclesiology' finds its origin in the claim that the eucharist constitutes the church, rather than *vice versa*[5]. The implication seems to be that the eucharist *alone* constitutes the church.[6] Thus a proper ecclesiology will find its object, the church, to be available for investigation as a function of eucharistic worship. Starting points for ecclesiology abound, reflecting a lack of theological wisdom and insight, but 'the fact remains that the church itself is established only by 'the upwards call of God in Christ Jesus', and that call is made concrete precisely in the eucharistic liturgy'.[7] Thus 'there is no place to ground serious thought about the church but the eucharistic assembly'.[8] We may wish to question this move to make the eucharist so specifically our focus, but the answer is plain:

> Where *shall* we begin if not at the very place where the bond between head and members is proclaimed, where the church's identity is renewed in memory and hope, where its unity is plainly set forth? The simple answer is that no other situation presents itself as an adequate alternative. All the various resources on which we must lean for insight into the church – scripture, creed, tradition, baptism, the experience of the faithful – live and move and have their being in a community knit together around a common table.[9]

Plainly, Farrow sees the eucharist as straight-forwardly determinative of the being of the church – it seems to be in eucharistic worship alone that the church is identifiable. The church is that community of people which sees and recognises Jesus as he meets them in this world, and 'the eucharistic assembly

---

[3] *Ascension*, p.1.

[4] *Ascension*, p.1.

[5] On p.1 of *Ascension*, Farrow mentions this idea as belonging to Zizoulas, and restrains himself from directly affirming it himself, however note 22 on p.7 appears to recommend Zizoulas' claim in more direct fashion.

[6] While it is true that Farrow does, in a very few places, recognise the place of the Word, in the end his affirmation of the Word seems to mean very little in the light of the great claims he consistently makes for the exclusive role of eucharist in ecclesial being.

[7] *Ascension*, p.2.

[8] *Ascension*, p.1.

[9] *Ascension*, p.2.

is to be the place where this will happen'.[10]   At the same time the term 'eucharistic' seems to be able to be used figuratively as well as directly. Firstly, ecclesiology needs to be eucharistic because it is in the eucharist that the church is constituted and becomes visible. But, secondly, ecclesiology must also be eucharistic in the more figurative sense that the eucharist displays and stands for patterns of Jesus' presence and absence – and therefore also the presence and absence of His kingdom – which must be at the centre of theological reflection.[11] Yet even here the sense remains that this ambiguity of the existence of the church – the fact that Jesus Christ is both present and absent, and that His people await His *eschaton* – is manifest at the least *primarily*, perhaps *only*, in the eucharist. 'For it is in its eucharistic ambiguity that the church is marked off from the world ontologically and not merely ideologically'.[12]

It is not the task of this essay to interact in detail with Farrow's eucharistic stance, but there is much that appears troubling in his opening chapter, and as the emphasis with which he begins is critical to his entire project, it is necessary to draw attention to some difficulties. Farrow does move to recommend the liturgy of the Word as the necessary partner of eucharistic liturgy – going so far as to recognise that eucharist without the Word, and Word without eucharist, 'would be unnaturally divided aspects of [Jesus'] self-giving to the church'.[13] Yet even here there are contentious assumptions involved. Word without eucharist is called 'disembodied word' and eucharist without word is 'mute substance' – but there is no indication of the origin of these descriptions. Why is the liturgy of the Word (however Farrow envisages it) 'disembodied'? Is an exposition of the Word by a preacher a 'disembodied' act, and if so, why? Moreover, where does the very distinction between 'disembodied word' and 'mute substance' come from? Do we look simply to a sacramental tradition with an emphasis on embodied forms of Christ's presence, or, for example, are there echoes of Hegel's phenomenology of spirit here?[14]   Moreover, and significantly, although Farrow says that the Word must partner the eucharist, the work he undertakes does not appear to reflect any further application of this assertion – the liturgy of the Word seems to play no part in determining Farrow's further thought about church and ascension.

---

[10] *Ascension*, p.8 (The *only* place where this will happen?!).

[11] See *Ascension*, p.3.

[12] *Ascension*, p.3.

[13] *Ascension*, p.4.

[14] Robert Jenson sees word as disembodied in that it is audible without being visible, and ties these notions to subjectivity and objectivity. For Jenson the audible has no objectivity, and thus can be described as an act of pure subjectivity which enslaves the listener by failing to offer the speaker as an object. Something similar appears to be assumed in Farrow. See, e.g., Jenson's *Visible Words: The Interpretation and Practice of Christian Sacraments* Philadelphia: Fortress Press, 1978. Chapter 8 will address this aspect of Jenson's thought in some detail.

The suspicion is that the eucharist is being loaded with more freight than it can safely bear – especially with any New Testament mandate.[15] Justin Martyr is quoted, in his explanation of Christians' worship taking place on Sunday, and from this some rather bold claims are extrapolated.

> Just here the eschatological character of the liturgy comes to the fore, together with its cosmic scope and ramifications, as Justin's conclusion indicates:
>
> > *But Sunday is the day on which we all hold our common assembly, because it is the first day on which God, having wrought a change in the darkness and matter, made the world; and Jesus Christ our Saviour on the same day rose from the dead.*
>
> This observation helps us to set the mystery of the church in a much wider context; that is, in the context of a more mundane ambiguity, the ambiguity of the whole world that is owed to the fall. The eucharistic event, as a movement from absence to presence, is as such a movement from chaos to order, darkness to light, death to life. It is an inventive, ordering event on the same plane as the act of creation, though its actual results are largely withheld from our view.[16]

Just how the move is made from Justin's rather innocuous statement to Farrow's declaration that the eucharist is 'on the same plane as the act of creation' is unclear. Moreover, Farrow seems to forget that Justin is not talking about eucharistic worship in isolation, but about the communal worship of God's people, which Justin himself has just described as including a liturgy of the Word, prayers, and eucharist. Farrow seems to assume that Justin's rather minimal description of the bringing of bread and wine, prayer, and distribution, actually describes a 'transformation of the contents of the liturgy of the word as they are ultimately caught up and fulfilled in the eucharist itself'.[17]

To return to the question of New Testament warrant for this emphasis on the eucharist, although it is (still) somewhat of a fashion in some quarters of biblical studies to see (rather coded) eucharistic passages throughout the New Testament, the interpretation of these passages remains contentious.   Of

---

[15] One is tempted to ask, rather facetiously, when the Spirit was poured out at Pentecost did the gathered believers immediately celebrate a eucharist together, as this seems the only activity in which they could gather as or act as 'church'?

[16] *Ascension*, p.5. Italics (for quotation of Justin) added.

[17] *Ascension*, p.5. Justin is quoted as saying: 'and when our prayer is ended, bread and wine and water are brought, and the president in like manner offers prayers and thanksgivings, according to his ability, and the people assent, saying Amen; and there is distribution to each, and a participation of that over which thanks has been given, and to those who are absent a portion is sent by the deacons'.   Once again, it is difficult to identify the source of Farrow's idea in this statement by Justin himself – how is Justin's rather simple description of the eucharistic action to be understood as claiming that everything that has gone before in the service is now 'caught up and fulfilled'?

particular note in comparing Farrow's ecclesiological determinations with the New Testament is the lack of interest he shows in external proclamation of any kind, although we may presume he sees the eucharist as a proclamation to and within the church. Yet surely the New Testament has a tremendous emphasis upon proclamation and witness – a task in which we might even argue that the church finds its vocation. Of course, this latter view is also that of Barth, and so we see indications of a foundational point of difference between Barth and Farrow.

But what of the relation between ascension and eucharistic ecclesiology in Farrow's construction? Farrow further describes the ecclesiological question of Jesus' presence and absence as turning on the divergence of two histories – Jesus' history and that of the world (including the church within the world). Jesus ascended is no longer accessible to us, and His ongoing history is no longer accessible to us, according to our normal modes of operation. Significantly, although 'the Easter events introduced a discontinuity into the life of Jesus which renders the kind of links we are used to impossible and irrelevant',[18] it is the ascension that finally breaks Jesus' history off from our own, and makes it altogether inaccessible. Jesus' resurrection appearances, such as that upon the Emmaus road, still involved a certain continuity with our normality,[19] but the ascension closes out even that limited continuity. 'For with the ascension the track of Jesus-history, still genuinely visible in some sense on the Emmaus road, passes beyond all ken'.[20]

It is this radical discontinuity – absence – of Jesus' on-going history from our own and from our perception that gives the church its particular shape – indeed that creates the church. Moreover, it is the eucharist which manifests this reality, and in which the absent Lord of the church makes himself present.

> It is the divergence of Jesus-history from our own that gives to the ecclesia its character and its name. It is the divergence of Jesus-history from our own that calls for a specifically *eucharistic* link: for the breaking and remoulding, the substantial transformation of worldly reality to bring it into conjunction with the lordly reality of Jesus Christ. ... Only with his establishment at the right hand of God – 'separated from sinners, exalted above the heavens' – did ecclesial being become possible. Only then did its eucharistic form become necessary, somehow anticipating a second and more profound 'change in the darkness and matter' that is yet to come.[21]

Thus the ascension lies at the heart of all Farrow's ecclesiology. In particular Farrow attempts to attend to the *absence* of Jesus, which arises from His ascension, noting with irony that the doctrine of the ascension is often used to

---

[18] *Ascension*, p.8.

[19] Although Farrow does not describe this continuity one might speculate that by 'normal' he means some sort of visible and audible presence of another human person.

[20] *Ascension*, pp.9-10.

[21] *Ascension*, p.10. Emphasis original.

uphold ecclesiologies that move in quite the opposite direction from his own. In particular, Farrow draws attention to what he calls the 'eucharistic ambiguity' of the church's being, by which he means the doubtful or tenuous nature of the church's existence given the absence of her Lord and Head. He claims that this tension is often resolved in favour of the church and at Jesus' expense. That is, certainty about Jesus as living and ascended Lord and concomitant awareness of the ambiguous existence of His (still all-too-worldly) church are inverted, with the outcome that certainty about the being of the church is combined with doubt about the being of Jesus Christ. For Farrow, the eucharistic tension in which the church exists is the tension between its rather obvious continuity with the world and somewhat hidden and more troubling discontinuity with 'universal history' on the basis of its mysterious union with its heavenly Head. Once again, ascension and eucharist provide the frame of Farrow's construction.

> Since the ascension the *only* thing standing in the way of the community's complete dissolution into the world (hence into what is called universal history) is its *eucharistic* reincorporation into the society of the one whose course is known to God alone.[22]

Irenaeus as the Ascension Theologian *Par Excellence*

Irenaeus, the second century Bishop of Lyon, is regarded by Farrow as the 'first theologian of genuinely catholic stature' and 'the great Christian champion against the Gnostics'.[23] Such was the quality of Irenaeus' work that 'his thoroughgoing repudiation of Gnostic and docetic revisions to the Christian message still rewards his readers nearly two millennia on, especially those who have an eye for the refined and subtle forms of those heresies which have gained so much ground again today'.[24]

It is not the purpose of this section to interact in any depth with questions regarding Farrow's reading of Irenaeus, or to scrutinize his estimation of Irenaeus' greatness. Suffice it to note that some of the same sorts of issues arise as were noted in relation to Justin Martyr. For example, early in his discussion Farrow asserts of *Adversus Omnes Haereses* that 'Irenaeus frames this first ever theological textbook with passages containing pointed references to the ascension'.[25] The quotations offered do indeed contain direct mention of Jesus' ascension, but in both cases only as one part of a summary of the events proclaimed as salvation history. This is not to devalue Irenaeus' attention to the ascension as one highly significant episode within the sum of the events of

---

[22] *Ascension* , p.11. Emphasis original.
[23] *Ascension* , p.44.
[24] *Ascension* , pp.44-5.
[25] *Ascension* , p.45.

Jesus' life and work, but at the same time it is unclear how the references are 'pointed', or especially significant.[26]

Nonetheless, Farrow sees Irenaeus' argument with second century gnosticism as to a large extent turning upon the doctrine of Jesus' ascension in the flesh – a point which certainly has something to commend it. The gnostics, as Farrow has it, were concerned with the matter of continuity and discontinuity between the world we presently inhabit and the world Christians await. Gnosticism 'was attempting in its own largely Hellenic way to cope with the basic antinomies of human existence which our world is always thrusting upon us'.[27] The way they did so involved salvation as entirely an overcoming and destruction of the old order of creation in the new order of Christ – but 'ascension in the flesh, as the bishop puts it, demands that we understand the former as something incorporated and perfected by the latter'.[28] Thus Irenaeus attempts to hold together both the notion of redemption overcoming fallenness (discontinuity between the ages) and of redemption as the taking up and perfecting of creation (continuity). In doing so, according to Farrow, he becomes the ascension theologian *par excellence*.

---

[26] This is the quotation of Irenaeus that Farrow offers from Book 1:

> [The Spirit] proclaimed through the prophets the dispensations of God, and the advents, and the birth from a virgin, and the passion, and the resurrection from the dead, and the ascension into heaven in the flesh of the beloved Christ Jesus, our Lord, and His manifestation from heaven in the glory of the Father 'to gather all things in one', and to raise up anew all flesh of the whole human race, in order that to Christ Jesus, our Lord, and God, and Saviour, and King, according to the will of the invisible Father, 'every knee should bow ...'.

Further he offers a quotation from the end of Book 5:

> For there is one Son, who accomplished His Father's will; and one human race also in which the mysteries of God are wrought, 'which angels desire to look into'; and they are not able to search out the wisdom of God, by means of which His handiwork, confirmed and incorporated with His Son, is brought to perfection; that His offspring, the First-begotten Word, should descend to the creature, that is, to what has been moulded, and that it should be contained by Him; and on the other hand, the creature should contain the Word, and ascend to Him, passing beyond the angels, and be made after the image and likeness of God.

Both quotations: Irenaeus *Against Heresies* ed. And trans. Alexander Roberts and James Donaldson. American ed. A. Cleveland Coxe. *The Ante-Nicene Fathers*, volume I, Grand Rapids: Eerdmans, 1987, cited by Farrow *Ascension* , p.45. The final clause of the second quotation seems to imply that Irenaeus envisages Jesus as being made after the image and likeness of God (the new Adam) only after His ascension.

[27] *Ascension* , p.43.

[28] *Ascension* , p.46.

Continuity and discontinuity are held in tension, and that tension – the very same that belongs to the eucharist – is what Irenaeus sought to preserve in defense of the Judeo-Christian hope. In doing so, and in particular in rejecting the gnostic's mythologizing treatment of the ascension for one with an historical dimension, he opened up vast tracts of fruitful theological discourse for us to explore, tracts regularly passed over by expositors whose eyes are elsewhere. So significant is his contribution that [it] ... will then stand as a measuring rod for the subsequent handling of the doctrine [in later theology].[29]

In Irenaeus' thought, therefore, in 'the ascension of Jesus the temporal and material dimensions of his being were affirmed and maintained, and by no means repudiated'[30] – in opposition to the *fleshless* ascension taught by the Gnostics. This yielded a radically reworked cosmology, as Greek cosmology was broken open by the fact of Jesus' ascension in the flesh, within the larger framework of the career of God incarnate.

It was time for the Christian faith to discover within itself a proper alternative even to that older and more reputable tradition of dualism which belonged to Plato and the rest, since it too was incapable of acknowledging the incarnation, or of answering to the climatic events of the life of Jesus and the promise they contained for the whole creation.[31]

Thus Irenaeus developed his well-known doctrine of recapitulation as a way of expressing the reality of Jesus' embodiment as the salvation of the entire creation and thus of its being lifted up and returned to God. In this Farrow identifies 'double descent' – Irenaeus was 'concerned in the doctrine of recapitulation not with one descent only, but with two'.[32]

This idea involves distinguishing between an *ontological* thesis, describing the necessity of the descent of the Son of God in taking flesh, and the *soteriological* thesis that 'the Son of God becomes the Son of Man in such a way that addresses our fallen condition'.[33] God's becoming flesh is not enough to save humans, a specific career is required of the incarnate One, and, given the fallen nature of those He sets out to redeem, that career must be a descent. 'The descent of the Son must be so arranged, then, as to meet that need as well. If he descends as God to man so that man may ascend to God, he also descends *as* man so that alienated man may not fail to ascend with him'.[34] As below, on this basis Farrow has difficulty with Barth, whom he recognises as 'wrestling' with the 'double descent' while failing to separate the ontological and soteriological necessities: Barth fails to recognise the contingent descent of Jesus as a man, preferring to see Jesus' career of suffering as simply the career

---

[29] *Ascension*, p.46.

[30] *Ascension*, p.47.

[31] *Ascension*, p.47.

[32] *Ascension*, p.57.

[33] *Ascension*, p.57.

[34] *Ascension*, p.57.

proper to His assumption of fallen flesh. This is what Farrow calls Barth's 'Chalcedonian clamp', seeing the ontological and soteriological aspects as one.

Irenaeus sees redeemed humanity, indeed a redeemed cosmos, as existing in the person of Jesus Christ who has descended and ascended in the flesh and thereby joins the creation He has assumed to the eternity of God. The new cosmology therefore involves a new anthropology, in which the definition of human being is reworked on the basis of Jesus' humanity. To be human is to be in Jesus, to exist in connection with God. The mode of this connection is via the second 'hand of God', the Holy Spirit. The fruit of Christ's descent and ascent is the gift of the Spirit:

> [If] Christ descends and ascends, incorporating the song of redemption into the melody of creation, he does so precisely in order to introduce the life-giving Spirit into the desert of human intransigence. Descending he accustoms the Spirit to dwell in an unreceptive environment, making room for him in the fallen creature; ascending he reconstitutes that environment by means of the same Spirit, and in so doing makes room for the creature in the Father's presence.[35]

As a function of his new Christian cosmology, Irenaeus' thought is eschatologically oriented. Rather like Barth he sees two times existing, with the time of Jesus functioning as the boundary of the fallen time of the old creation – as Jesus has ascended to the Father, thus remaking humanity, He has remade time, yet while the *parousia* is yet awaited the old time of sin continues to abide.

> Now humanization with Christ in the Spirit is just what Irenaean eschatology is all about, as the doctrine of ascension in the flesh suggests that it should be. When Christ ascended 'to the height above, offering and commending that man which had been found,' he made 'in his own person the firstfruits of the resurrection of man,' opening up the time of increase which will answer to the present time of decrease and condemnation.[36]

This cosmological and anthropological reordering is 'an attempt to press through to a coherent Christian world view ... in which the mediation of Christ is backed by a relational ontology based in the perichoretic power of the Spirit, so that in his ascension he does indeed fill and fulfil all things ...'.[37] This leads Farrow to offer his own name for Irenaeus' world view: 'Is it not essentially a *eucharistic* model of reality ...?'[38]

---

[35] *Ascension*, p.60. Note the sequential movement, in that the reconstitution of the human occurs in Jesus' ascent – by which is meant the event of His ascension – a point of contrast with Barth's Chalcedonian reading of descent/ascent, and a point of similarity with Torrance and Milligan. Farrow may well be open to a similar critique as that offered of Torrance in respect of the *extra Calvinisticum*.

[36] *Ascension*, p.63.

[37] *Ascension*, p.66.

[38] *Ascension*, p.66. Emphasis original.

From here Farrow moves into a discussion of the nature of the church and what he calls 'ecclesial time'. Given that we have already seen his emphasis on eucharist it is not surprising that Farrow chooses to entitle this section of his book 'Eucharistic Ecclesiology', for he claims that: 'Irenaeus sees in the eucharistic prising open of man to the possibilities of ecclesial life the very stuff of the kingdom'.[39] Against the Gnostic rejection of the world Irenaeus sees the function of the church as transformation of the world through its participation with the life of the Son in the Spirit.

> The eucharistic frame of reference in which he contemplates the ecclesial vocation affords a bold Christian ethic which sharply contradicts the deviant *praxis* of his opponents. How so? The true Gnostic ... denies all obligation to the world ... But the church, believing in the renewal of creation, offers an oblation which commits it to a life of responsible engagement with the world for the sake of its transformation.[40]

This, 'the cruciform life of the church, in the witness above all of its martyrs, is the evidence of an unrelenting devotion'.[41]

Finally Irenaeus' thinking is gathered under the heading of the 'two histories'. Jesus' history diverges from general history and He cannot be made to fit any of the various Gnostic versions of that history: the ancient notion of the entire destruction of general history is disallowed, but so also is the modern idea (*à la* Hick) of the complete continuity of Jesus' time and time as we know it. At the centre of this lies the doctrine of ascension in the flesh.

> If his ascension, as ascension in flesh, is not a vertical or atemporal affair, neither is it a horizontal one. It is not an extension of this time of ours. It is indeed a *new* beginning from an old place. Christ's identification with our time, which runs into the abyss, is the time of his descent not his ascent. Ascension time (which cannot be grasped by us) is the renewal or re-opening of time through genuine converse with God.[42]

Thus Irenaeus' thought is taken up, with particular emphasis on Jesus' ascension, as a source of material for a conflict with modern day projects (such as that of John Hick), which break down the eschatological tension of Christian existence in favour of a gradualism or religious evolutionism.

---

[39] *Ascension*, p.71.

[40] *Ascension*, p.72. Although the church works for the transformation of the world, Farrow is sure that Irenaeus knows well that only God can accomplish this task.

[41] *Ascension*, p.73.

[42] *Ascension*, p.78. Emphasis original. Throughout this section, and frequently through his discussion of Irenaeus, Farrow is attempting to refute the belief that Irenaeus taught a doctrine of the general ascent of man via the transformative work of the Spirit (in the church). Whether he is successful is not finally a matter to be decided in the present discussion.

Clearly there are significant parallels between Farrow's attention to the dynamic of presence and absence and the reading of Barth developed in the present work. However, as indicated earlier, Farrow remains unconvinced by Barth's understanding of the ascension. Moreover, Farrow's emphasis on the eucharist is foreign to Barth's scheme. At this point we may note a significant point for later discussion: the ascension is significant for Barth, but it is only one of a number of doctrines and affirmations related to Jesus' transcendence and otherness – for instance in Jesus' Lordship over the church. Farrow seems to rely more exclusively on the ascension to introduce the discontinuity between Jesus' history, and the history of the church, and his theology diverges from Barth's in numerous ways. Thus, a number of points of criticism arise in Farrow's interaction with Barth, which in turn lead into a critique of much of Barth's theological project – many of the key doctrinal moves for which Barth is well known are reviewed and rejected by Farrow as he traces their influence through into ascension theology. The breadth of Farrow's critique often makes his comments difficult to penetrate, as he appears to assume in the reader an untoward level of prior understanding. At times he seems to assume an existing agreement with what he thinks, and therefore a comprehension of the full nature of his complaint without a thorough explication of his argument. However, the task before us is to attempt an exposition of the key complaints Farrow makes, and the basis he finds for them in Barth's work.

The Failure of Barth's Ascension Theology

Farrow has two central complaints about Barth's ascension theology, around which we can find clustered a large number of critical comments. Firstly he believes that Barth's project does not allow Jesus any meaningful history beyond the cross, so that resurrection and in particular ascension do not add anything significant to the picture of Christ's work, and Jesus ascended has little or nothing to do. Secondly Farrow believes that Barth misappropriates the motif of descent and ascent, failing to maintain the (Irenaean) model of descent and ascent of a human, with the attached criticism that Barth does not allow the human Jesus any freedom to choose the way of the cross.[43] He wants to maintain a level of contingency in the history of Jesus of Nazareth, and believes that Barth's doctrine of election does away with the freedom of the human Jesus. Barth's key moves in regard to election and his (so-called) actualism come under fire as Farrow takes issue with what he perceives to be their fruit in relation to Jesus' ascension.

---

[43] Contrastingly, Colin Gunton likens Barth to Irenaeus in holding a doctrine of *recapitulatio*: 'a strong conception of the second Adam fulfilling the promise to and of the first'. 'Salvation' in Webster, John B. ed. *The Cambridge Companion to Karl Barth* Cambridge: Cambridge University Press, 2000, pp.143-58, p.146.

Soteriology and Ontology: the 'Chalcedonian Clamp'

Both of the above criticisms centre on Barth's radical identification of Jesus' saving work with His being as the God-man. For Barth, the fact that Jesus saves is fundamentally a matter of the incarnation – remembering that the movement of incarnation finds its goal and fullness in the cross, and that the cross therefore remains the centre of the reconciliation Jesus achieves.[44] The cross is always the goal of the incarnation of the Son of God, for the cross is precisely the place of judgement and rejection *by God* that belongs to sinful humanity, and Jesus Christ is God entering fully into the place of sinful humanity and accepting the judgement that belongs to those whom He saves. Jesus is 'the Judge judged in our place'. The cross completes, and in so doing illuminates and explicates, the entire life of Jesus of Nazareth as 'the way of the Son of God into the far country'.[45] According to Barth's doctrine of election, therefore, Jesus is the man elected to the cross, and to the vindication of the Father, from all eternity – His course is decided from beyond all created time. As the Son of God united with the Son of Man, Jesus can do no other than He does, particularly given the unity of His being and act (in contrast to the disunity of being and act proper to fallen humanity). Further, as explored at some length in earlier sections of this work, the shape of the course of Jesus' life with its emphasis on the cross means that the resurrection and ascension take on the character of revelation of the salvation present in Jesus' very being.

It is precisely these central features in the whole architecture of Barth's theology that cause Farrow to have doubts about Barth's exposition of Jesus' ascension. We will attempt to take each point in order, examining Farrow's criticism, and assessing the merits of his claims alongside possible defences of Barth.

Descent and Ascent 'of a Man'

As above, Farrow credits Irenaeus with emphasising and working through Jesus' history as the history of descent and an ascent of a man – the model Farrow claims best fits with the New Testament. In taking up this way of talking about Jesus' career he criticises Barth for assigning descent to the Son of God, and ascent to the Son of Man. Just where Farrow follows Irenaeus' sequential reading,[46] Barth overturns the traditional reading of humiliation and exaltation as sequential movements, and rather assigns them both to the whole of Jesus' life, interpreting them in relation to the two natures of Christ, and seeing both as reaching their peak at the cross. However, Farrow's claim is

---

[44] Given the exposition of Barth's thought in other parts of this work, this section will for the most part lack specific references to Barth's texts, except for occasions when interaction with Farrow leads to the examination of particular passages of Barth.

[45] For more on this see Chapter 6 above.

[46] Farrow is very similar to Torrance at this point. We may refer the reader back to the critique of Torrance's sequential reading in Chapter 6.

that Barth overturns the tradition at the wrong point, or at least fails to overturn it at the most important point. For it is not the sequential movements of descent and ascent that are the problem – in fact on Farrow's account this description is essential – but the assigning of the two movements to God and humanity respectively. Indeed, Farrow claims that all his 'criticism reduces to this one point, even if other points must also be made'.[47] There is an immediate terminological issue in relation to this discussion, for Barth prefers to speak of *humiliation* and *exaltation*, presumably in order to get away from a too rigid alignment of these aspects of Jesus' history with the (sequential) events of incarnation and resurrection-ascension. Nevertheless, Farrow chooses to see Barth's use of *humiliation* and *exaltation* as equivalent to his own use of *descent* and *ascent*. How much this is an accurate assessment of Barth's use of humiliation and exaltation is a question to which we will return.

For Farrow, the descent of Jesus the man is one aspect of what he calls 'double descent', which is tied to the notion that the particular history of the man Jesus of Nazareth, the incarnate Son of God, is a *contingent* history. Thus the suffering and death of Jesus are not determined in His eternal election as Saviour, but are contingent events in an 'open' history – events that Jesus therefore experiences in freedom *rather* than determination, and in obedience to the will of the Father as a *free* response to their contingency. Thus Barth's entire scheme of salvation, with all his derivative anthropology, comes under fire. For Barth the description of human freedom is derived from his analysis of the determination of the Son from all eternity as the Crucified One. Human freedom is precisely the freedom to find oneself in the determination of one's being by God. Significantly for our discussion, Farrow claims that for Jesus' life to be *humanly obedient*, in any meaningful sense, the events of His life must involve contingency, and therefore grant space for His own *freedom* in response to them. But Barth in no way feels the need to tie contingency and freedom together in this way. Creaturely freedom and determination by God are not mutually exclusive on Barth's account, but rather synonymous. Tied in to this is Barth's understanding of Jesus' suffering and death as belonging naturally to his humanity, but as quite foreign to His divinity. Thus, for Barth, Jesus cannot be said to descend as a human – as outlined above – even in accepting the depths of despair and suffering associated with His cross, for as a *human* He simply occupies the place which belongs to fallen humanity before the holy God. It is on this basis that Barth describes the soteriological nature of Jesus' human acts as residing in the fact that the *subject* of these human acts is the eternal Son of God, who in the form of the Servant reconciles His own flesh to the Father through total obedience. Jesus' humanity is exalted in its union with His obedient and divine Sonship, as this is realised throughout His career, culminating upon the cross.

Thus Farrow argues that for Barth Jesus has a 'closed' history that terminates at the cross, and therefore that Barth's doctrines of resurrection,

---

[47] *Ascension*, p.243.

ascension, and heavenly session are empty of content. On Farrow's reading of Barth the latter simply gives the risen and ascended Lord too little to do – or more accurately, too little *new* to do. The failure to assign descent to Jesus as human as well as God breaks down the high-priestly model of Jesus ministry, and empties the ascension of significance as the ascent of the High Priest to the presence of God, taking His people with Him. Farrow compares Barth's account with Irenaeus' doctrine of recapitulation and finds Barth's version lacking.

This complaint is focused upon Jesus' *munus triplex*. Farrow sees Jesus' role as priest as degraded via a 'reduction' of His history beyond the cross to revelation, and His ascended ministry to that of prophet. Farrow's concern is that Jesus' humanity is devalued – as in the lack of human freedom exercised in Jesus' journey to the cross, at least on Farrow's account – and so concern with *our* genuine humanity in the scheme of salvation is also reduced. The final assessment of damage done remains beyond Farrow's consideration, but nonetheless he is frank in his assertion that Barth's scheme ultimately distorts the gospel.

> What is perfectly clear is that it shifts the focus away from what happens to and for Jesus, in his own humanity, to the question of his revelation to us. And with the loss of attention to his humanity goes a loss of attention to ours. The biblical story itself begins to peter out.[48]

Following Torrance, Farrow perceives a '"suspicion of doceticism" even in Barth'.[49] Barth may fully and even strongly affirm the humanity of the ascended One, but it is a humanity trapped within a 'circle' – that is the circle of ascent and descent as a closed history. The force of this complaint is that as prophet, and in the forty days, Jesus can only *repeat* the history of His humiliation and exaltation, because on Barth's account nothing can be added to this history – particularly as this history is tied into the very being of Christ as the God-man. All this is gathered up in Farrow's concern that God alone is the agent of salvation, and that Jesus' humanity, if not made accidental, is at least conceived of in utilitarian fashion.

> A final question combines the previous ones: If Jesus' pre-history terminated in the cross, can his post-history go further than the ascension, or must it simply repeat or re-establish itself in ever-widening spheres of influence? Again Barth denies it, but his doctrine of a threefold parousia and his universalist leanings suggest otherwise.[50]

---

[48] *Ascension*, p.248.

[49] *Ascension*, p.248. Although he does not cite Torrance, the phrase 'suspicion of doceticism', which Farrow places within quotation marks, is Torrance's. See *Karl Barth* ... p.134.

[50] *Ascension*, p.249.

As earlier, Barth anchors Jesus' being as Lord of the church, as the transcendent One (in the difference between His history and ours), in a complex of doctrinal work which includes Jesus' ascension, but Farrow has the ascension do a great deal more work on its own. This yields, for example, differing approaches to eschatology. As explicated in greater detail earlier, Barth sees the *eschaton* as proleptically present in the resurrection and ascension, and the present age as created by a delay between inauguration and fullness of the new age. Thus follows the doctrine of threefold *parousia* – in resurrection-ascension, in the outpouring of the Spirit, and in the *eschaton* itself. The present age can only exist as a space that Jesus creates within His own time – eschatological time – for the continued being of the old time of the world, and for the being of the church as His body within that old time. On this basis Jesus is not described as needing to achieve anything new as regards salvation, but rather as exercising His authority to reveal Himself as the Lord and thereby to bring about the redemption of those who belong to Him. Barth can therefore even describe this age 'between' as an extension of Jesus' passion, in that He continues to suffer the existence of sin and evil, and actively to engage it in His church. During this 'time between' everything becomes eschatologically focussed, with resurrection-ascension and the promise of the Spirit both finding their meaning in the orientation of the Crucified One toward His *eschaton* and the fulfilment of His being and action in the unveiling of the fullness of the kingdom of God. Thus if we are to look for a 'new beginning' to Jesus' history, beyond the cross, it would seem to be found in the *eschaton* itself, partially present in the first two forms of *parousia*.

Farrow is right, therefore, when he claims that for Barth the ascension does not (quite) mark a new phase of Jesus' history, and that all that Jesus can do is what He has already been doing. Does this, however, necessarily indicate a static or 'closed' history? For Barth, the continuation of Jesus' activity beyond His ascension is surely always new, as He acts in the Spirit to bring about the redemption of His people. Although Farrow recognises that Barth's account of Jesus' self-revelation is more than simply noetic, he does not seem to finally take this into account. Thus he regards Jesus' high priesthood as diminished in being gathered up into His office as prophet. Yet, given that Jesus' self-revelation is the mediation of salvation achieved once for all in His obedience from cradle to cross, His prophetic ministry can readily be understood as also His work as high priest.

Of course the differences in approach between Farrow and Barth are too deeply founded for a comparison on the level of individual statements to offer very much that is useful. This is a problem which dogs Farrow's own treatment, but he at least is able to recognise, as noted, that despite large-scale agreement the differences nonetheless trace all the way to the foundations.

Presence and Absence – Agreement and Difference

Having glanced at aspects of Farrow's critical stance toward Barth, let us now turn to a previously noted area of large-scale agreement, yet still with a view to eliciting greater understanding of the critique. Both Farrow and Barth identify Jesus' ascension with the key motif of His absence – both with regard to 'universal history' and the particular history of the church. The present work has put forward the argument that it is Barth's attention to Jesus' absence, as one form of expression of His Lordship, that enables Him to attend to Jesus' presence in a way that makes sense of the present age as the 'time between'. However, Farrow claims that Barth's reading of this dialectic finally dissolves in the direction of pure presence.

Farrow considers the question of the presence of Jesus to be the central question of Christian theology (following Dietrich Ritschl[51]), but he considers the question of *absence* to exercise the proper control over that of presence. His discussions of the themes of *Christus praesens* and *Christus absens* involve his establishment of the interconnection of the two poles, with a moderate emphasis upon the *absens*. The latter emphasis follows his establishment of Irenaeus as his primary theological source. Ireneaeus' work was directed primarily at the Gnosticism of his age, and Farrow finds in him the resources to counter the gnosticising, docetic, thread running through theology. It is with his maintenance of Jesus' risen and ascended humanity that Irenaeus attacks Gnosticism, and Farrow finds here a significant link to the *Christus absens* – Jesus ascended in the flesh cannot be subsumed into a docetic scheme of 'universal presence', whether as spirit/mind, or the more modern 'moral influence'.

The question is therefore, 'What manner of description of Jesus' presence is appropriate?'. Drawing on the eucharist, Farrow offers a description of Jesus' presence that is eschatologically grounded – the 'eucharistic tension' in which the church exists is the tension of the 'already and not yet'. As above, the absence of Jesus, which will not be resolved until His parousia in the *eschaton*, means that we cannot speak of Him as simply present in the church – let alone of His unqualified presence in the world, or history. Farrow quotes Zizoulas' very high treatment of the church, but he qualifies it by maintaining the necessity of the distinction between Jesus ascended and the church within the world. To quote at some length:

> *Here the Holy Spirit is not one who aids us in bridging the distance between Christ and ourselves, but he is the person of the Trinity who actually realizes in our history that which we call Christ, this absolutely relational entity, our Saviour ... All separation between Christology and ecclesiology vanishes in the Spirit.*

---

[51] *Ascension*, p.8.

Now if the church is indeed, as Ephesians asserts, τὸ σῶμα αὐτοῦ, τὸ πλήρωμα τοῦ τὰ πάντα ἐν πᾶσιν πληρουμένου, will we not want eventually to say something very like this? And if so, would we not be better to eschew protracted talk of ascension in the flesh, for fear of throwing up a narrow and competing meaning of σῶμα – of getting stuck on what Zizoulas calls the biological hypostasis rather than the ecclesial? ... Let us not be hasty, however. ... All that has been ruled out [in attending to ascension in the flesh] is any construal of [Jesus'] union with the church as a denial of his absence, hence of the eschatological qualification of ecclesial being.[52]

Thus Farrow maintains what might be called a high ecclesiology, while holding the being of the church in tension with its eschatological hope.

The presence of which we rightly speak is Jesus' presence in the Spirit, as an outworking of ascension in the flesh. 'On this view 'the divine as it presents itself to us in our time' is the Holy Spirit, who does not in fact present Himself but the absent Jesus'.[53] A view of absence that leaves the field free for humanity in general to take His place and a view of His presence that identifies Him without remainder with His church are both ruled out. As earlier, for Farrow this dialectic of presence and absence is a matter of the separation of Jesus' history from our own, which ultimately occurs in the ascension.

Much of this seems, on the face of it to agree readily enough with Barth's treatment of presence and absence. Yet as we have already noted this is a place at which Farrow is strongly critical of Barth, claiming at once that Barth's ascension theology dissolves into a theology of too much presence in the world, and of not enough presence in the church. How does this criticism function?

Barth's interpretation of resurrection and ascension causes Farrow to see the absence removed in favour of presence. Jesus' victory at the cross, witnessed to in the resurrection, means for Barth that Jesus' time is the time of the new age, and this time, as *the time of God*, is therefore the only real time. As we have seen, Jesus' time is the only time with a future – His is the only reality – and so the world and even the church only exist as He graciously makes space for them in this age between. Thus for Barth, as Farrow notes, the task of the church is to bear witness to the salvation – the new creation – present in Jesus and universal in scope. Farrow asks:

What in particular is the effect of making resurrection time into ascension time, and thus into the ground of ecclesial time? What in other words is the effect of contemporaneity with Jesus that is not properly qualified by his departure? Is it not to misconstrue the very problem of presence and absence ...? Not to put too

---

[52] *Ascension*, p.268-9. The quotation is from Zizoulas' *Being as Communion: Studies in Personhood and the Church* Crestwood: St Vladimir's Press, 1985, p.110f. Italics added.

[53] *Ascension*, p.257.

fine a point on it, the effect is simply too much real presence. In Barth, as in the Origenist tradition, the eucharistic possibility is generalized.[54]

At the same time, this willingness to see Jesus as in some sense present to the world downplays the emphasis on the church that Farrow wants to maintain.

> In other words, it is still a matter of Christ's hidden co-existence in and with the world, which must be proclaimed and celebrated and brought out in the open. But that means, conversely, that in the *church* there is too little real presence. The distinction between church and world gravitates once again towards the noetic.[55]

At this point a very significant strand of Farrow's criticism comes to the fore: his assessment of Barth's theology according to the criteria of the eucharist – as he perceives it. On the page immediately following that from which the above quotations are drawn, Farrow recognises that Barth *does* in fact distinguish quite clearly between church and world, but he does so on the basis of the *Word*, not eucharist *per se*. 'Barth's insights here are often quite profound, as we have tried to notice elsewhere; what we did not notice is the dislocation of the entire discussion from the eucharistic ground of ecclesial life'.[56] Thus the heart of Farrow's difficulty with Barth comes into view. The corollary of Farrow's desire for the ascent and descent of a man is desire for the particular focus on the eucharist which seems to drive his own theological programme.

The fundamental difference in approach to the question of Jesus' presence and absence – given that many of Farrow's statements regarding this dialectic could well have been made by Barth – is the difference in approach to the eucharist, and only thus to ecclesiology. This is made particularly plain when we encounter a passage such as the following description of the irony of Jesus' absence, which confronts every person as a question directed at his or her very existence:

> But who understands the divine irony? Who is really aware of this absence? As an absence without parallel it is little noticed … Indeed, it would not be noticed or identified at all but for the work of the Spirit, who here and there tantalizes us with a real presence so that we may discover what real absence is, thus learning to love and long for Jesus' appearing.[57]

Such a statement seems quite consonant with the exposition of Barth attempted in this work. Farrow's preceding statements even refer to Jesus ascended as God's questioning of the being of *every* human person, just as we might expect of Barth. Yet in the subsequent elaboration the eucharist comes forward to take centre stage once again, and the breach with Barth is clear, for

---

[54] *Ascension*, p.250.

[55] *Ascension*, p.250.

[56] *Ascension*, p.251.

[57] *Ascension*, p.271.

it is the eucharist *alone* which tells the church that 'this is the man', and that He is absent yet returning: 'The *Ecce homo!* must be repeated eucharistically, then, if it is to be heard where it needs to be heard. But what if the church which hears it begins to forget the absence?'[58] Farrow himself acknowledges (although only in a footnote) that in understanding Jesus' presence as the basis of our knowledge of His absence Barth is quite correct. 'Here too is the right and necessary footing for our own claim that the real absence must on no account be glossed over'.[59] Yet the perceived failure of Barth's view of the ascension is measured by his (weak) approach to the sacraments. 'To the extent that neglect of the ascension as a distinct episode in the story of Jesus weights his Christology in favour of presence (that is what we had in mind when we spoke of overcorrecting Kierkegaard) a eucharistic understanding of the church eludes him'.[60]

Eucharist and the Determination of Farrow's Critique

The key role the eucharist plays in Farrow's thought, apparently dominating his ecclesiology, has already been made plain. However, as we seek to fully comprehend Farrow's interaction with Barth we need an understanding of the way the eucharist plays this determinative role. At significant points Farrow criticises Barth for failing to give due place to the eucharist in his theology, as above. But how does the eucharist come to dominate Farrow's theology, and thereby to fuel his debate with Barth? For although we find very occasional references to the role of the word alongside the eucharist, they remain peripheral, and seem to play no part in Farrow's programme. He can say of the Spirit, whom Jesus promises His disciples, that this 'is the Spirit who through word and sacrament also unites us to the absent Jesus, so that it is we who are grasped or seized, ἐκ τοῦ κόσμου'.[61] But the vast majority of comments take the form of the following: 'For the eucharist ... means precisely that we who are not contemporaries of the historical Jesus can become so in the Spirit'.[62] Farrow criticises Barth for a 'too-narrow Protestant conception of the church as *creatura Verbi*',[63] and then goes on to make plain how he sees this as linked to loss of Jesus' priestly office, with a consequent loss of 'the eucharistic nature of the church'.[64] Indeed, the Word itself cannot be understood as a sacramental reality, for that is where Barth went wrong in over-emphasising the Word.

---

[58] *Ascension*, p.272.

[59] *Ascension*, p.241, note 358.

[60] *Ascension*, p.252.

[61] *Ascension*, p.257.

[62] *Ascension*, p.258.

[63] *Ascension*, p.253.

[64] *Ascension*, p.253.

Barth developed his elaborate doctrine of the Word of God (*CD I*) in such a way as to secure the dependency of the church's knowing, and hence its being, on Christ's own sovereign act of self-proclamation. In doing so he treated the liturgy of the word as a kind of substitute sacrament.[65]

On what basis does the eucharist function in such a fashion within Farrow's theology? Returning to the material from his opening chapter, which we examined earlier, we can trace a movement from the key question of presence and absence to the establishment of eucharist as (perhaps) *the* controlling feature of his work. As noted already, Farrow quotes Dietrich Ritschl to the effect that the question of Jesus' presence 'lies at the center of Christology itself, and of all theology'.[66] Yet attention to Jesus' presence (*Christus praesens*) can only find a way forward in 'attending more seriously to the *Christus absens*',[67] and this leads us immediately to Jesus' ascension and the bifurcation of His history from 'universal history'. This set of moves lays down the justification for a book about the ascension – only an ecclesiology that pays due heed to the dialectic of presence and absence can do justice to itself, and presence and absence automatically involve the ascension. Further, as explicated above, only as Jesus is present can we become even aware of His troubling absence – only as He comes to us can we realise that He is in no way our possession, and that our being as church remains in the eschatological tension of the 'already and not yet'. 'Not the ascension by itself, but the ascension and the parousia together, constitute the *Ecce homo!* which in the eucharist is heard and repeated'.[68]

The outstanding question remains that of a justification for the weight the eucharist bears. Ecclesiology provides the measure for theological work:

> Ecclesiology is, or ought to be the, the conscience of biblical studies, by which we seek to clarify our reading of scripture; of dogmatics, by which we strive to comprehend the faith embodied in the creed; of practical theology, through which we hope to translate the prayers of God's people into a thoughtful course of action consistent with the upwards call.[69]

But, in turn, it is the eucharist which provides the heuristic track along which ecclesiological reflection must run. As quoted earlier, this move is plainly stated at the very head of the work: 'there is no place to ground serious thought about the church but the eucharistic assembly'.[70] Thus, it appears that the eucharist provides the decisive *locus* for all theological enquiry, via ecclesiology.

---

[65] *Ascension*, p.251

[66] *Ascension*, p.8

[67] *Ascension*, p.9

[68] *Ascension*, p.272

[69] *Ascension*, p.7

[70] *Ascension*, p.1

This means that the key moves in Farrow's critique of Barth are somewhat circular. Reading in one direction: Barth's theology of the ascension fails because Barth does not grant the ascension a place as an altogether new event in the history of Jesus, and the ascension cannot therefore exercise the proper control over notions of Jesus' presence and absence. The proof of this is found in the fact that presence and absence resolve in the wrong directions – too much presence in the world, too little presence in the church. But the basis for the complaint is the expectation that the eucharist is the (one and only) place where Jesus becomes available,[71] (and is therefore also recognised to be absent) and so Jesus must be present to and in the church in a way that He is not present to and in the world. 'For it is in its eucharistic ambiguity that the church is marked off from the world ontologically and not merely ideologically'.[72] Yet the other key argument runs something like this: The church can only be the church when it lives out of its ground in the presence of the absent Lord. Thus ecclesiology is properly shaped by attention to Jesus' absence via ascension, and the eucharist embodies that tension for us – it is in the eucharist that the fact of Jesus' absence is made plain – and thus the eucharist is established as the key. 'It is the divergence of Jesus-history from our own that calls for a specifically *eucharistic* link …'[73] So that, as we have seen, Barth's failure is seen as the failure to write an adequately eucharistic theology of the church, and therefore his failure to write a eucharistic theology *per se*.

Barth fails because He does not have the correct idea of ascension, and the eucharist provides the basis for the claim, and yet Barth is also said to fail because he does not have a eucharistic approach, and the ascension provides the justification for this claim! At the bottom of this circularity lies the priority of the eucharist in Farrow's thought, and, as we have seen, this priority is never given a dogmatic justification, but rather is offered using a mixture of assumption and a somewhat liberal re-reading of Justin Martyr. It is quite true that in his chapter upon the ascension in the New Testament Farrow claims that John the Evangelist intentionally links ascension and eucharist, and this leads Farrow to make explicit his view 'that the ascension is the greater mystery on which the lesser mystery of the eucharist rests, such that we must

---

[71] Again, as earlier, the church is the people with the challenge and joy before them of encountering Jesus – and it is in encountering Him that they are a people at all – but: 'The eucharistic assembly is the place where this will happen'. *Ascension,* p.8.

[72] *Ascension,* p.3.

[73] As quoted more fully earlier. *Ascension,* p.10.

interpret each in the light of the other'.[74]   But that the eucharist is a mystery that is grounded in Jesus' ascension need not lead to the establishment of eucharist as *the* hermeneutical guide in ecclesiology, and thereby throughout Christian theology.

This brings us back to the issue which Farrow names as the central matter of his disagreement with Barth, namely the ascent and descent of a man. As Farrow himself notes, 'few theologians are as defensible, even when they are in error, as Karl Barth'.[75] Defence of Barth on this count might well begin with an examination of that key section of *Church Dogmatics* volume IV, section 59 'The Obedience of the Son of God'. For in spite of the title, Barth's reading of Jesus of Nazareth as the Servant in whom the disobedience of Israel is reversed and overcome involves and relies upon His obedience precisely as a man.[76] Farrow himself seems to recognise this when he acknowledges that Barth 'reckons courageously with the double aspect of the descent of the Son, that is with his assumption of fallen humanity, …'.[77] But Farrow still believes that Barth fails to grapple with the fact that this is the descent and ascent of a man.

Farrow's concern over the descent and ascent of a man works through into his unhappiness that Barth does not consider Jesus' ascension to 'change' Jesus in any way. Barth's failure to allow that the ascension is a new event for Jesus would seem to lie behind Farrow's dissatisfaction with Barth's alignment of ontology and soteriology. But what is it that Farrow feels Barth loses at this point? Alongside the claims that Jesus' genuine humanity becomes under-weighted, and that our humanity therefore has diminished significance,[78] there stands the significant question; *What does Farrow have the ascension achieve within his scheme?* The answer is that where Barth in no way chooses to see the ascension as Jesus' exaltation, or as adding to His transcendence, or as establishing Him as Lord over the church or the world, this is exactly what Farrow has the ascension achieve.

---

[74] *Ascension,* p.38 The passage Farrow has in view is Jesus' response to the dispute about His claim to offer His flesh as food and his blood as drink in John 6. Jesus says: 'Does this offend you? Then what if you were to see the Son of Man ascending to where he was before?' (John 6[61-62] NRSV). It seems quite reasonable to understand here a link between Jesus' ascension and His giving of Himself to us so that we may share His life, and to recognise that this self-giving lies at the centre of eucharistic worship, but equally it seems less reasonable to see an authorisation to make the eucharist the central reality of ecclesial existence.

[75] Farrow, Douglas 'Karl Barth on the Ascension: An Appreciation and Critique' *International Journal of Systematic Theology* 2 (2000) p.148.

[76] That is, Barth's grounding of the entire possibility of reconciliation in the covenant. See §57.2 'The Covenant as the Presupposition of Reconciliation', *CD* IV/1, pp.22-66.

[77] *Ascension* , p.244.

[78] 'The charge is that Barth has spoken the name of Jesus so loudly that other names cannot even be heard; that the problem of abstraction reappears in another form; that once again humanity is being swallowed up, if not by God directly then by 'the humanity of God''. *Ascension,* p.243.

For Farrow, the bifurcation of Jesus' history from universal history, and therefore the bifurcation of His path from that of all other humans, occurs in the ascension.[79] It is in the ascension, as the church is confronted by Jesus' absence, that the troubling fact of His utter difference from us is established. The eucharist fits into this complex – perhaps, as above, grounding the entire project – for it is in the eucharist that Jesus' new history interrupts the old history of this world, 'breaking and remoulding, [in] the substantial transformation of worldly reality ...'.[80] But for Barth it is the entirety of Jesus' history that involves His difference from us – Barth and Farrow share the dictum that it is only in His presence (or nearness to us) that we apprehend Jesus' absence (or distance), but Barth works this out in relation to the incarnation as a whole. Jesus' difference from us is found precisely in His life of obedience as the Son of God taking our flesh (*sinful* flesh), which is exactly where He draws closest to us. Thus the cross, as the culmination of that journey, is both the place at which Jesus draws closest to us in our fallen alienation from God, and the place where He is found to be most different from us – here is the high point of His offering of Himself in the obedience of which we are incapable.

Farrow complains that the gnostic streak in Christian theology, by doing away with the distinction between resurrection and ascension, breaks down the idea of ascension as an historical event, and thereby loses sight of the *parousia* as the return of 'this same Jesus'. 'That in turn puts in jeopardy the proper discontinuity between Jesus-history and common history, leading to the substitution of our own story (the story of man's self-elevation) as the real kernel of salvation history in the present age'.[81] In one sense this complaint would not appear to apply to Barth, as he certainly opts to see the ascension as a real event in Jesus' history, but nonetheless Farrow does believe that Barth fails to fully overturn the tradition he is criticising here. As above, Barth is accused of finally having 'too much real presence' in relation to the world (and not enough in the church). This criticism would seem to belong with the complaint directed at those who see too much continuity between Jesus-history and common history.

Yet Barth's reading of Jesus' history emphasises from the very beginning the divergence of this history from our own, as we have attempted to show. This divergence is a central theme in Barth's work – one that more often produces the complaint that it is far too strong! Once again, on the positive side, Barth and Farrow would appear to have a great deal in common, precisely in the key area of presence and absence and the divergence of Jesus' history. That being so, we ask once again what it is that Farrow wants from Barth and does not get, and once again we are lead to conclude that it is simply

---

[79] As quoted earlier: 'For with the ascension the track of Jesus-history, still genuinely visible in some sense on the Emmaus road, passes beyond all ken'. It is this 'passing beyond' that bifurcates Jesus-history and common history. *Ascension*, p.9-10.

[80] *Ascension*, p.10.

[81] *Ascension*, p.29.

the eucharistic emphasis that is missing, but which Farrow himself struggles to justify rather than assume.

Soteriology and Ontology

Finally, following on from dialogue with Torrance's thought a set of questions may be brought against Farrow's own treatment of Jesus' incarnation, and the relation between human and divine action in His work. The key matter is the relation of soteriology and ontology in Jesus' incarnate history. Farrow complains that Barth clamps ontology and soteriology together too strongly, and the obvious implication is that Farrow wants to separate them to some degree. What does this separation entail, and what implications does it have for Farrow's thought regarding the incarnation, and the history of Jesus' acts? We will not finally decide against Farrow's reading of the incarnation – ultimately there is not enough material to permit such a decision – but we will indicate an apparent difficulty of significant degree.

Although Farrow wishes to acknowledge a greater distinction between *ontology* and *soteriology* in the incarnation, he does not want to separate them altogether. The ontological reality of Jesus' being as both divine and human forms the necessary presupposition for soteriology. On this basis soteriology is a matter of Jesus' incarnate acts, and in particular His acts as a man. This has already been established in relation to the 'double descent' Farrow describes. Thus Farrow sees the 'clamp' which Barth applies to Jesus' history as doing away with the saving power of Jesus' history as such. The claim is that the dynamic history of Jesus' suffering, death, resurrection, and ascension is swallowed by the static reality of His being as the God-man and His election from eternity.[82] According to this Barth has ontology (and protology) overwhelm soteriology.

We have already had cause to question this reading of Barth. Thomas Torrance describes Barth as balancing the *ontological* and *dynamic* poles of Jesus' saving history.[83] That is, according to Torrance Barth has *soteriology* comprehend both *ontological* and *dynamic* aspects of Jesus' incarnational history. This is a more accurate reading of Barth than Farrow's, and it is of great significance in responding to Farrow's critique. As we argued in relation to Torrance, Barth does not see Jesus' incarnate being as saving being at the expense of seeing His acts as saving acts, rather he sees the two together.[84] As George Hunsinger puts it:

> The incarnation, Barth argued, is best understood as a concrete history, not as an abstract state of being. ... The incarnation, the meeting of the two natures in Christ, is what occurred as he enacted his saving history. Although his deity and

---

[82] See above, 'Descent and Ascent "of a man"'.
[83] See *Karl Barth* ..., pp.197 and 201.
[84] See above Chapter 6.

his humanity were actual from the very outset ... their union was never essentially static. It was a state of being in the process of becoming.[85]

Farrow misreads Barth and thus applies a clamp which Barth does not, making a dynamic history into a static one. Barth does not make ontology rule over soteriology, but rather the unity of Jesus' being and act necessitates that soteriology comprehend both the ontological and dynamic poles of Jesus' incarnation.[86] Jesus' being and His acts are both saving – they are inseparable.[87]

All this is clear enough in our earlier discussion. But, again, what of Farrow's own thought as he separates ontology from soteriology? (Even if the separation is only partial, for Jesus' being does remain the presupposition of His saving acts.) Farrow moves to align soteriology and act – his criticism of Barth implies that he identifies the dynamic pole exclusively with soteriology. Moreover, as we have seen, that dynamic reality of Jesus' acts appears to be understood more in terms of Jesus' humanity than His divinity. Thus, as earlier, Farrow's great interest is in 'double descent' – the descent of God in becoming creature, and the descent of the creature in suffering. But the force of this is somehow to abstract the action of Jesus the man from the being and action of God.

The problem here is not with the emphasis upon Jesus' human action – that is right and essential – but with the implication of separation between Jesus' human action and the action of God in Him. This casts the incarnation itself in a difficult light. Farrow overturns Barth's reading of Jesus' suffering and humiliation as that of the Son of God – for as the Son of Man, as sinful flesh, such suffering is proper to Him – but in doing so he implies a very different reading of the incarnation. The humanity of Jesus is assumed to suffer contingently – that is, it is not a necessary consequence of His humanity that He suffers. If this is so then His humanity must be regarded as in some

---

[85] 'Karl Barth's Christology: Its basic Chalcedonian character' in Webster, John B. ed. *The Cambridge Companion to Karl Barth* Cambridge: Cambridge University Press, 2000, pp.127-42, pp.134-5.

[86] Hunsinger notes that Chalcedonian thought is largely concerned with *soteriology*. See 'Karl Barth's Christology ...', p.127.

[87] Hunsinger argues that Barth self-consciously alternates between christological statements which sound more Alexandrian on the one side, and more Antiochian on the other, in order to maintain a fully chalcedonian recognition of full deity and full humanity. Barth does not believe the two can be said and understood together, and so one is emphasised at one turn, and the second at another. This may explain the way in which Barth may be read as having, for example, a docetic tendency, because docetic sounding statements can be found. The reality however is that those statements must be understood within the framework and pattern of speech Barth adopts, and thus balanced against the intentionally opposing emphasis found elsewhere. See 'Karl Barth's Christology ...'. The title of this essay involves an intentional allusion to one of Hunsinger's targets, Charles Waldrop's *Karl Barth's Christology: Its Basic Alexandrian Character* Berlin: de Gruyter, 1984.

sense unlike ours – He must in fact be godlike to the degree that suffering and alienation from the Father, which is the lot of all other humans, is not naturally His lot.

In many ways this appears to be exactly right, and just what the New Testament describes.   Jesus' obedience is human obedience, and His Gethsemane decision to embrace the cross must be seen as a human decision.[88] But the question remains as to why the action of God in all this is somehow to be isolated out from the human action?   Why is the human Jesus to be seen as the active subject in such a way that, as earlier, His humanity is only united to the Father in the ascension and not throughout His career?   What sort of *kenosis* is involved in the incarnation in order for the eternal Son of God not to be seen as the active subject in the suffering obedience of the man Jesus (as Barth would have us see Him to be)?

The seventeenth century *kenotic* debates relied upon a sequential reading of Jesus' exaltation and humiliation – a reading such as Farrow's.   As Wolfhart Pannenberg notes, the central matter of the Lutheran debate over *kenosis* was an explanation of the delay in the exaltation of Jesus' humanity (until His resurrection and ascension) given the union of the eternal Logos and human nature in Him at the incarnation itself.[89]   It was in trying to deal with this issue that *kenotic* theory separated divine and human action in Christ, attributing a *kenosis* to Jesus' humanity as He underwent His career of suffering and death. Farrow's notion of 'double descent' seems to describe a very similar movement, and thus a criticism which was offered within that old debate may well apply to him too.   If Jesus' humanity is thus regarded as somehow involved in a *kenosis* that is separate from the activity of God, and Jesus' suffering is predicated of His humanity in this way, then it reflects upon the union of God and humanity in Him.   'Separate activities mean separate persons'.[90]

Where then does this leave Farrow?   It is not finally clear how he conceives the incarnation, for there is not enough direct incarnational material to enable a decision.   It is true, however, that there are strong indications that (following on from Torrance) he overemphasises the human action of Christ in such a way that the ontological reality of Jesus as God and man in one acting subject becomes endangered.   If that is so, then at the foundation there lies a sequential reading of exaltation and humiliation, and an attempt to give Jesus' ascension too much to do, with strong links to an intense prioritisation of the eucharist. Farrow attempts to correct Barth by making Jesus' ascension the act in which He is installed as Saviour and High Priest, but in doing so he attempts

---

[88] Barth's comments on Jesus' anguish in Gethsemane and His sense of abandonment upon the cross are illustrative of his intent to hold together Jesus' radical human obedience, forged in the fire of human decision, and the eternal will and decision of God. See *CD* IV/1, pp.238ff.

[89] See Pannenberg, Wolfhart *Jesus – God and Man* Lewis L. Wilkens and Duane A. Priebe translators, London: SCM Press Ltd, 1968, p.307ff.

[90] Pannenberg, *Jesus – God and Man* p.309.

too much and overemphasises both ascension and eucharist. The result is that he finds it difficult to justify his decisions and may even end up with a distorted theology of the incarnation.

Chapter 8

Robert Jenson: Trinity, Ascension, and Ecclesiology

Robert Jenson is renowned as a writer of trinitarian theology and ecclesiology.[1] At the heart of Jenson's work lies a clear concern for ecumenical discussion and *rapprochement*, and areas of ecumenical debate are therefore often to the fore in his writing. Clearly, ecclesiology and sacramental theology are crucial areas of ecumenical discussion and debate, and Jenson has a great deal to say upon these themes.[2] Although Jenson does not display a great interest in Jesus' ascension, he does attend to it in brief but significant passages, and importantly, his Trinitarian and ecclesiological thought have substantial, although largely implicit, links with his view of Jesus as ascended. As might be expected, Jenson's conception of both ascension and heavenly session are closely linked to his ecclesiology, and in particular his very strong sacramentology. Although his early work focussed upon Barth, and he is often regarded as following Barth in significant ways, Jenson's work diverges markedly from Barth's in regard to these very issues of resurrection, ascension,

---

[1] Although Jenson has written at length upon themes of Trinity and of church, there is very little secondary literature available, and the task of this chapter is to focus upon the primary sources. A recent addition to the secondary material is a festschrift: Gunton, Colin E. ed. *Trinity and Time: A Response to the Theology of Robert W. Jenson* Grand Rapids: Eerdmans, 2000.

[2] See for example *The Triune God* Philadelphia: Fortress Press, 1982; *Visible Words: The Interpretation and Practice of Christian sacraments* Philadelphia: Fortress Press, 1978; *Unbaptized God: The basic flaw in ecumenical theology* Minneapolis: Fortress Press, 1992; 'The Church and the sacraments' in Gunton, Colin ed. *The Cambridge Companion to Christian Doctrine* Cambridge: CUP, 1997, all of which are strongly influenced, perhaps driven, by ecumenical concerns. See also *Systematic Theology* vol.s I and II Oxford: OUP, 1997-1999 (hereafter *ST*).

and ecclesiology with sacramentology, and thus he is critical of Barth's ecclesiology.[3]

The notion of Jesus' embodiment, especially as risen and ascended, will be of considerable significance to our discussion, and provides a locus of interaction with the breadth of Jenson's thought. Jenson's interpretation of the notion of body is crucial to the shape of his ideas, and, allied to his distinct view of personhood, underpins his theology at every point. Jenson's treatment of body will be explored with a view to Jesus' ascension, which will in turn provide a contrast to Barth's treatment as we have explored it.

Due to Jenson's complex analysis, it is remarkably difficult to treat any one theological theme in isolation from his compendious reworking of theology as a whole, and in particular from his doctrine of the Trinity. Jenson's approach to the body – including Jesus' body – and thus to ascension and ecclesiology, thoroughly interpenetrates his trinitarian thought, and they must be understood in reliance upon each other. In order to approach Jenson's reading of Jesus' ascension, it is necessary to first explore Jenson's trinitarian thought and then his ecclesiology. Some critical comment will appear in these expository sections, but the bulk of critical interaction will appear in the sections that conclude the chapter.

The Doctrine of the Trinity

Jenson draws on Gregory of Nyssa in order to radically reform the western theological tradition – indeed, Jenson desires to undo our 'usual metaphysics',[4] which he believes to be essentially pagan. He believes that the metaphysics of timeless eternity fails utterly to do justice to the being of God, and so he seeks a fully trinitarian metaphysic. The key to beginning this journey is to adopt Gregory's use of the word God as a *predicate*.

What does this mean? The move is to see the word God as describing the mutual activity of the Trinity, rather than a static entity.

> ... 'God', according to Gregory, refers to the mutual *action* of the identities' divine 'energies', to the perichoretic triune *life*. And since all divine action is the singular

---

[3] Jenson criticises Barth for overemphasising the discontinuities between creation and redemption, in terms of the relation between God's time and human time, and therefore for underplaying the Spirit's work within the church and sacraments. See, *Unbaptized God*. As James J. Buckley notes, 'Barth was not unsympathetic towards pneumatological critiques of his theology. But he also wondered whether pneumatology can do the synthetic job some hope for without falling back into Hegel's or at least Schleiermacher's Spirit.' ('Community, Baptism, and the Lord's Supper' in in Webster, John B. ed. *The Cambridge Companion to Karl Barth* Cambridge: Cambridge University Press, 2000, pp.195-211, p.208). Significantly, Hegel will appear as an important background figure in Jenson's thought.

[4] *ST* vol. II, p.215.

mutual work of Father, Son, and Spirit, there is only one such life and *therefore* only one subject of the predicate 'God'.[5]

This introduces the notion of time into the equation. God is not a static, timeless entity, but rather a '*going on*',[6] and that means that God moves from a past, via a present, and into a future. In fact the relation between these three poles of time is the basis of Jenson's description of the three-ness of God. The Father is described as the origin, or past, of God, the Son as the present, and the Spirit as God's future.[7]

The next significant move is to align this thought with what Jenson calls 'the Augustinian-Hegelian discovery of God's personhood' in order to develop his theory of self-consciousness. A person is a subject who has oneself as an object.[8] In order to unpack this subjectivity and objectivity Jenson turns to the matter of embodiment, and of spiritual life. To be subject is to be spirit, but to have oneself as an object requires embodiment. Thus the incarnation becomes the basis upon which God is a *personal* agent, with subjective knowledge of God's own objectivity in historical embodiment. So the 'one in whom the Father intends himself is Jesus, an item of and subject in our history'.[9] God's self-knowledge is therefore knowledge of the history of the man Jesus of Nazareth. God's action toward us in Jesus is radically constitutive of God's being.

In fact, on the subject of revelation Jenson can not only claim that God towards humanity is the same as He is in Himself, but also that God's knowledge of Himself must be identical with our knowledge of him. Otherwise we will be required to recognise some other God who knows Himself, but not as we know him.[10] God does is not revealed in any partial fashion, or selectively, 'God *is* the Word he speaks; and the word he speaks is an embodied Word'.[11] '... Jesus, the body who dwelt in Palestine is "one of the Trinity"'[12].

Furthermore, in that God has a body we find that 'God *transcends* himself, that he has history'.[13] Jenson description of the Trinitarian being of God, pointing with 'time's three arrows', and so forth, relies completely upon the incarnation of God in Jesus. God has a body, and body mediates the past – my availability is as the one I have thus far become. 'In that I give myself as body, I give the one I already am, I give the product of my deeds and sufferings

---

[5] *ST* vol. I, p.214. Emphasis original.
[6] *ST* vol. I, p.214. Emphasis original.
[7] See *ST* vol. I, p.218. See also Philadelphia: Fortress Press, 1982, pp.24-5.
[8] *ST* vol. I, p.144.
[9] *The Triune God,* p.146.
[10] See e.g. *Visible Words*, pp.28ff.
[11] *Visible Words*, p.32.
[12] *Visible Words*, p.35.
[13] *Visible Words*, p.35. Emphasis original.

to date. The only available self is the so-far-achieved self'.[14] Does this mean that we do not therefore have access to God as He will be? Or that God may turn out in the future to be other than we now know? No, because Jesus is the one who has died, and who is risen, He is therefore the one who both transcends death and creates the future.

God defines His being in ultimate futurity, not in stasis with the ultimate past. Indeed, it is futurity that defines God's past and present. Jenson claims that, as God is His own final future, and as Jesus risen is a member of the Trinity, so He has *always been* a member. God's anteriority is in fact the priority of His futurity. 'Since the Lord's self-identity is constituted in dramatic coherence, it is established not from the beginning but from the end, not at birth but at death, not in *persistence*, but in *anticipation*'.[15] Thus God is not eternal in the sense that God begins as 'all he ever will be; he is eternally himself in that he unrestrictedly anticipates an end in which he will be all he ever could be'.[16]

Ecclesiology: Where and How is Jesus 'Bodily' Ascended?

What then is the doctrine of the church that Jenson builds upon this foundation? He utilises several key terms: church as 'polity', 'people of God', and 'the body of Christ'. Commensurate with his ecumenical interest, and his willing engagement with Roman Catholic theology, Jenson emphasises the church as the 'body of Christ', and this designation dominates his thinking.[17] His exploration of the theme of body within his Trinitarian thought flows on into ecclesiology, with direct import for Jesus' ascension: the church is developed as the realm into which Jesus is 'bodily' ascended.

The Body of Christ

The church as Jesus' body functions in the same way that Jesus' earthly body functioned before His resurrection. The church, with her sacraments, is now the availability of Jesus ascended. So, 'is', in 'the church is the body of Christ',

---

[14] *Visible Words*, p.23.

[15] *ST* vol. I, p.66. Emphasis original.

[16] *ST* vol. I, p.66.

[17] David Yeago offers an interesting discussion of the Lutheran context for Jenson's thought, with a particular focus upon the notion of church as 'polity'. Of particular note is Yeago's description of a standard Lutheran view of the visible church as wholly secular – a view which Jenson seeks to overturn. Nonetheless, we argue that the image of the church as Christ's body is dominant, even as Jenson utilises the language of polity. See Yeago, David S. 'The Church as Polity? The Lutheran Context of Robert W. Jenson's Ecclesiology' in Colin E. Gunton ed. *Trinity and Time: A Response to the Theology of Robert W. Jenson* Grand Rapids: Eerdmans, 2000, pp.201-37.

straightforwardly denotes the being of the church, and does not posit a metaphor or other comparison.[18]   Indeed, while Jenson does speak of Jesus rising bodily, ascending bodily, and even of His awaited bodily return, the relationship between this body and the body that is the church remains clouded.   They seem to be identified in a way that eludes simple logic: 'The church is the "body" of that Christ whose bodily departure to God's right hand his disciples once witnessed and whose return in such fashion we must still await'.[19]   Or, 'the Lord's past life in Palestine and his present in the congregations make one coherent life, and the body in Palestine and the body in the congregations one body'.[20]   Jenson's argument for the church as the *only* body the risen Christ has or needs is outlined below, but how that argument accounts for Jesus' resurrection appearances and bodily ascension is unclear.

A ground of the church's existence as both 'body of Christ' and 'people of God' is offered in the futurity of God, as 'it is what creatures may anticipate from God that is their being'.[21]   The church is Jesus' body and His people in *anticipation*, but not the less genuinely because of it.   Rather, because God Himself is future, so creaturely being in anticipation is the truest and highest form of creaturely being.   Ultimately, however, the church *is* the body of Christ simply because God wills for it to be so.   That is, Jesus elects this community as the one in which He is His own and the Father's object, and for this to be true 'all that is needed is that the risen Christ's personal self-understanding determine what is real, that is, that he be the *Logos* of God'.[22]   No further argument is required.

Thus, the object of God's self-knowledge, the ascended Lord Jesus Christ, is formally the *totus Christus*; the man Jesus, risen and incorporated with the community that is His.   God knows Himself in this community!   'Where does the risen Christ turn to find himself?   To the sacramental gathering of believers'.[23]   Jesus is the 'transcendental subjectivity' and the church is His 'objective self', the Risen Christ's 'Ego'.[24]   Whatever resurrection body Jesus was when He appeared to His followers, and when He ascended, seems to disappear in Jenson's treatment, either replaced by or conflated with the

---

[18] Susan Wood notes that Jenson's identification of Jesus' risen body and the church exceeds a Roman Catholic view, with the result that the church tends to become equal to a fourth person of the Godhead, and also that the eschatological 'not-yet' becomes minimised or lost. See Wood, Susan K. 'Robert Jenson's Ecclesiology from a Roman Catholic Perspective' in Colin E. Gunton ed. *Trinity and Time: A Response to the Theology of Robert W. Jenson* Grand Rapids: Eerdmans, 2000, pp. 178-87, especially pp.180-84.

[19] *ST* vol.II, p.172.

[20] *Visible Words,* p.47.

[21] *ST* vol.II, p.172.

[22] *ST* vol.II, p.214.

[23] *ST* vol.II, p.214.

[24] *ST* vol.II, p.215.   This usage of 'Ego' seems strange – the usual definition of this term is a person's subjectivity, although a lower ranking dictionary definition is 'a person's self-image', and presumably this is the sense in which Jenson is using it.

church and sacraments as 'instantiations' of Christ's body. It is in fact unclear quite how Jenson views this relationship, as he never really explicates it. Perhaps he is happy for Jesus to have more than one body – one the basis that body is simply a form of physical availability, and plurality of this sort of body is not problematic for him. However, it is quite unclear how the unity of spirit and body can be properly maintained alongside a plurality of bodies. How Jenson conceives that *identity* can be mediate in more than one body is an open question.[25]

Whatever the case, Jesus takes the availability (body-ness) of these things and makes them His own availability. To quote at length:

> The object – the body – that the risen Christ is, is the body in the world to which this word calls attention, the church round her sacraments. He needs no other body to be risen man, body and soul. [26]

This is clearly contrary to usual thought, which sees the church as very much a secondary embodiment of Christ.

> There is and needs to be no other place than the church for him to be embodied, nor in that place any other entity to be the 'real' body of Christ. Heaven is where God takes space in his creation to be present to the whole of it; he does that in the church.[27]

The church as Christ's ascended body is not only the object in which God knows Himself, but also the object in which God is visible to His creatures. Moreover, without this *visibility* God cannot be known to Himself, whether the visibility we are speaking of is that of Christ in the church or in the sacraments. 'The embodiment of the gospel, presented to us as the body of Christ, is *truly* his body for us if and only if it is that also for him'.[28] But why is it necessary for Christ to be in some way *visible* in order for genuine knowledge to occur? Again, this development implicitly relies upon a prior phenomenology, (which might be argued to *intrude* upon the nature of the theological discussion at this point!)

---

[25] When discussing the identity of the risen Jesus with the man of Nazareth, Jenson indicates that this identity turns upon the Holy Spirit who rested upon Jesus on earth and who raised Him from the dead, and in turn the Spirit is the spirit of the Father. Thus identity in more than one body is here made a function of the unity of the Trinity. (See *ST* vol.I., p.200). However, once again it starts to look as if what is important is subjectivity, and that objectivity is more or less instrumental – but in that case how is embodiment anti-totalitarian?

[26] *ST* vol.I, p.206. Note how that to which the Gospel draws attention is the church and sacraments – as the presence of God – but not the mighty acts of God in Jesus, His cross, and so forth.

[27] *ST* vol.I, p.206.

[28] *Visible Words* p.46.

According to Hegel, were someone to be present to me as subject only and not also as my object in turn, I would just so be that someone's object only and not a subject over against him/her. Thus such a personal presence, even were the person the risen Christ, would enslave me.[29]

So it is that this requirement upon God to become objectively available is worked out with reference to the eucharist:

Why do we need the eucharistic bread and cup? Why must Christ be present to us 'bodily'? Now we have an answer: because a disembodied presence of Christ would be enslaving rather than liberating.[30]

Spirit is pure subjectivity, therefore pure spirit has no objective availability. Any person who relates to me as pure spirit cannot be an object in turn for me, and I am denied the possibility of *personal* relation or interaction. The effect of this is to make me a slave, in that I am an object for the other, but an object *only*, and not subject in turn. I cannot be subject unless I am permitted an object, and the approach of pure spirit is precisely the denial of any objective availability for me – the denial of my personhood. To continue, this dialectic of subject and object, paralleled in spirit and body, must also be aligned with *audible* and *visible*.

Audible and Visible Words

Jenson divides all communication into audible and visible words, and these two basic forms of communication map onto the basic division in our being – our subjectivity and objectivity. Audible words are the realm of spirit, and of the subjective, while visible words are embodied communication and therefore express our objectivity. Thus language as a function of our subjective selves involves openness to the future, and to new possibilities – that is what being spirit is all about. But equally the only self we can offer to another is the self that is the product of our history to date, and this requires embodied words – objective words. True personal communication must therefore involve *both* audible and visible words. Disembodied words are the stuff of propaganda and of totalitarian enslavement.[31]

Thus, God *is* His self-communication. How else could God's word of address achieve the grant of God as object? 'The event that God is and the event that we are addressed in Christ are but one occurrence; God's act of self-communication is the act of his reality as God'. Bearing in mind that the object of human knowledge of God needs must be the same object as which

---

[29] 'Autobiographical Reflections on the Relation of Theology, Science, and Philosophy; or, You Wonder Where the Body Went' in *Essays in the Theology of Culture* Eerdmans: Grand Rapids, Michigan, 1995, pp.216-224, p.220.

[30] 'Autobiographical Reflections ...', p.220.

[31] See *Visible Words*, p.28.

God knows Himself, God's act of self-revelation cannot be an action *ad extra*, but rather the activity *as which* God is God.[32]

That the church is the body in which Jesus is manifest, or object, is therefore a miracle of the Spirit, who comes to this community, and who is the communal spirit that is its life. At first glance, this mention of Spirit looks to alter the balance of discussion, as the agency of the Spirit might appear to soften the total identification of the church as Jesus' body. If it is recalled, however, that the Spirit is Jesus' spirit in the same sense that everyone has a spirit, then no real shift from earlier talk has actually occurred.[33] Jesus takes the church and her sacraments as His body, which is effectively to say that His spirit takes these things as a form of availability, and this can equally well be expressed as the work of the Holy Spirit. The being and work of the Spirit have already been defined by the spirit/body definition of personhood within which Jenson chooses to theologise.

As the spirit of Jesus, the Spirit is the futurity of God, and thus the Spirit creates a community that is *anticipation* of that future. The church is founded within the space created for it by God, a peculiar time of interruption or postponement within which the dominant theme is mission. The triune God acts to institute the church 'by *not* letting Jesus' Resurrection be itself the End, by appointing the 'the delay of the Parousia''.[34] The church is not the 'End' – she is not the advent of the new age – but she is the anticipation of the new age. She is *anticipated* eschatology, not *realised* eschatology, 'an eschatological *detour* of Christ's coming', and 'an event *within the event* of the new age's advent'.[35]

The church as anticipated reality is worked out in greater detail in the dialectic between church and sacraments. Jenson draws heavily upon his exegesis of Paul's use, in the First Letter to the Corinthians, of 'body' to refer to both the community and the Eucharistic elements that they share.[36]

Church and Sacraments

Jenson claims that his use of 'body' to denote a person's availability, or objectivity, is actually Pauline usage. 'In Paul's language, someone's 'body' is simply the person him or herself insofar as this person is *available* to other persons ...'.[37] Thus, when Paul speaks of the church as the body of Christ he is

---

[32] Does this mean I am the ink on this page? As an 'embodied' form of communication is this chapter my 'body'?

[33] This view of Jenson's was documented above.

[34] *ST* vol.II, p.170. Emphasis original.

[35] *ST* vol.II, p.171. Emphasis original.

[36] Jenson reads 'you fail to discern the Lord's body' (1 Corinthians11[29]) as a failure to discern the body present in *both* bread and wine *and* gathered community. He is insistent that 'this is the only possible exegesis'. Other commentators are not, however, quite so emphatic.

[37] *ST* vol.I, p.205. Emphasis original.

using the term as a 'proper *concept*',[38] a statement of correspondence. But this only applies because the bread and wine are also properly the body and blood of Christ. 'The church, according to Paul, is the risen body of Christ. She is this because the bread and cup in the congregation's midst is the very same body of Christ'.[39] That is, it is only because Jesus is objectively available to the congregation as something other than itself that it can be His objectivity. Only confrontation with Jesus as Word and as Body creates the possibility of the community embodying that Word also. Thus, the ascended Christ's transcendence of the church is safeguarded in the same moment as the church's being as His body is affirmed.

> The object that is the church-assembly is the body of Christ, ..., just in that the church gathers around objects distinct from herself, the bread and cup, which are the availability *to her* of the same Christ.[40]

It is the eucharist that provides for an exteriority of Christ to the church, as well as interiority.

> Within the gathering, we can intend Christ as the community we are, without self-deification, because we jointly intend the identical Christ as the sacramental elements in our midst, which are other than us.[41]

Christian faith is therefore 'essentially a communal reality and not an individual possession: the sacramental presence of the gospel's particular God is not separable from the community it creates'.[42] The embodiment of God to me is essential to His self-communication, and His embodiment is in a community of human persons. 'Thus the address of the gospel's God is always also the address of my fellows; and the presence of the gospel's God is always also their presence'.[43]

Why is it necessary for Jesus to be embodied for the church in this way? Why must the bread and wine be seen as objectively Christ's body? Clearly the answer lies in all that has gone before, regarding spirit and body, audible and visible. Jenson turns to Luther:

> Were Christ's presence in the assembly disembodied, it would be his presence as God but *not* ... as a human, for as a human he is a risen body. And to the posit of

---

[38] *ST* vol.I, p.204. Emphasis original.

[39] *ST* vol.I, p.205. Emphasis original.

[40] *ST* vol.II, p.213.

[41] *ST* vol.II, p.213. It should be recalled, however, that the differentiation here is eschatologically conditioned – in the eschaton the church will simply and straightforwardly become Jesus' body.

[42] *Visible Words*, p.38.

[43] *Visible Words*, p.39.

Christ's presence as sheer God ... Luther can react only with horror: 'Don't give me anything of *that* God!'[44]

Thus Jenson turns to Hegel, referring directly to his *Phenomenology of Spirit*. 'If in the meeting between us you are subject of which I am an object but are not in turn an object for me as subject, you insofar enslave me'. [45] And so, by extension: 'Were Christ not embodied in his community, were his presence there merely to and in thoughts and feeling, he would be the community's destruction ...'.[46]

The *promises* that Jenson discerns in the eucharist are the cup that is 'a new covenant in my blood', and the 'body which is for you'. He identifies the 'new covenant' as that of Jeremiah chapter 31, and Jesus' shed blood as the sacrificial seal upon that covenant. 'The promise that "comes" to the cup is therefore Israel's entire eschatological hope, as it is now sealed by Jesus' sacrifice'.[47] The promise that 'comes' to the bread is simply that it *is* Jesus' body, His availability. These promises, and their variants in the New Testament, together promise one thing: that the church is Jesus' risen body, the community in which He is objectively present.

> The Eucharist promises: *there is* my body in the world, and you here eating and drinking commune in it. It promises: *there is* the actual historical church, and you are she. That the risen Christ is not present merely 'spiritually' is itself a vital promise of the gospel, ... made specifically by the bread and cup.[48]

In the eucharist, God's people receive not only Christ, but also each other. The body on the table, and the community gathered around it, are forms of *one reality*, they are both the body of Christ. Participants 'at once receive Christ and the church in which we receive him'.[49] God does not communicate an individual parcel of some grace or other to each believer; rather God in communicating Himself communicates the Trinitarian love which is His being. The church exists as the anticipation of creation's incorporation into the triune communion, the fellowship of God's final future, the end that He is bringing and that He is. 'The church exists to become that fellowship; the church's own communal Spirit is sheer *arrabon* of that Community'.[50]

This treatment involves a very strong interweaving of church and eucharist, predicated once again on Jenson's tireless emphasis on the church as the body of Christ, while acknowledging the elements of the eucharist as 'also' Christ's body. Christ cannot be present in either only as 'spirit', because,

---

[44] *ST* vol.II, p.214. Emphasis original.

[45] *ST* vol.II, p.214.

[46] *ST* vol.II, p.214.

[47] *ST* vol.II, p.219.

[48] *ST* vol.II, p.220. Emphasis original.

[49] *ST* vol.II, p.222.

[50] *ST* vol.II, p.222.

according to Jenson's phenomenology, pure spiritual presence is by definition an evil. Jesus must be physically – objectively, visibly – present in church and sacrament or else not be present at all. At the heart of that phenomenology is the link between body and objective communication, and the insistence upon the necessity of such objective communication for a word to be that of any God we could name as such.[51] But what does this mean for Jesus as ascended?

Jesus' Ascension into Heaven, and His Resurrection Body

Jenson's identification of the church as Jesus' body clearly has major implications for the way in which he views Jesus' embodiment *per se*. As already indicated, Jesus' embodiment as the *risen* Son of Man becomes a matter of some interest – He is regarded as 'ascended into heaven', and is understood as located at the right hand of the Father. However, the relationship between these statements and Jesus' embodiment in church and eucharist drives a particular understanding of heaven and indeed of the ascension itself.

Jesus' 'Bodily' Ascension into Heaven

Jenson is quite direct in seeking to redescribe heaven, particularly in relation to what he regards as outmoded and inappropriate cosmological presuppositions. Following the Swabian Lutherans, and Johannes Brenz in particular,[52] heaven as a localised space within the creation is 'demythologised', with a particular view to the doctrine of Jesus' embodiment in the sacraments. The idea that Jesus ascended to a realm of space beyond the earth – in the Ptolemaic universe, the outmost sphere – had always made it hard to think of Jesus as bodily present in the eucharist.

> Thus throughout theological history, at least in the West, there was constant pressure, exerted by the way in which heaven was conceived, to attenuate the understanding of Christ's bodily presence in Eucharistic. Surely Christ is only 'spiritually' present on the eucharistic altar, or something like that.[53]

But Jenson finds that the Swabians overcome this difficulty through a radical rethink of the notion of heaven.

---

[51] 'The word in which God – for the present, *any* God – communicates must be an embodied word, a word with some visible reality, a grant of divine objectivity.' *Visible Words*, p.28.

[52] It is interesting to note that Brenz was a key figure in the theology that produced the *kenotic* debates to which we referred in relation to Farrow and Torrance.

[53] 'Autobiographical Reflections ...', p.218.

Luther and others were lead by their concern for Christ's sacramental bodily presence to deny that heaven is any *other* place than the places of Jesus' sacramental presence to us, that is, that it is a 'place' strictly speaking at all. Thus there is no spatial separation needing to be overcome, between heaven and the eucharistic altar. ... All the created universe, said Brenz and then Luther, is simply *one* place before God ...[54]

What then is the notion of heaven which Jenson, following Brenz, recommends? Jesus is risen into the glory of God – that is the meaning of the resurrection – this is the same as saying that Jesus is risen as the future, that He is risen into the kingdom *of heaven*. 'Thus he is himself the presence of God in heaven; he is what makes it heaven'.[55] For the apocalyptic prophets the kingdom of heaven is ever a future reality, but for Jesus it is already accomplished reality – and thus where He is simply *is* heaven. 'In ontological finality, the space that is heaven is the space defined by the risen Son's location at the right hand of the Father'.[56] The 'where?' of Jesus' ascended state thereby once again comes to rest with the matter of His *availability*, *à la* Jenson's reading of Paul, and thus Jenson seeks to advance upon Brenz and his colleagues.

We must learn to say: the entity rightly called the body of Christ is whatever object it is that is Christ's availability to us as subjects; by the promise of Christ, this object is the bread and cup and the gathering of the church around them.[57]

The key question becomes focussed on Jesus' availability to creatures. Thus, once again: 'Heaven is where God takes space in his creation to be present to the whole of it; he does that in the church',[58] and we may add, in the sacraments.

Any picture of God ruling the hearts of his believers from the church's table, font, and pulpit, and ruling the rest of creation from someplace *else* called heaven is ... radically inappropriate.[59]

Jesus' ascension into heaven is therefore His ascension into church and sacraments, and his bodily presence both with the Father and to the world is as these realities. Ascension is really about the withdrawal of Jesus' availability according to the manner of the resurrection appearances, so that He can be made available in these other forms. At the same time these forms of Jesus' embodiment remain, as earlier, somewhat provisional. In the eschaton there

---

[54] 'Biographical Reflections ...', pp.218-19. Emphasis original.

[55] *ST* vol.I, p.201.

[56] *ST* vol. II, p.123. As we have seen, this is Barth's position too. See *CD* III/3, pp.443-4.

[57] *ST* vol. II, p.205.

[58] *ST* vol. II, p.206. Cited earlier.

[59] *ST* vol. II, p.206.

will no longer be any need for Jesus' sacramental presence to His community as anything other than the community itself.

> Christ will know himself as his people with no more reservation; ... the head of a
> body that he does not need to discipline. Thus he will eternally adore God *as* the
> one single and exclusive person of the *totus Christus*, as those whom the Father
> ordained ... and whom the Spirit has brought to him.[60]

This brings us to the matter of embodiment in the *eschaton*. Given the treatment of 'body' he has developed, and the emphasis on the community as the *corporate* body of Jesus, what does Jenson have to say about embodiment in the *eschaton*?

Eschatological Embodiment

There is a sense for Jenson that Jesus ascended is also caught in the 'not yet' of the present age, and that He awaits His resurrection body. Jesus' eschatological body will be the perfected community, which in the meantime only exists proleptically and imperfectly in the church.

> There is even a sense in which Christ, *insofar* as his body is still an association also
> and not purely a community, possesses his risen body only in anticipation; thus the
> Lord's own resurrection awaits a future also.[61]

Thus the risen and ascended Christ Himself may be said to await His true embodiment, for the body of which He is head is still only partially united to Him. In the embodiment He undertakes in church and sacraments God anticipates the embodiment which will be His in the *eschaton*, when the community is so united with the Son that together they are the second person of God, without ceasing to be creatures. 'Because we become God, we do not cease to be creatures; we will be those creatures who are indissolubly one with the creature God the Son is'.[62] But the question then becomes, what sort of body the corporate community of the risen saints can be? If Jesus risen is only embodied in the church, then how are the saints embodied in their union with Him? Moreover, how may the saints be understood as seeing or hearing God – a usual expectation of the age to come – given that they themselves are to be God's embodiment? The answers Jenson offers are significant, and lead into the critical engagement which follows.

To take the last question first, Jenson is quite sure that to attend to God the risen saints will simply attend to the other saints.

---

[60] *ST* vol. II, p.339. Emphasis original.

[61] *ST* vol.II, p.347. Emphasis original.

[62] *ST* vol. II, p.341. For the logic of 'deification' which this involves see *ST* vol. II, pp.340f.

The great eschatological transformation has this at its center: the dialectic of Christ's presence to and by the church will end, the people of God will directly be Christ's availability also for her members, and Christ will be directly our availability to each other.[63]

Thus, in the 'perfected Community I will intend the body of God by intending the Community'.[64]

This also provides the basis upon which Jenson thinks of individual Saints as embodied in resurrection. The Saints' histories are brought before God in Jesus they become the availability of the Saints to God and to each other.

The redeemed histories are complete in their deaths. And they are brought into the history of God as those for whom the Son died; they appear in God's life because and as Jesus' love infinitely interprets them. They are brought into God as the *interpretandum* of the inner dialogue of the Son's actual triune life.[65]

This availability of the redeemed into eternity is therefore dependent on nothing more or less than God's adoption of them into the internal life of Father and Son.

Therefore the reality in God of all the redeemed's past, and its mutual availability between each of them and Christ and so between all of them, again need nothing more than full congruence with the eternal *perichoresis* of the triune life.[66]

According to Jenson, materiality is defined by the reality of God bringing creatures together in such a way that they are 'other' to one another, and therefore what we have in the availability of our histories is 'body' and in this sense 'material'. Materiality in the age to come will be altogether other than it is now – the present age will cease and there will be a new heaven and a new earth – but availability remains the dominant notion linked to materiality.

Critical Engagement

As stated at the beginning of the chapter, much turns upon the notion of body Jenson develops – and considerable space has been devoted to the explication of this idea. The outstanding question is still 'Does such a reworking of the idea of a body finally succeed?' This question may be applied in a number of ways, for instance at the level of consistency and internal coherence, but we may also enquire into in the shape such reworking has given to key doctrines. We will attempt to address something of this below. Although Jenson's thinking about 'bodies' cannot be claimed to derive directly from his notion of

---

[63] *ST* vol. II, p.340.
[64] *ST* vol. II, p.340.
[65] *ST* vol. II, p.348.
[66] *ST* vol. II, p.348.

ascension, it is nonetheless true that his belief that Jesus ascends into the church gathered around the eucharist is pivotal. Moreover, holding a different understanding of ascension – centrally, a different notion of 'where' we may locate Jesus ascended presence with the Father – would force Jenson to think very differently about 'bodies' and therefore the Trinity, Jesus, and the church, both now and in the *eschaton*. On the one hand Jenson's thought exhibits considerable consistency in applying ideas across the breadth of his doctrinal work. However, as Farrow has commented, this also means that any fundamental move will tend to bear distinctive fruit throughout the enterprise.[67]

Phenomenology of 'spirit' and 'body' dominates the whole discussion, and drives Jenson's ecclesiological decisions at every point. In fact, it rather appears that Jenson's commitment to the 'real presence' of Christ in the eucharist, and in the church, may drive his decisions about the nature of personhood, and his description of the Trinity. Jesus' being as ascended, and the nature of His bodily resurrection, are interpreted in such a way as to place no obstacle in the way of His complete identification with the church and sacraments.

Much of Jenson's divergence from Barth is surely a function of this decision. Barth will not allow sacramentology to govern ecclesiology, nor ecclesiology to shape Christology. The ascension of Jesus and the way in which His ascended existence is conceived is not necessarily the foundation of the differences between Barth and Jenson, but we can claim that Jesus' ascended life provides a *locus* for discussion of key issues. Moreover, if Jenson felt obliged to maintain something like Barth's reading of Jesus' ascension he would would not be able to make many of the moves that he does.

In interacting further with Jenson we will focus on foundational issues: his adoption of subject – object, spirit – body, language for trinitarian and ecclesiological purposes; and following on, his treatment of 'body' with regard to the incarnation, resurrection/ascension, and the being of the church and sacraments. The emphasis upon the church and sacraments as the totality of divine availability for humans, and also for God Himself, may be linked to a loss of genuine three-ness within God, and will be strongly challenged. Links to Jesus' ascended life will be made at points throughout the discussion.

Trinitarian Concerns

When Jenson borrows human phenomenological categories and directly applies them to the Trinity, the categories do not appear able to cope. God is 'spirit', as Jenson affirms, but because God is assumed to have a structure of personal knowing like to that of humans, God must also become an object.

---

[67] 'Robert Jenson's *Systematic Theology:* Three Responses' *International Journal Of Systematic Theology* 1.1, 1999, pp.89-104. See p.89.

That is, God must become embodied in order to have self-knowledge. This occurs in Jesus, the incarnate One.

This approach leads to considerable difficulties in explicating the internal relations of the Trinity, difficulties that Jenson does not appear to be altogether aware of. If we apply this definition of personhood, which Jenson carries over from humanity to God, then God the Trinity can be thought of as *person*, but not the three 'identities' within God, as Jenson calls them. A person is a union of spirit and body, and thus God *becomes* person in the incarnation. As quoted earlier: Jesus' human body is in fact the body in which 'God has himself as his own Object', and the 'one in whom the Father intends himself is Jesus, an item of and subject in our history'.[68] But, as there is only *one* body here, there can be only *one* person. The difficulties associated with this need to be worked out in some depth. That Jenson develops the notion of body to mean 'the availability of a history' does not alter the difficulty here.

God's embodiment is important, because it prevents us from viewing God as an enslaving pure subject. But this move itself creates a significant difficulty. We may ask: if Jesus of Nazareth is the embodiment of God, then what can be said of His relationship with the Father? Surely Jesus can only apprehend the father as pure subject, disembodied spirit, as Jesus' own body is the only objectivity the Father has. Either the Father is pure subject in relation to Jesus, or the Father cannot be seen as having any significant *otherness* in relation to the Son at all. We have already seen the antipathy Jenson has to the notion of pure subjectivity.

Jenson therefore has a genuine difficulty in distinguishing the Father and Son when talking about Jesus as the objectivity of God – God's embodiment. Furthermore, this difficulty rolls over into ecclesiology and eschatology.

From this it follows that talk of any sort of relationships within the being of God must break down. Jenson identifies God as an event of love, but within his own scheme love does not seem possible without otherness, without objectivity in relationship, and by definition there is only one object in God, the man Jesus and His risen body the church. The Father cannot give Himself in love to the Son when He has no objectivity to give apart from the Son's own body![69]

We will argue further below that Jenson is able to talk of God taking on bodies on a more or less *ad hoc* basis. God's words upon the tablets of stone could be just as much God's body as Jesus' flesh, or Aaron's staff that budded,

---

[68] *The Triune God*, p.146.

[69] Of course, the Christian tradition has often spoken of the Father, in the Spirit, giving Jesus His body the church – that is, in thinking of Christians as those given to Jesus by the Father – but that in no way helps Jenson to overcome the difficulties we are highlighting.

or Moses' staff which became a snake, or the burning bush, and so on.[70] Thus, if anything objective to us can serve as the body of God because whatever God says 'just is', then the incarnation becomes unnecessary, at least from a stand point of revelation. In the same way, the necessity of God's embodiment in Jesus of Nazareth is thrown into question by the description of availability in Jenson's treatment of the risen life of the community of the saints. 'Body' is a term that has simply become a too general for it to do the work that Jenson really wants it to do for him. Jenson may respond that it *just is* the case that God chooses to become incarnate, and this is a good response, but in that case there is no reason to insist that God must be limited to know Himself *only* in exactly the same form that humans know Him. God *just does* reveal Himself, and so is truly known, whether His self-knowledge is restricted in this way or not.

Ecclesiological Concerns

As we have noted, Jenson's treatment of ascension and ecclesiology is so shaped around his trinitarian thought that our critique has so far focussed upon trinitarian issues, with little reference to ascension or church. However, the conception of embodiment that is subsequently brought to bear on Jesus' ascension has particular ecclesiological impact, and it is the task of this section to explore that impact.

Jenson's spirit – body description of God and the church, already problematic, becomes even more difficult when Jenson begins to address Jesus' being as resurrected and ascended, and His appropriation of church and sacraments as His body. Jenson does not appear to recognise all the difficulties. He obviously attempts to explain how he thinks that Jesus *can* take these other 'bodies' as His own – an explanation based as we have seen on the designation of 'body' as no more or less than 'objective availability', and finally resting on the claim that Jesus simply 'says that this is so', and Jesus' words are reality.[71]

The problems here are simply an extension of the problems explored above with relation to the incarnation of the Son. When Jesus rises, He takes the church and her sacraments as His body – but then all the issues surrounding the embodiment of the Trinity, and divine self-knowledge, find a new locus in God's embodiment in the church. Furthermore, the description of Jesus

---

[70] As above, Jenson is happy to speak of 'such bodies as the inkwell and pen, or the body of water in which we baptize, precisely and insofar as they ... are drawn into personal communication, and so come to belong to personal embodiment'. *Visible Words*, p.21.

[71] As earlier: for the church to be Jesus' risen body 'all that is needed is that the Christ's self-understanding determine what is real, that is, that He be the *Logos* of God'. *ST* vol. II, p.214.

personhood appears to become even more confusing. The reworking of Jesus'
ascension – so that He ascends into the church and sacraments – is deeply
problematic.

Jesus' Ascended Body

It is difficult to think of Jesus' as ascended *person* when He is embodied in
various objects, in what a harsh reading might describe as an *ad hoc* fashion.
Furthermore, if the church and sacraments are the embodiment as which
Christ knows Himself, then they are the embodiment as which the whole
Trinity knows itself. Thus the issues surrounding the identification of Father,
Son, and Spirit as the *one* subjectivity of the earthly body of Jesus are
intensified in the apparent disposability of Jesus' resurrection body in His
ascension, (or the disposability of His physical existence in resurrection).

Moreover, if God is the spirit who knows himself in the body of Jesus,
then when Jesus rises and is seemingly able to take this or that body as His
chosen objectivity, does that mean that He is risen as pure *spirit*? How can we
think of Jesus' transition from His existence as object to (seemingly) pure
subject in relation to the church and sacraments as His own objectivity? And
what might that mean for the being of God – once again, is God's triunity
somehow to do with three spirits and one body?

As we have noted, Jenson does affirm bodily resurrection, and, 'very
cautiously' even the empty tomb.[72] However, the reason he affirms the empty
tomb is merely that Jesus' corpse would have become a *relic* – a form of
availability that would have created altogether the wrong sort of devotion.
Bodily resurrection is not maintained in a fashion which would tie the
ascended Jesus to a particular resurrection body, and therefore a particular
form of availability. Jesus, ascended and present in church and sacraments,
'needs no other body to be a risen man, body and soul. There is and needs to
be no other place than the church for him to be embodied, nor in that other
place any other entity to be the 'real' body of Christ'.[73] According to this way
of talking, Jesus' embodiment appears rather accidental – for all that Jenson's
earlier descriptions of body imply the opposite. The ascended Jesus so
transcends His body that the genuineness of His availability may be called into
question.

If Jesus' human body is unimportant in the resurrection and the ascension,
then what *is* important is His spirit.[74] 'Body' appears to take on rather

---

[72] See: *ST*, vol.I, p.206.

[73] *ST*, vol.I, p.206. Previously quoted above.

[74] We might well ask what actually did happen to the corpse. Did Jesus rise bodily and
then discard this body? Or did he rise spiritually and the angels dispose of the corpse
to prevent the 'wrong sort' of availability? What are we to make of gospel accounts
of empty graveclothes, touching, eating, and so forth? Read in the light of at least
some Old Testament thought, such a 'spiritual' resurrection would equate only to life
in Sheol!

instrumentalist connotations. Especially when Jenson can talk of inkwells and pens as 'bodies' in as much as they are used in personal communication. According to Jenson's phenomenology we certainly can call the church and her sacraments Jesus' body, but at the same time the claim seems emptied of much of its content, so that it is hard to see how this description of Jesus' availability implies very much, and how deeply Jesus becomes objectified for us. We get a sense that the 'real' Jesus is not a body elsewhere, but that He *is* a transcendent spirit effectively elsewhere.[75]

The Authority of Jesus over the Church

On the other hand we might compare Barth's approach to Jesus' ascension with Jenson's and note that for Barth the significance of scripture as authoritative over the church relates strongly to his conception of Jesus' ascended being and agency. In Chapter Three of this work Barth's ecclesiology was discussed in relation to Jesus' ascension. A central claim of that chapter was that Jesus' continued creaturely existence *elsewhere* than in the church – that is, in a heaven that is other than the church – causes Barth to limit the sense in which the church can act as its own authority, even if that authority is formally described as belonging to the Spirit of the Lord. Scripture is the form of authority the ascended Lord adopts over His church. For this reason Barth offers conscious and direct criticism of those theologies which may formally recognise the authority of Jesus over the church, but practically deny it by failing to acknowledge the form of that lordship in the rule of Holy Scripture. To repeat an apposite citation:

> [The] rule of Jesus Christ may be seriously acknowledged in form, but it is represented as a direct leadership of the Spirit, and it is only a secondary question whether the point at which this leadership of the Spirit touches and seizes the Church is supposed to be an infallible Pope or Council, or the office of an authoritarian bishop, or that of a hypostatised pastor, or a free leadership or inspired individuals in the community, or finally the whole community as such. The false thing in all these types of Church government is the ambiguity with which the rule of Jesus Christ is (perhaps very seriously) asserted, but scripture is ignored as though it were not the normative form of this government for this intervening period.[76]

There is no doubt that Jenson does in fact point to Scripture as the canon of the church – of the church's gospel – and that he grants scripture a normative role in theology.[77] Scripture is the norm of the 'church's attempts to speak the gospel'[78] and is authoritative in relation to dogma, liturgy, and all other tradition. However, as he works out the relation between Jesus ascended

---

[75] Clearly this is exactly the reverse of Jenson's intention.

[76] *CD* I/2, p.693-4. Cited above in Chapter Three.

[77] See the 'Prolegomena' of *ST* vol.I.

[78] *ST* vol.I., p.29.

and the church the only way he describes Jesus' otherness to the church is in the sacraments of bread and wine, and this can hardly be a description that would satisfy Barth. Jenson's theology does not reflect the priority of scripture, and the vast weight of his emphasis is upon the church as the objective reality of Jesus. For Barth, although the church is the earthly historical 'body of Christ' it is *not* the primary form of His creaturely embodiment – His ascended body is other than the church, and other than the eucharist – and it is thus that scripture stands in authority over the church, even though it is not a form of 'embodiment'.

> How else, then, can the Church be ruled except by this witness? Any other rule can only turn the Church into that which is not the Church. Any other rule can only lead the Church back to the sovereignty of man as he is autonomous in the strength of his false faith. It can consist only in a denial of the character of our time as the time between the ascension and the second coming.[79]

The Church and the Gospel

An outcome of all this is that for Jenson the gospel is now focussed on the church and sacraments, as the objectivity of God. To repeat part of a significant quote:

> The subject that the risen Christ is, is the subject who comes to word in the gospel. The object – the body – that the risen Christ is, is the body in the world to which this word calls attention, the church round her sacraments.[80]

And so, again: 'Heaven is where God takes space in his creation to be present to the whole of it; he does that in the church'.[81] Yet, an examination of significant New Testament descriptions of the referent of the gospel might raise some questions for Jenson at this point. Jenson holds that the church and sacraments as Christ's embodiment are the *objectivity* of the Saviour and of His cross, and are appropriately therefore the objects to which the gospel points, but this view would be hard to reconcile with the message of the apostles. The preaching of the apostolic church does not appear to have *primarily* focussed on the church, but on the church's Lord, and particularly His identity as Messiah, and the cross and resurrection through which His messianic mission was fulfilled.[82]

---

[79] *CD* I/2, p.693. Cited above in Chapter Three.

[80] *ST* vol.I, p.206.

[81] *ST* vol.I, p.206.

[82] Thus: witness Paul's discussion of his proclamation as focussed on Jesus' crucifixion, in 1 Corinthians 1, 2 Corinthians 4, and references to Christ revealed as crucified, e.g. Galatians 3[1]. This is not to claim that the community was in any way unimportant for the apostolic church, but that the church was not the referent of the word of the gospel.

For Barth, in line with His emphasis upon the absence of Christ ascended as the condition of His presence, the objectivity of Christ in the gospel is maintained through scripture. The object of Christian faith is Jesus Christ as He is attested by scripture and *proclaimed* by the church.[83] But the word of scripture is authoritative in this regard, and the church's proclamation is authentic to the degree that it rests upon scripture and flows out of hearing Jesus Himself through it. Faith in Jesus is faith in 'Him as attested by Scripture and proclaimed by the community', but the word of proclamation is derivative: thus genuine faith in Christ 'always takes place in the sphere of Holy Scripture which attests Him and in the community which proclaims Him *in obedience to Scripture*'.[84]

The Mission of the Church

Flowing out of the orientation of the gospel to the church as its object, it is very interesting to note the lack of treatment Jenson gives to the church's missionary nature. Given his Lutheran background and the occasional mention that mission receives, perhaps we can assume that he sees external proclamation of the gospel as important and necessary, but he offers no significant discussion of it. In the seven chapters of his *Systematic Theology* that make up his section on the church, encompassing some 138 pages, there is no section or subsection devoted to the being of the church in mission. Two pages are offered in recommending the institution of the *catchumenate*, but even there the discussion is more concerned with the socio-cultural situation of the church 'in the midst of her divorce proceedings from the culture',[85] than with any explication of how the church might be involved in proclaiming Christ to those who then might become catechumens. Some sort of mission is of course assumed, as elsewhere in the two volumes of the *Systematic Theology*,[86] but the assumption does not receive any explication and therefore cannot be claimed to exert much influence.

Thus, when Jenson tells us that scripture is the norm of the church's gospel speech the weight of his theology indicates that the speech he is thinking of is the *internal* speech of the community – proclaiming the story of Jesus upward to God in praise, and horizontally, seemingly, to each other.

Perhaps a parallel within Jenson's thought – that is, between the nature of the promises associated with the eucharist and the referent of the gospel – can lead toward an explanation of his lack of missiological interest. As we have

---

[83] That Jenson too believes in the proclamatory role of the church does not alter his emphasis upon the church as also the object of the gospel's intention, although it appears to alter and minimise his conception of the church's mission. See below.

[84] *CD* IV/1, p.762. Emphasis added.

[85] *ST* vol. II, p.305.

[86] So Jenson can call Christianity a 'missionary faith' (*ST* vol. I, p.35), but it remains an isolated saying.

already noted, the promise 'which 'comes' to the bread' is that church and sacraments are Christ's body:

> The Eucharist promises: *there is* my body in the world, and you here eating and drinking commune in it. It promises: *there is* the actual historical church, and you are she. [87]

At the same time, Jenson claims, the gospel points us to the church around the sacraments. The eucharist and the gospel declare the same thing: that Jesus Christ is here present and available in the church as the body He has redeemed. That this is the *only* body Jesus has, and the only form in which He makes Himself available, gives the eucharist the priority we have noted, and perhaps this clarifies the lack of outward focus in Jenson's ecclesiology. It is therefore unproblematic for Jenson to see the primary form of gospel proclamation as the eucharist, with its referent in the church it nourishes. This combination turns the gospel more in the direction of an inward and churchly word, rather than an outward missionary word. Of course, there is no requirement that these two variants of proclamation – inward and outward – be mutually exclusive, quite the reverse is true, but in Jenson's case one seems to have all but swallowed the other. If participation in the eucharist is restricted to the believing community, and the eucharist is the particular *locus* of gospel proclamation, then the exposition of the gospel comes to be for and within the church.

On the other hand, Barth's reformation conception of the church as *creatura verbi* enables a much more mission oriented ecclesiology. The church exists for the one purpose of serving Jesus' mission, which itself is conceived of in terms of a movement from the realm of God into the world – a movement which continues that of the incarnation itself, as the reality of salvation in the eternal election of Jesus invades the realm of sin and death and reveals the victory of God over that which is 'nothing'. As above, by refusing to conflate Jesus' ascension with His being in the church with her sacraments Barth is able to understand the being and mission of the church very differently from the way in which Jenson must in order to maintain his phenomenological understanding of the Trinity.

Outcomes of the Ecclesiological Concerns

In conclusion, flowing out of Jenson's Trinitarian thought, the church and her sacraments come to carry too much weight as the full availability of God in the world – and more than that, the full availability of God to God. Jenson's emphases upon the church as truly the body of Christ, and upon the reality of the incarnation, are to be highly commended. But the way in which he develops his doctrine of God, and subsequently of the church does not function well to protect the threefold being of God from collapsing into something that

---

[87] *ST* vol. II, p.220. Emphasis original.

looks very much like modalism. The term 'God' ultimately designates an event which does not involve three persons in mutual self-giving, but rather an event in which one spirit, temporally (but not effectively) differentiated, takes on embodiment and thereby becomes person. Jenson finally identifies God with church and sacraments in a way that reduces God's self-knowledge to knowledge of these entities, and again, does violence to any notion of intra-trinitarian communion. The gospel comes to be about the church and sacraments, as the objectivity of God, and we might wonder if in the end we should not be worshipping these objective realities of God's presence? Jenson tells us we should not, but can he maintain the injunction?

In the last analysis, *body* itself becomes such a weak notion, that contra to Jenson's intention, all that has power and significance is spirit. Perhaps this is why we do not worship the church or sacraments *per se*, but the result is that God appears to secretly be pure spirit all along, and for Jenson this means that God is an enslaving, hidden presence, absent in the ways that count the most. The emphasis on an *ad hoc* embodiment leaves us with real problems with God's presence, the very thing Jenson seems to want to guarantee.

In contrast, Barth maintains that Jesus' resurrection involves an empty tomb, and an embodiment apart from the church – even though he is prepared to call the church the ascended Jesus' 'earthly-historical form'. For Barth this has a great deal to say in relation to anthropology, eschatology, and the shape of redemption as it takes place in the time between. In a section that is focussed on the physical life of the Christian, Barth emphasises the physicality of Jesus' being,[88] and of the redemption revealed in Him.

> The exalted man Jesus, from whom the power of this life derives, is the One who is exalted in the totality of His soul and body, just as he is the One who is humiliated in the totality of His outer and inner life. He is flesh and blood in His being and therefore in its revelation. It is inevitable, then, that the power which proceeds from His resurrection, and He himself as the resurrected, should sow a seed which is not only psychical but physical ... Eternal life as it is applied to man by this power is the declaration and pledge of his total life-exaltation, from which not a hair of his head or a breath that he draws can be excluded.[89]

The shape of Barth's theology is thus quite different, and not least in regard to the church as related to Jesus' ascension, as we have seen.

---

[88] Barth follows Paul (1 Corinthians 15) in seeing the resurrection body as a 'spiritual'. This does not mean a lack of physicality, however, but rather involves a hope for embodiment according to another order of physicality.

[89] *CD* IV/2, pp.316-17.

Eschatological Issues

As we have explicated above, in the eschaton Jesus' will finally become embodied in the community of the saints, with no separation or remainder. Jesus will be the subject and the community His body. Jesus' lordship will cease, for He will be united to the saints in such a fashion that together they form one person. Jenson here holds out a wonderful vision of the union of Jesus with His people – a genuinely eschatological vision of hope. Yet the same problems regarding personhood and embodiment that dog his treatment of the Trinity and of the church return in much the same form here also.

Personhood in Eternity

Just as question marks hang over the triune being of God in His embodiment in Jesus of Nazareth, and then in Jesus' body the church, so they hang over God's eschatological embodiment in the community of the risen saints. Once again the Father, Son, and Holy Spirit appear to form the one subject of the single corporate body. The logic of deification is so strong that to intend the body of God the saints will turn to the community they form – they need only look at each other. 'In the perfected Community I will intend the body of God by intending the Community'.[90] The saints will be deeply involved in 'the eternal *perichoresis* of the triune life', but hanging over this claim is the perpetual difficulty in speaking of God's 'three-ness' given that there is still only the one body, and Jenson's notion of personhood inextricably links body, objectivity, and relationship.

When we turned to the question of the individual embodiment of the saints similar questions arose: how can the triune God be the subject who knows Himself in the single corporate body of the redeemed, and at the same time the saints know themselves and each other as subject-bodies? In seeking to answer this question Jenson appears to overturn his entire project by claiming that the eternal life of God allows for an availability of persons one to another which in no way relies upon spatiality or materiality. The latter realities are now tied to fallen temporality in such a way as to see them as overcome simply in the union of the saints histories with the eternity of God.

But from the very beginning of his project Jenson has relied upon the distinction between subjectivity and objectivity, audible and visible, and indeed has applied that distinction to the inner life of God. God is said to have Himself as His own object in that Jesus is His body, and therefore God is claimed to know Himself only as this body. But in the above it appears that the structure of subjectivity and objectivity in God is altogether other than for humans in this age after all. Where the structures of personal being and self-knowledge were earlier applied directly from human phenomenology to the life of God, now it appears that the matter of self-knowledge, with the attendant

---

[90] *ST* vol. II, p.340. Cited above.

issue of embodied and disembodied communication, is a function of the problematic temporality of fallen creatures. Pure subjectivity is a problem because it does not involve the body as the sum of the individual's past, but in God past, present, and future cohere, and so a form of subjectivity that is temporally conditioned does not now appear possible. Why then does God originally need a body in order to have self-knowledge? Either Jenson's solution to the question of the individuality of the saints in eternity fails, or his entire project is predicated on a disposable notion of personhood! He claims that the saints loving intention of each other, within the eternal relations of the Trinity, can constitute their mutual availability, but if so, then why can we not speak of the Father so intending the Son and the Spirit, and *vice versa*, without the necessity of the incarnation as God's act of self knowledge?

Ascension in the 'Body' and Deification

To follow this line further we may ask, 'What difference does Barth's idea of ascension make to the logic of deification?' If Jesus' bodily ascension is not simply into the church and sacraments and thence into the community of the risen, then how are we to think of the union of the saints with Christ in eternity?

Whether or not we hold something like Jenson's description of the being of God as person, which Barth does not, certain implications would seem to flow from the identification of Jesus as embodied apart from, as well as in, the communion of the saints. Jesus would be distinguishable from the community, as well as united to it. However, this need not imply a limitation upon the union of Christ to His people *per se*, for it does not seem impossible that Jesus be intendable simply as the one who is united to those who are His, and that His being as a person in His own right need not imply His independence. In fact, it seems likely that Barth would move to say that it is precisely as the Son of God who is also the Son of Man, the embodied second person of the Trinity in His own being, that Jesus can and does take to Himself those whom He has redeemed. That the second reality (the union of Christ with His people) is derivative upon the first (His continued being as the incarnate Son) does not in any way imply that His union with His own is false or even lesser. Rather the absolute reality of the God-man – in the union of resurrected soul and body, albeit a 'spiritual body' – is the guarantee of the absolute reality of His union with the saints. Although Barth cannot be cited as making these claims, something like this would appear to be required by Barth's doctrine of election, his firm commitment to the being of humans as a unity of soul and body, and his insistence upon Jesus' bodily resurrection.

Moreover, if Jesus is recognised as ascending 'in the body' then, *à la* Paul, His resurrection body may be recognised as the first fruit of the resurrection of our bodies. The notion of eschatological embodiment for the saints takes an entirely different shape, and the confusion over personhood may be avoided.

What it might mean to receive new bodies, within an entirely new creation, cannot be described, but that need not matter particularly.

Barth and Jenson on Jesus' Ascended: The Lord and the Church

Finally, what then may be said regarding Barth and Jenson's divergent approaches to Jesus' ascension? As with Barth's theology, it would be quite inappropriate to claim that Jenson's conception of the ascension is the controlling feature within his thought. Like Barth, Jenson works across a wide doctrinal front, and any single doctrinal determination only functions within a complex of decisions and affirmations. Nonetheless, the difference between Jenson and Barth's treatment of the ascension does point up significant aspects of the wide-ranging divergence in their thought.

Although both Barth and Jenson seek to describe Jesus' Lordship over the church, they do so in a quite different fashion, and to a large degree the shape of that difference resides in the distinct notion each has of Jesus' ascended life. Although he does not attempt to describe the way in which it is a reality, Barth is committed to bodily resurrection and ascension in such a form that Jesus is 'physically' located somewhere other than the church and sacraments, and this absence conditions the way in which Jesus' transcendent Lordship is expressed. Jenson on the other hand views Jesus' Lordship over the church as a temporary matter, exercised via His presence in the eucharist. When the eschaton occurs Jesus will no longer be Lord of the church – He will simply be united to it. The key to this is Jenson's appropriation of Hegelian phenomenology. Jesus' ascension can be described as into the church and sacraments, and His future body as simply the community of the saints, because body has been radically redescribed as 'availability'. The fundamental move is the reworking of the notion of 'body', but nonetheless it is only as he is prepared to reinterpret what it means for Jesus to ascend that Jenson can claim that church and eucharist are the only body Jesus has or needs.

Chapter 9

Conclusion: The Ascended Lord

In the conclusion to Part I (Chapter Five) we argued that Barth's theology of Jesus' ascension and heavenly session has particular significance within his project as a whole. No attempt was made to give Jesus' being as the ascended One any priority over other important doctrinal affirmations within Barth's theology, and so the ascension *per se* was not granted a significance that it does not have for Barth – such as the mechanism of Jesus' glorification, or of the unification of His humanity with God's divinity. Rather, Jesus' ascension and session with the Father were shown to function in partnership with other doctrines, as together they combine in a larger dogmatic framework. So, in line with Barth's Chalcedonian reading of the incarnation, Jesus' resurrection and ascension *reveal* His glory and exaltation, but do not create or even initiate them – Jesus is always glorious, and always the exalted One, precisely as He is the humiliated One. Yet this role of revelation is itself crucial – in union with the resurrection the ascension sheds an extremely important light upon Jesus' very being and work from Bethlehem to Golgotha, and even back upon His eternal election. Without the revelation of Jesus' identity and work as the Son who belongs with the Father no saving significance could finally be attached to His career. For Barth, revelation and reconciliation are two aspects of the one event and reality. Moreover, within the complex of Barth's theology, it was found that Jesus' ascension and heavenly session also play out a constructive role beyond that of revelation, particularly in relation to the nature of the present age, which Barth conceives to be the 'time between' ascension and eschaton. What follows is a brief summary of conclusions drawn in Chapter Five, and it is in that chapter that a full treatment of these matters is undertaken.[1] From that summary we will move to draw together the conclusions made in dialogue with other theologians, and then to make some final comments on Barth's treatment of Jesus as ascended. Finally a brief recommendation of the importance of theological reflection upon Jesus' ascension and ascended ministry completes the thesis.

Recapping Part I: Barth on Jesus Ascended

Barth's description of the *form* of Jesus' agency, transcendence, and lordship, are all at least partially shaped by the awareness that He is ascended and seated

---

[1] No textual support will be offered for the following statements relating to conclusions drawn in Part I of this work – the reader is referred to Chapter 5 above.

at the Father's right hand. A dynamic of the presence and absence of the ascended Lord is worked out in Barth's doctrine of the Spirit, and subsequently in both his ecclesiology, with the related doctrine of Holy Scripture, and in his description of the Christian life. Due to the absence of the risen Saviour these realities are shaped by the utterly eschatological thrust of Jesus' ascended work, as He Himself moves toward the fulfillment of His *parousia* in the coming *eschaton*. While Jesus is absent – ascended to the Father's side – and while all creation awaits His return in glory, the church and her members live in the age of penultimate reality. This is the age in which reconciliation is truly and genuinely present in the redemptive work of the Spirit, but nonetheless is present only in the form of promise, and of hope. The dynamic of presence and absence inherent in this situation is itself only possible upon the basis of the genuine presence of the heavenly Lord in the agency of the Spirit. Jesus is truly present in the Spirit – Barth identifies the Spirit wholly with the mediation of the ascended ministry of Jesus – but at the same time there is a limitation of that presence due to Jesus' lack of immediacy. Jesus is not immediate to this age, but absent and located at the Father's right hand, from where He breaks into the current age in the Spirit as He Himself moves toward His coming in the *eschaton*.

Thus Barth's pneumatological determinations in relation to the present age – that the Spirit's mode of presence is in the form of promise, that His work is always eschatological in direction, and thus that the redemption He brings is ever a 'coming' reality – may be argued to be christologically determined. The One who is present and absent in the Spirit is Jesus Christ the ascended Lord. Pneumatology, and indeed the doctrine of revelation and of Holy Scripture, is therefore shaped by the christological reality of Jesus' presence and absence, and of the form of His transcendent Lordship as it is expressed in the 'time between'.

The church therefore appears as the earthly-historical form of Jesus' continued existence, and the place wherein the Spirit creates knowledge of God and genuine human response to Jesus as God's Word. Barth is firm in his designation of the church as Jesus' body, and the present form of His earthly-historical life, but nonetheless, the church is never allowed to take centre stage. The way in which Barth conceives of Jesus' ascension and heavenly session – indeed, of heaven itself – will not allow the church to assume any of the place of His humanity. That is, Jesus is bodily ascended and 'located' at the Father's side in a heaven which is *within creation* and so the church cannot assume the role of Jesus' *only* body, or of His *only* creaturely existence. The church genuinely and really exists as Jesus' body, the earthly-historical *soma* in union with the heavenly Head, but precisely and actually *only* in union with the heavenly Head who is bodily ascended to the Father. Thus the church's embodiment of Jesus is always penultimate, and derivative upon His heavenly embodiment – the church can never be the primary body of Christ, because He lives as the risen man Jesus of Nazareth in the presence of the Father.

At this point the doctrine of Holy Scripture – as the concrete presence of Jesus' self-witness – provided a particularly clear example of the influence of Jesus' ascended state upon Barth's thought. The role of Scripture as the form in which Jesus exercises His authority *over* the church, and the way in which this forbids any reduction of Jesus' authority over the church to the authority *of* the church is highly significant in Barth's ecclesiology. By no means was this move traced solely to Jesus' ascension and heavenly session, but nonetheless, Jesus' ascended presence and absence were found to underpin Barth's thought about Jesus' presence in Holy Scripture in an important fashion.

As the members who make up the church, a similar dynamic applies to the being of Christians as those who are being redeemed by Jesus Christ in the Spirit. Christians exist in the tension of the 'already and not yet' which characterises the present age of the world as the 'time between'. On the basis of all Jesus achieved on the way from Bethlehem to Golgotha, and thus of His ascended life and agency, Christians are those who live now the eschatological redemption which objectively applies to all creation. Yet due to the absence of Jesus – in the sense of the lack of His immediacy, which was worked out in terms of the presence and absence of His time – Christians also live as sinners who are only invisibly the redeemed.

Still, as we have argued, Barth is not at all denying the full reality of human existence with and before God, or denying the way in which Jesus Christ takes hold of human beings and unites them to Himself. Precisely the opposite is in fact the case. Barth's interest is to establish, as fully and concretely as possible, the true and genuine reality of redemption as an event and experience within the *human* world, but to do so he insists upon finding and maintaining the correct basis upon which to build. Thus it is the absolute reality of justification achieved in and by Jesus Christ that forms the foundation of all Barth seeks to say.

Many highly significant doctrinal affirmations inform Barth at this point: the transcendence that is proper to Jesus as the Son of God; the inability of humans to offer even the slightest degree of assistance in the work of salvation as a result of the radical nature of sin; the application of this radical fall to the whole of creation; and so forth. Yet as Barth seeks to speak fully and concretely of the reality of human redemption the dynamic of presence and absence exercises a considerable role, particularly as Jesus' ascended being shapes the present age. So, for instance, the nature of the dual command to love God and love the neighbour was explicated and developed entirely in relation to the present age as the 'time between' and the age of Jesus' presence and absence. An explanation of Barth's pneumatology, ecclesiology, and ethics is therefore possible on the basis of his ascension theology, and, for those who are troubled by Barth's approach to these matters, attention to the way Jesus' ascended life functions may help explicate Barth's treatment of these areas of theology.

As we now turn to gather up the conclusions drawn in the dialogues that make up Part II of this work, we aim further to justify our claims regarding the role of Jesus' ascension and heavenly session in Barth's thought. Moreover, we aim to develop more fully the claim that an understanding Jesus' ascended life must play a role in shaping theological descriptions of His being, of the church as His body, and of the reality of salvation for individual Christians in this 'time between'. But, of course, not any role or description of Jesus ascended will do. Jesus' ascension and heavenly session can be either overplayed or underdeveloped, or simply poorly understood, as may be shown with reference to our dialogue partners.

Drawing upon the Dialogues

In attempting to place Barth in dialogue with other theologians we have tried firstly to hear their critiques of Barth's theology and to evaluate their constructive proposals. In the case of Jenson, rather than attend to a critique of Barth, we have tried to listen to the alternative proposal that he offers, in spite of the fact that he does not attend very closely to ascension theology *per se*. In response to this initial act of listening, we have then attempted, firstly, to defend Barth from the critiques offered, and then, secondly, to demonstrate how the three dialogue partners all run into difficulties of their own – specifically in relation to Jesus' ascension and heavenly session. The point of this has not been simply to defend Barth at every point, heedless of the worth of the criticisms and alternatives that are offered, but rather to defend Barth on the basis that his theology makes the best sense and is the most faithful to the gospel of Jesus Christ.[2]

Within the three dialogues two formal lines of debate may be found, with some significant material links, and indeed apparent theological agendas, crossing over between the two. Thomas Torrance and Douglas Farrow have been argued to form an axis of dialogue with Barth. Farrow takes up Torrance's critique of Barth's ascension theology and seeks to further it by embracing a stronger reading of the ascension – and a more thoroughgoing critique of Barth – than Torrance does himself. Farrow places great weight upon the ascension and Jesus' ascended humanity, and so attempts to develop a theology that largely turns upon his reading of Jesus' history as finally achieving saving reality in Jesus' ascension into heaven. Jenson, on the other hand, belongs to a somewhat different strand of theological thought, at least with regard to the ascension, and in distinction from Farrow he places little weight upon the event of Jesus' ascension, effectively if not actually removing *bodily* ascension from his theology. Interestingly, however, both Farrow and Jenson display considerable interest in the eucharist as the primary form of Jesus' ascended presence in and to the church, and moreover, both are eager

---

[2] The material for this section is drawn from the dialogues of Chapters 6, 7, and 8, and the textual justification and references that underlie the claims made here are to be found in those chapters.

for the church to have a stronger role in the work of salvation than Barth is prepared to allow.

We have noted that a lack of ecclesial action is often the substance of complaint against Barth, and at times this is tied to the complaint that Jesus' humanity – even humanity itself – is undervalued, and the Holy Spirit's role underdeveloped. In this sense both Jenson and Farrow may be said to reiterate an existing position in relation to Barth, although very much in their own distinctive ways. Although Farrow and Jenson (and, to a much lesser degree, Torrance) have this emphasis on ecclesiology in common, together with an even stronger likeness in their shared emphasis on the eucharist, the way that they approach Jesus' ascension is rather different. For this reason we cannot treat them together, but must see them as representing two quite different attempts to achieve strongly eucharistic theologies. Thus, in what follows we will first of all draw upon Torrance and Farrow, with the weight falling upon our dialogue with Farrow, and then take up the results of the dialogue with Jenson.

Torrance and Farrow: Ascension, Incarnation, and Eucharist

As we argued in Chapter Six especially, Thomas Torrance offers a critique of Barth that Douglas Farrow takes up and attempts to apply more rigorously. Torrance himself believes that Barth fails to give adequate space and attention to Jesus' ascended humanity, and therefore to Jesus' ascended work as high priest. However, Torrance's criticism is mild, and for the most part his position is rather similar to Barth's. Although we noted that Torrance draws upon William Milligan and takes up Milligan's sequential reading of Jesus' humiliation and exaltation, this does not result in Torrance reading Jesus' incarnation or the history of reconciliation in a manner significantly different from that in which Barth does. The result of this is a certain inconsistency on Torrance's part, as Farrow also notes. There is an apparent difficulty for Torrance in attempting to uphold both the *extra Calvinisticum* and a sequential reading of exaltation and humiliation, as he seems to want to do. The latter move involves the claim that Jesus' humanity is only fully united to the life of God in the ascension, but such a claim cannot sit easily with a refusal to see any *kenosis* of the divinity of the Son in His incarnation. Nonetheless, our final judgement is that Torrance's theology is different, but largely not divergent from Barth's, with whom he is normally in agreement.

When Farrow takes up Torrance's line of critique he applies it far more strenuously, and strives to work out its implications in greater detail within his own programme. Thus Farrow censures Torrance for failing to criticise Barth's theology of the incarnation (Torrance in fact defends it) and Farrow himself works to overturn what he calls the 'chalcedonian clamp' in Barth's description of the incarnation. On this basis the greatest difference between Barth and Farrow lies in their understanding of what Jesus' ascension achieves for Him – that is, what role it takes within His history.

Farrow, like Milligan and Torrance, sees Jesus' ascension as introducing His exaltation, and for Farrow this means that Jesus' ascension is the point at which Jesus' history finally diverges from the general history of all other humans. For Barth, however, Jesus' ascension *reveals* that His history has diverged from general human history, from the history of fallen humanity, at every point. Jesus fully enters into fallen human history – and so His history is fully united to our human history – but it is exactly in this unity with our flesh and history that Jesus diverges so radically from all other humans. This is because in every aspect of His life, subjected to temptation and fallen flesh even as we are, Jesus does not sin and thereby turns fallen humanity back to God. For Barth, Jesus' divergence from us is most evident in His very unity with us – it is as He takes up our sinful flesh and *does not sin* that He diverges from us. On the other side, Farrow's reading of Jesus' history seeks to do justice to this same reality of Jesus' 'recapitulation' of fallen history, but Farrow insists that this movement requires Jesus' ascension as the event that unites perfected humanity to the life of the Father, and that yields the heavenly ministry which is our salvation. The relationship between the deity and humanity of Jesus of Nazareth, and the relative action of the two appears to be conceived in different terms, as Farrow appears to somehow separate the activity of God and humanity in Jesus.

At the centre of this is the matter of the relation between the *ontological* and *soteriological*, or in Barth's case the *ontological* and *dynamic* poles of Jesus' incarnate ministry. Farrow separates the ontological and soteriological poles of Jesus' history, and criticises Barth for failing to do so. There is a terminological issue at this point, which is itself representative of the deeper difference between these two thinkers. With Torrance and Hunsinger, we interpret Barth as describing the ontological and dynamic poles of *soteriology*: that is, Barth sees Jesus' *being* as the God-man and His *acts* as the God-man as inseparable, and so *both* being and act are 'saving'. Soteriology thus comprehends both the being and the act of the incarnate one. Barth's reading of Jesus' entire history is shaped around the ontological and dynamic poles of the one saving event – an event that begins at Bethlehem (or perhaps Jesus' conception) and culminates upon the cross at Golgotha. Moreover, the acting subject throughout is the eternal Son incarnate – which is to say, the acts of Jesus of Nazareth are the acts of the eternal Word of God, but the acts of this Word *incarnate.* Thus these acts are also fully human acts, but only as they are the acts of the Son of God. Thus ontological and soteriological poles of the incarnation cohere and no separation of human and divine action is permissible.

For Farrow the ontological reality of Jesus' being as the Son of God in union with the Son of Man does not function soteriologically *per se*, but rather is the presupposition of soteriology. Farrow's reading of the saving history of Jesus is centrally concerned with His acts alone, and indeed with those acts as belonging to Jesus as a human, rather than to Him as God. Whether such a conception of Jesus' incarnation and life can be sustained remains an open question.

Throughout Farrow's work the key issue was found to be the eucharist, and in particular the relation between the eucharist, Jesus' ascended life, and the being of the church. Farrow finds in the eucharist the tools to interpret Jesus' ascended relationship to general, continuing, history, drawing upon his belief that it is the eucharistic assembly which furnishes the one ground upon which to base ecclesiology – his project is directed toward the production of what he calls a 'eucharistic ecclesiology'. At the same time there is a circularity in Farrow's thought, as we noted. Jesus' ascension is named as the event which establishes the possibility of eucharistic presence, and on this basis not only does the eucharist offer Farrow the appropriate framework within which to attend to Jesus' ascension, as above, but the ascension itself is also claimed to be the proper ground upon which to base eucharistic thought.

Barth, of course shares the view that it is only as Jesus is present that we are made aware of His absence, but Barth does not choose to locate this event so strongly around the eucharist, and this is what finalises Farrow's complaint against him. 'To the extent that neglect of the ascension as a distinct episode in the story of Jesus weights [Barth's] Christology in favour of presence (that is what we had in mind when we spoke of overcorrecting Kierkegaard) a eucharistic understanding of the church eludes him'.[3] However, Farrow struggles to justify his emphasis on the eucharist, and at the same time problems arise in his own theology.

Thus, in opposition to Farrow we claim that Barth's approach to Jesus' ascension and heavenly session shows a better balance – particularly in resisting the temptation to have the ascension do too much work. Much of the material in Farrow regarding Jesus' presence and absence is similar to Barth, (*except* as Farrow locates that material solely in relation to the eucharist and therefore accuses Barth of devaluing both eucharist and church as the (only) places of Jesus' presence). However, Barth does not and will not have the ascension exalt Jesus, nor even introduce His ministry before the Father *per se*, and it is here that Farrow may run into difficulties with the doctrine of the incarnation. His emphasis on Jesus' human action may come at the cost of Jesus' full and active divinity. This brings us back to the matter of the eucharist once more.

Overall, therefore, Farrow's dual emphasis on ascension and eucharist unbalances his theology. His desire to pay due heed to the ascension is praiseworthy, but in the end he cannot sustain the programme he develops. Farrow criticises Torrance for failing to overturn Barth's theology of the incarnation and fully embrace the ascension as Jesus' glorification, but we hold that Barth's theology is in fact stronger than Farrow's and less likely to run into difficulty, while remaining able to maintain the importance of Jesus as ascended in this age between.

---

[3] *Ascension* p.252, cited earlier.

Jenson and the Loss of Jesus' Bodily Ascension

In contrast to Farrow's emphasis upon the ascension as the centre for theological reflection (in union with the eucharist), Robert Jenson has been shown to give very little role to the doctrine of Jesus' ascension at all. This allows Jenson to develop a particular vision of Jesus' being and ministry in the present age – what Barth calls the 'time between'. We did not argue that the ascension itself was instrumental in shaping Jenson's theology – in fact his adoption of subject-object language and appropriation of that language to a phenomenology of body and spirit is far more influential. Nonetheless Jenson's conception of Jesus' ascended existence, and his lack of interest in any ascension body apart from the church and sacraments, are significant within the programme he undertakes.[4]

Unlike Farrow, Jenson does not explicitly tie ascension and eucharist together, but we contend that a link is implied by the nature of his approach to each – particularly in relation to Jesus' embodiment. Thus, while Jesus is present *in* the church as His body – indeed the church is strictly His *only* risen embodiment – the (only) way in which He is present *to* the church, as an object of the church's intention, is in the eucharist. Indeed, it is only as Jesus is objectively present to the church as another, that is, in the eucharist, that the church exists as Christ's body at all. At the same time, Jesus is not assumed to rise or ascend bodily, and so He may well be described as rising and ascending into the church gathered around her sacraments. Indeed, heaven is described as the church around her sacraments, and so Jesus' ascension into heaven is straightforwardly His ascension into the church. Jenson's treatment of Jesus' resurrection and ascension seems tailored to clear the way for his very strong identification of the church as Jesus' ascended body. So we argued that a different reading of Jesus' resurrection and ascension – such as Barth maintains – would force Jenson into a different ecclesiological position: he would have to be more reserved in his identification of Jesus and the church *without remainder*, and indeed in his description of Jesus' personhood. As above, Barth holds that Jesus' ascent into heaven is not simply His ascent into the church – heaven is the invisible Godward side of creation, and Jesus remains an embodied human there. This is a significant move for Barth, as Jesus' heavenly existence apart from the church functions as check upon overdeveloped ecclesiology.

For Jenson, Jesus – indeed God – is person in that He is embodied. To be a person is to be subject and object, spirit and body. But after the resurrection, and in His ascension, Jesus is no longer to be thought of as embodied in this way – Jesus is embodied in the church and her sacraments. Significant questions were raised in relation to God's personhood and Trinity within such an arrangement, and it is here, around the foundational matters of Trinity and

---

[4] As earlier, despite disagreeing over the ascension and the form of Jesus' heavenly session, Jenson and Farrow largely agree in their approach to the eucharist, and their vision of the church as constituted by sacramental mediation of the presence of Jesus.

incarnation that our criticism of Jenson focused. His theology of the Trinity breaks down into a description of God as an 'event' which is temporally but not effectively differentiated, so that God appears to be either three spirits identified by one body (Jesus' body) or one person (one spirit-body) identifiable in threefold form due to the threefold nature of time as past, present, and future. Due to Jenson's adoption of spirit-body phenomenology it becomes very hard to see how God may be seen as threefold in any meaningful fashion – except as temporally distinguished as past, present, and future. To be a person – to have identity – is to be a spirit and a body, but God has only one body, the body of the man Jesus, and then the church. Moreover, even the spiritual distinctions within God appear to break down as Jesus' spiritual being becomes utterly identified with the Holy Spirit, and the Father too is said to be the Spirit who knows Himself in the body of Jesus. Again, debate between Barth and Jenson over these moves by no means need be restricted to the matter of Jesus' ascended being. However, Barth's treatment of the ascension clearly exhibits the altogether different set of commitments he makes in relation to Jesus' embodiment, humanity, and personhood. At the centre there remains Jenson's particular interpretation of the church and sacraments as the objective reality of Jesus, which Barth strenuously rejects in his attacks on Roman Catholic ecclesiology.

In further contrast to Barth, for Jenson the gospel comes to refer to the church – for the church is Jesus' embodiment and therefore His objective availability to humans – and so, in contrast to Barth, the external mission of church fails to receive any significant treatment from Jenson. Indeed, the chief weight of proclamation seems to fall internally within the church, as the form of that proclamation is the eucharist itself, which declares that Jesus is present and embodied in the church.[5] Barth's treatment of Holy Scripture as the concrete presence of the ascended Lord stands in marked contrast to Jenson's view of the church itself as Jesus' ascended embodiment.

Barth's divergence from Jenson is therefore particularly plain. Barth conceives God's triunity and the nature of the incarnation in rather different ways, and moreover, he will not allow sacramentology to found ecclesiology or ecclesiology to dominate his theology. Barth does give both the church and the subjective human appropriation of the Gospel an important place in His theology, and Jesus' heavenly session is key to this, but not in the way Jenson moves. Jesus' bodily ascension, and His ascended existence in a heaven that is not reducible to the life of the church, is a key element within Barth's thought at this point, and his treatment of Jesus as ascended that contrasts so strongly with Jenson's. Crucially Jenson must encounter great difficulties within his

---

[5] Jenson names scripture as a key source of the life of the church, and of proclamation, but in practice his exposition focuses almost exclusively on the sacraments as Jesus' presence to the church. Within the phenomenology of audible and visible communication (as tied to subjective and objective, spirit and body) the sacraments are *visible words* in which Jesus makes Himself present, and thus they become the objective presence of the Gospel. On this basis the Scriptures simply cannot compete.

programme, and so his adoption of spirit-body phenomenology, and his emphasis on the church as Jesus' ascended body, cause his theology to founder. The difficulties encountered, as above, are foundational and widespread throughout his thought: what could be more basic than the doctrine of the Trinity?

On the other hand, Barth's theology offers a strong alternative to Jenson, especially in his understanding of Jesus' ascension and heavenly session, and in the way that this understanding informs his ecclesiology. It is not that the ascension is the decisive issue between Barth and Jenson, but nonetheless, the very different ways in which they conceive of Jesus as ascended are highly significant within their disagreement. If Jenson were to attend more to Jesus' bodily ascension, then other key issues with relation to embodiment – Jesus' relationship to the church and the form of His transcendent Lordship in the time between, the witness of the church and even trinitarian theology – would all need to be approached very differently.

Jesus' Ascension and Heavenly Session

In investigating the role of Jesus' ascension and heavenly session within Barth's thought we found that Barth does attend to Jesus' ascended state, and that in doing so he finds important tools for understanding the present age as the 'time between'. Jesus' presence and absence in that time, the mission of the Holy Spirit as Jesus' agent, and thus also the being of the church and the life of the Christian, are all understood within the framework founded upon Jesus' ascension to the Father's side and life there for us. So too, the important matter of eschatology takes shape in the light of Jesus' ascended being and awaited return.

Through dialoguing with Torrance, Farrow, and Jenson we have been further able to explicate the particular role of Jesus' ascension in Barth's theology, and moreover, make a case for the superiority of Barth's approach to those of these other theologians. In broad outline, Farrow – as he extends in the direction indicated by Torrance – may be claimed to place too much weight upon Jesus' ascension. With an agenda to prioritise theological reflection upon the eucharist, Farrow attempts to give Jesus' ascension a controlling function that is unsustainable. This is particularly clear in two ways. Firstly, Farrow's emphasis upon the soteriological function of the ascension requires the separation of ontological and soteriological aspects of the incarnation, with a resulting threat to the theology of the incarnation itself. Secondly, the place given to the eucharist is not able to be justified except (partially) by reference to the ascension and the bifurcation of Jesus' history and general history which it finalises. But this argument is in turn rather circular, for the ascension is argued to have the significance it does because the eucharist is so central to ecclesiological reflection, and thus to theological reflection *per se*.

On the other hand, Jenson may be broadly described as attending too little to Jesus' ascension and heavenly session, and therefore as overplaying both the church and the eucharist as Jesus' ascended body and availability. Jenson's theological programme runs into difficulties in many places and on many levels, but certainly his lack of interest in Jesus' ascended embodiment, *apart* from the church round the sacraments, plays a role within his thought.

Jesus Ascended, the Church, and the Christian

Both Farrow and Jenson are, at least to some degree, driven by a desire to elevate the status of the church (and sacraments) within protestant theology. Although they approach Jesus' ascension and heavenly session in opposing ways, nonetheless, in both cases the treatment of Jesus' ascended life, and of Jesus' ascension as an event within His history, is tailored to fit an ecclesiological stance. Barth's direction of thought is the opposite, as he moves from the New Testament description of Jesus as ascended (including the event of His ascension) to the dogmatic outworking of that description, but always in clear partnership with an entire complex of dogmatic material. This is the strength of Barth's approach. He attends to Jesus' ascended being on its own (New Testament) terms, firstly in partnership with other dogmatic claims and secondly without succumbing to the temptation to establish a previously determined ecclesiology or sacramentology, or to seek to 'make more of' the human before God. This has the result that Jesus' ascension and session play an important role in conditioning Barth's understanding of the nature of the entire present age, but do so in a dogmatically defensible fashion.

Thus Jesus' ascended being, and the interplay of His presence and absence, causes Barth to *affirm* strongly the being of the church, and the reality of subjective justification – that is, the reality of the Spirit's work in the human world. Far from lacking interest in the church and human response to God's reconciliation in Christ, for Barth the being and work of the church – human response to God in thanks and mission – is the meaning and purpose of this entire age of the creation. It is for the church and to allow for further human history that the Father creates the time of Jesus as ascended, the space between ascension and *eschaton*. Moreover, therefore, Jesus' agency in the Spirit – His ascended work in the exercise of His authority at the 'right hand of the Power' – is focussed upon the reality of subjective human appropriation of, and response to, His grace.

Yet at the same time Barth places equally strong limits around his descriptions of the church and Christian response to God, seeing these realities as entirely penultimate pending the *eschaton*. The church's embodiment of Jesus, and the various forms of human response Jesus creates are genuine, but always partial. Jesus' ascension and heavenly session create a space for further human history before God, and response to God's justifying work in Christ, and moreover, Jesus in His lordship empowers that history and the response to be made. But at the same time Jesus as ascended is not immediately present, and His *parousia* in the Spirit is not His *eschaton*, so that His ascension and heavenly session also impose limits upon the description of the present age and define it as penultimate.

Barth's incorporation of Jesus' ascended state into his theology is therefore highly successful, and it bears fruit in making sense of the present age as the 'time between'. On this basis we recommend Barth's approach to Jesus' 'post-history' as a useful, and indeed necessary, aspect of theology. In particular we recommend Barth's scheme – in the face of the criticism it receives – in the way he conceptualises the work of the Spirit, and thus the being of the church and the Christian. Attending to Jesus' ascension and heavenly session involves attending to His presence and absence, and so to the particular shape of His transcendent Lordship in the 'time between' as it defines the nature of the present age of the creation. This *locus* of thought ought to command the attention of theologians in the future.

Ascension, Heavenly Session, and the Incarnation

Further, if Jesus' ascension and 'location' at the Father's right hand are to be affirmed, in line with the testimony of the New Testament, then this affirmation has implications for christology, and theology as a whole. This is particularly clear in relation to the incarnation. Barth's reading of Jesus' ascension is closely tied to the way in which he understands the incarnation, and the continued being of the incarnate one. In one sense, the way in which Jesus' ongoing existence as the ascended incarnate One is conceived highlights the key moves in incarnational theology. This has been particularly clear in the limited discussions of *kenosis* and the *extra Calvinisticum* above. Both Farrow and Jenson embrace theologies of Jesus' ascension and heavenly session which are tied to particular visions of Jesus' incarnation, and in both cases difficulties arise. Torrance too runs into issues related to the incarnation, although in Torrance's case it is simply that a certain degree of inconsistency accompanies his resistance to *kenotic* theory.

It would be a mistake to claim that a theology of Jesus' ascension and heavenly session should control incarnational theology – along with other key dogmas these two areas of reflection must condition each other, rather than the one always conditioning the other. To this degree affirmation of Jesus' bodily ascension and rule on the right hand of God should be permitted to exercise a role in shaping incarnational theology – as it does not in Jenson's thought.

On the other side, it is also the case that dogmatic material relating to the incarnation must exercise some control over the ways in which Jesus' ascension is conceived, and over any understanding of His heavenly ministry – as evident in our defence of Barth and criticism of Farrow. Any manner of ascension, or of glorification and installation as priest in ascension, which threatens the doctrine of Jesus' full humanity and deity, united as they are in one person and one history of action, is to be rejected. On this basis the link between sequential readings of Jesus' humiliation and exaltation, as a human, and the seventeenth century *kenosis* debates should not be forgotten.[6]

Jesus as the Ascended Lord

Thus Jesus' ascension and heavenly session provide a useful and important *locus* of theological investigation. Ascension theology, and Jesus' heavenly session, does not merely offer a point of comparison between theologies and theologians, but, more significantly, it enables dogmatic reflection upon the living reality of Jesus Christ and the relation between His past, future, and His current life for us. Jesus' ascension marks the beginning of the present age, and while His being and work as the ascended Saviour is veiled, nonetheless it remains the ultimate reality of this age. As the Lord of all, and the firstborn of the new creation, Jesus' movement from ascension to *eschaton* is the secret meaning of current history and the basis of His own eschatological drive toward the age to come. Jesus' presence and absence, the form of His Lordship and relationship to church, world, and Christian are all shaped by His ascended life.

Failure to attend to Jesus' ascension and heavenly session, and the particular shape that this gives the present age, will result in theological distortion, as will an overdeveloped theology the event of the ascension itself (that is, by having the event accomplish too much). If Jesus' ascended being is not given proper place, then theology is all the more prone to overdevelop the subjective pole of justification, and to make either the church or the Christian the centre of theological reflection and truth. Proper attention to Jesus as ascended, as a necessary aspect of attention to the entirety of His history, will help to ground a genuine awareness of the subjective reality of justification in Jesus Christ – as grounded in the objective reality of Christ Himself – while enabling an understanding of the penultimate nature of that subjective reality prior to the *eschaton*. Thus we may say that Jesus' ascended being and work shape the way in which eschatology must be conceived, and in doing so shape the present age accordingly. Neither over-realised, nor over-remote notions of eschatology – involving as it does our full being in Christ – are able to fit with Jesus' ascended presence and absence, and so neither option can function within a theology that attends to that presence and absence.

That Christians are those who watch, wait, and seek, is also a function of the 'time between', and of the penultimate nature of incorporation into Christ.

---

[6] In regard to Jenson's strong notion of the communication of attributes in the incarnation, Colin Gunton has identified a tendency for this to allow Jesus' humanity to be swamped by His divinity. This may apply to the way in which Jenson conceives of Jesus' ascended embodiment. See Gunton's 'Creation and Mediation in the Theology of Robert Jenson: An Encounter and a Convergence' in Gunton, Colin E. ed. *Trinity and Time: A Response to the Theology of Robert W. Jenson* Grand Rapids: Eerdmans, 2000, pp.80-93, especially pp.83-5.

Christians exist as the 'not yet visibly redeemed', and rely upon the mediate presence of Christ in the Spirit, Scripture, and the church – the presence of Jesus as 'promise' – while hoping and praying and seeking for the immediacy of His presence which is our future. This 'time between', with all the frustration involved in the continuation of sin, evil, and suffering, is nonetheless the time of grace. It is the age in which the new creation and the new time of God, established in Jesus Christ, are with Him in heaven while the old time of the world is allowed to continue so that grace and faith may reign, and so that Jesus' work of self-witness itself may be completed. Thus the mission of Jesus – in self-witness – which characterises this age also characterises the work and mission of Christians and the church. The 'time between' is specifically the time of outreach, of the church as *creatura Verbi* and as servant of the Word, and of the Christian as necessarily the servant of Christ's mission to the world.

Once again, such an understanding of the present age and the being of Christians within it – and of this age as the age of grace and mission – relies upon the nature of Jesus' ascension and of His heavenly session. It is the withdrawal of His time, and the fact of His mediacy rather than immediacy – the fact of the gap between the ascension and the eschaton – which creates the conditions within which His mission of self-witness continues in this particular way, and incorporates the work of church and Christian within it. It is also this withdrawal that leaves the Christian watching and seeking for Jesus, and His kingdom, as He remains the ever 'coming' Lord. Consequently, failure to attend to Jesus' ascension and ascended ministry may allow theology to lose sight of the particular character of the age and of the mission and task of both church and Christian within it. Mission may be lost in favour of maintenance of the church itself and the church and its life may come to be seen as an end in itself. Similarly, the work of the Christian may be lost in favour of an ethic of divine contemplation, or alternatively, the coming kingdom – held with Christ in heaven – may be reduced to an outcome of the processes of this age and therefore the attempt may be made to bring it about within fallen history. But neither of these options is available when Jesus' ascension and heavenly session are understood as we have suggested.

Thus attention to Jesus as ascended – bodily ascended, and in some way located at the Father's side, absent, but also present in the Spirit – has a key role to play in shaping an understanding of Jesus' identity, work, and continued life in the present age, and in shaping hope for the age to come. This role is not independent of, but functions alongside of and in partnership with the rest of the church's doctrines, so that an understanding of the ascension and heavenly session of Jesus is informed by other dogmatic material, and so that Jesus' ascension and session informs that material in return. In this way theology may benefit from reflection upon the present age as that in which Jesus is ascended, and seated on the right hand of the Father, from whence we await His return.

Bibliography

Barth, Karl

The Epistle to the Romans second edition, trans. E.C. Hoskyns, London: Oxford University Press, 1933.

Church Dogmatics volumes I-IV, Edinburgh: T&T Clark, 1936–1969.

Knowledge of God in the Service of God, trans. J. Haire and I. Henderson, London: Hodder and Stoughton, 1938.

Dogmatics in Outline, London: SCM Press Ltd., 1949.

Evangelical Theology: An Introduction, Grand Rapids, Michigan: Eerdmans, 1963.

Credo, London: Hodder and Stoughton, 1964.

Protestant Theology in the Nineteenth Century: Its Background and History, London: SCM Press, 1972.

The Christian Life: Church Dogmatics IV/4. *Lecture Fragments*, Edinburgh: T&T Clark, 1981.

Biggar, Nigel

The Hastening that Waits: Karl Barth's Ethics, Oxford: Clarendon Press, 1993.

'Barth's trinitarian ethic' in Webster, John B. ed. *The Cambridge Companion to Karl Barth*, Cambridge: Cambridge University Press, 2000, pp.212-27.

Bonhoeffer, Dietrich

Christ the Center, trans. E.H. Robertson, San Francisco: Harper and Row, 1978.

Buckley, James J.

'Community, baptism, and the Lord's Supper' in Webster, John B. ed. *The Cambridge Companion to Karl Barth*, Cambridge: Cambridge University Press, 2000, pp.195-211.

Farrow, Douglas

Ascension and Ecclesia: On the Significance of the Doctrine of the Ascension for Ecclesiology and Christian Cosmology, Edinburgh: T&T Clark, 1999.

'Karl Barth on the Ascension: An Appreciation and Critique', *International Journal of Systematic Theology* 2, 2000.

Farrow, Douglas, David Demson, and J. Augustine Di Noia	'Robert Jenson's *Systematic Theology:* Three Responses', *International Journal Of Systematic Theology* 1.1, March 1999.
Gorringe, Timothy	*Karl Barth: against hegemony*, Oxford: Oxford University Press, 1999.
Gunton, Colin	'The triune God and the freedom of the creature' in S. W. Sykes ed. *Karl Barth: Centenary Essays*, Cambridge: Cambridge University Press, 1989.
	Christ and Creation, Carlisle: Paternoster Press, 1992.
	'Creation and Mediation in the Theology of Robert Jenson: An Encounter and a Convergence' in Gunton, Colin E. ed. *Trinity and Time: A Response to the Theology of Robert W. Jenson*, Grand Rapids: Eerdmans, 2000, pp.80-93
	'Salvation' in Webster, John B. ed. *The Cambridge Companion to Karl Barth*, Cambridge: Cambridge University Press, 2000, pp.143-58.
Gunton, Colin E. ed.	*Trinity and Time: A Response to the Theology of Robert W. Jenson*, Grand Rapids: Eerdmans, 2000.
Hart, Trevor	'Revelation' in Webster, John B. ed. *The Cambridge Companion to Karl Barth*, Cambridge: Cambridge University Press, 2000, pp.37-56.
Healy, Nicholas M.	'The Logic of Karl Barth's Ecclesiology: Analysis, Assessment and Proposed Modifications', *Modern Theology* 10:3, July 1994, pp.253-70.
Hunsinger, George	'Karl Barth's Christology: Its basic Chalcedonian character' in Webster, John B. ed. *The Cambridge Companion to Karl Barth*, Cambridge: Cambridge University Press, 2000.
	'Karl Barth's doctrine of the Holy Spirit' in Webster, John B. ed. *The Cambridge Companion to Karl Barth*, Cambridge: Cambridge University Press, 2000, pp.177-94.
Hütter, Reinhard	'The ecclesiastical ethics of Stanley Hauerwas: a Lutheran responds', *Dialog* 30 Summer 1991, pp.231-41.
	Evangelische Ethik als kirchliches Zeugnis: Interpretationen zu Schlusselfragen theologischerEthik der Gegenwart, Neukirchen-Vluyn: Neukirchener, 1993.

'Karl Barth's "Dialectical Catholicity": Sic et Non', *Modern Theology* 16:2, April 2000, pp.137-57.

Irenaeus

Against Heresies ed. and trans. Alexander Roberts and James Donaldson. American ed. A. Cleveland Coxe. *The Ante-Nicene Fathers*, volume I, Grand Rapids: Eerdmans, 1987.

Jenson, Robert

God after God: The God of the Past and the God of the Future, Seen in the Work of Karl Barth, New York: The Bobbs-Merrill Company, 1969.

Visible Words: The Interpretation and Practice of Christian Sacraments, Philadelphia: Fortress Press, 1978.

The Triune God, Philadelphia: Fortress Press, 1982.

Unbaptized God: The basic flaw in ecumenical theology, Minneapolis: Fortress Press, 1992.

Essays in the Theology of Culture, Eerdmans: Grand Rapids, Michigan, 1995.

'The Church and the Sacraments' in Gunton, Colin ed. *The Cambridge Companion to Christian Doctrine*, Cambridge: Cambridge University Press, 1997.

Systematic Theology, volumes I and II Oxford: Oxford University Press, 1997-99.

Johnson, William Stacy

The Mystery of God: Karl Barth and the Postmodern Foundations of Theology, Louisville, Kentucky: Westminster John Knox Press, 1997.

McGrath, Alister E.

Iustitia Dei: A History of the Christian Doctrine of Justification: Volume II, from 1500 to the present day, Cambridge: Cambridge University Press, 1986.

Milligan, William

The Ascension of Our Lord, London: Macmillan, 1894.

Nicholson, G. C.

Death as Departure: The Johannine descent-ascent schema, Chicago: Scholars Press, 1983.

Pannenberg, Wolfhart

Jesus – God and Man, Lewis L. Wilkens and Duane A. Priebe translators, London: SCM Press Ltd, 1968.

Rosato, Philip J. (S.J.)

The Spirit as Lord: The Pneumatology of Karl Barth, Edinburgh: T&T Clark, 1981.

Thacker, Anthony

Karl Barth's Understanding of the Resurrection: Analysis, discussion and contrast. Unpublished dissertation, University of Oxford, Faculty of Theology, 1983.

Thompson, John   *The Holy Spirit in the Theology of Karl Barth*, Allison Park, Pennsylvania: Pickwick Publications, 1991.

Torrance, Thomas F.   'Royal Priesthood', *Scottish Journal of Theology Occasional Papers* No.3, 1955.

'Introduction' in *The Incarnation: Ecumenical Studies in the Nicene-Constantinopolitan Creed A.D. 381* Thomas F. Torrance ed., Edinburgh: The Handsel Press, 1981.

The Trinitarian Faith: The Evangelical Theology of the Ancient Catholic Church, Edinburgh: T & T Clark, 1988.

Karl Barth, Biblical and Evangelical Theologian, Edinburgh: T&T Clark, 1990.

Space, Time and Resurrection Edinburgh: Handsel Press, 1976, republished by T & T Clark, Edinburgh, 1998.

Waldrop, Charles   *Karl Barth's Christology: Its Basic Alexandrian Character*, Berlin: de Gruyter, 1984.

Webster, John B.   *Barth's Moral Theology: Human Action in Barth's Thought*, Edinburgh: T&T Clark, 1998.

Barth, London: Continuum, 2000.

Webster, John B. ed.   *The Cambridge Companion to Karl Barth*, Cambridge: Cambridge University Press, 2000.

Williams, Rowan D.   'Barth on the Triune God' in S. W. Sykes *Karl Barth: Studies of his Theological Method*, Oxford: Clarendon Press, 1979.

Wingren, Gustaf   *Theology in Conflict: Nygren, Barth, Bultmann* trans. Eric H. Wahlstrom, Edinburgh: Oliver and Boyd, 1958.

Wood, Susan K.   'Robert Jenson's Ecclesiology from a Roman Catholic Perspective' in Colin E. Gunton ed. *Trinity and Time: A Response to the Theology of Robert W. Jenson*, Grand Rapids: Eerdmans, 2000, pp. 178-87.

Yeago, David S.   'The Church as Polity? The Lutheran Context of Robert W. Jenson's Ecclesiology' in Colin E. Gunton ed. *Trinity and Time: A Response to the Theology of Robert W. Jenson*, Grand Rapids: Eerdmans, 2000, pp.201-37.

Zizoulas, John D.   *Being as Communion: Studies in Personhood and the Church*, Crestwood: St Vladimir's Press, 1985.

Index